DECOLONISING DESIGN IN AFRICA

Decolonising Design in Africa offers a groundbreaking exploration of design education in Africa through a decolonial lens. By examining the colonial legacies that have shaped design education in Africa, it foregrounds the problematic ways that current pedagogical approaches primarily reflect western values and priorities. This book advocates for integrating Indigenous knowledge, cultural practices, and philosophies into contemporary African design education. It spans a wide geographical and temporal range, from historical analyses of colonial influences to envisioning decolonised African design futures. It delves into diverse aspects including spirituality in design, cultural symbolism, sustainable practices, and the ethical dimensions of decolonising design.

Pioneering in its interdisciplinary approach, the book weaves together theoretical discussions, methodological innovations like storytelling, and practical strategies for curriculum reform. It presents inspiring case studies of designers and educators who are actively decolonising their practices. *Decolonising Design in Africa* is a vital resource for design educators, students, practitioners, and policymakers, not just in Africa but worldwide. It makes a compelling case for reimagining design education in a more inclusive, contextually relevant and socially conscious way. The book's ultimate aim is to cultivate a new generation of designers equipped to address the complex challenges of a decolonising world.

Yaw Ofosu-Asare is a Teaching Associate at the University of Melbourne and Associate Research Fellow at Southern Cross University. With extensive experience in Ghana, Africa, and Australia in visual design and marketing, his research focuses on African philosophy, decolonisation, and design education.

"*Decolonising Design in Africa* is a powerful work that contributes significantly to the global discourse on design and education. It is a testament to the resilience, creativity, and innovation of African design and a call to action for more inclusive and respectful design practices. This book is not just about decolonizing African design; it is about reimagining and reshaping the future of design. It is a journey of discovery, reflection, and transformation that invites us to see design differently. It celebrates African design in all its splendour and diversity as an emancipatory process. It is a call to action for a more inclusive, equitable, and sustainable design practice. It is a testament to the power of design as a tool for social change and cultural preservation. It is, in essence, a love letter to African design."

—**Nick Stranger**, *Senior Lecturer, Faculty of Education, Southern Cross University*

"It has been my pleasure and my privilege to read the first book of esteemed academic Dr Ofosu-Asare. In his rich and palpable African voice, Ofosu-Asare takes the reader on a textured and interesting adventure of decolonising Ghanaian design education. This thoughtful and arresting book assembles decolonising ideas and strategies that seek to embrace African ontologies, epistemologies and axiologies in ways that are authentic for not only African students and professionals of design, but the scholarly field of design education more broadly. It is a profound exploration of the transformation potentials of African design education. Full of cultural methods, styles and positionings, the book takes us into Africa, into African classrooms, with African people. It offers a suite of perspectives, stories and speculative positionings to take design education into new horizons and futures. I highly recommend this book; may there be more to come."

—**Professor Alexandra Lasczik**, *Director, Professional Experience, Southern Cross University*

"This book is a book every African SHOULD read and every African creative MUST read. It's a true mindset changer and carries design philosophy that is good to know as you start your design journey. It digs deep into our identity as Africans, how design shaped our past and how if we pay closer attention, it will shape the future. Great thoughts of reflection for both new and seasoned African designers. I will recommend as a reading material for our design institutions. It is both a cultural and commercial masterpiece."

—**Daniel Ampofo**, President, *dEX Ghana*

DECOLONISING DESIGN IN AFRICA

Towards New Theories, Methods, and Practices

Yaw Ofosu-Asare

NEW YORK AND LONDON

Designed cover image: David Malan

First published 2025
by Routledge
605 Third Avenue, New York, NY 10158

and by Routledge
4 Park Square, Milton Park, Abingdon, Oxon, OX14 4RN

Routledge is an imprint of the Taylor & Francis Group, an informa business

© 2025 Yaw Ofosu-Asare

The right of Yaw Ofosu-Asare to be identified as author of this work has been asserted in accordance with sections 77 and 78 of the Copyright, Designs and Patents Act 1988.

All rights reserved. No part of this book may be reprinted or reproduced or utilised in any form or by any electronic, mechanical, or other means, now known or hereafter invented, including photocopying and recording, or in any information storage or retrieval system, without permission in writing from the publishers.

Trademark notice: Product or corporate names may be trademarks or registered trademarks, and are used only for identification and explanation without intent to infringe.

Library of Congress Cataloging-in-Publication Data
Names: Ofosu-Asare, Yaw, 1990– author.
Title: Decolonizing design in Africa : towards new theories, methods, and practices / Yaw Ofosu-Asare.
Description: New York : Routledge, 2024. | Includes bibliographical references and index.
Identifiers: LCCN 2024012752 (print) | LCCN 2024012753 (ebook) | ISBN 9781032692630 (hardback) | ISBN 9781032692654 (paperback) | ISBN 9781032692647 (ebook)
Subjects: LCSH: Design—Study and teaching—Africa. | Africa—Colonial influence.
Classification: LCC NK1487 .O35 2024 (print) | LCC NK1487 (ebook) | DDC 744.071/06—dc23/eng/20230320
LC record available at https://lccn.loc.gov/2024012752
LC ebook record available at https://lccn.loc.gov/2024012753

ISBN: 978-1-032-69263-0 (hbk)
ISBN: 978-1-032-69265-4 (pbk)
ISBN: 978-1-032-69264-7 (ebk)

DOI: 10.4324/9781032692647

Typeset in Times New Roman
by Apex CoVantage, LLC

restructuring and reforming. It is about cultivating a design ethos that embraces multiplicity and fosters a global dialogue, enriching our collective understanding and appreciation of design in all its forms. In this context, the book aims to navigate these complex waters, offering insights and perspectives that provoke thought, inspire change, and contribute to the ongoing discourse on how we can collectively build a more inclusive and balanced design world.

PROLOGUE

Dear Reader, the narrative awaiting your exploration has evolved from its initial incarnation as a doctoral thesis into the book that now lies in your hands. This transformation is not merely a shift in format, but a deepened and broadened inquiry that aims to reach beyond the academic realm, inviting a wider audience into a critical dialogue around decolonising design education in Africa. The thesis, a rigorous exploration of design pedagogies through a decolonising lens within Ghana's educational landscape, has blossomed into a narrative enriched with further reflections, dialogues, and a ceaseless aspiration to contribute to the ever-evolving discourse around decolonisation in African design education.

In the heart of Ghana, amidst the rhythmic ebb and flow of life, my narrative finds its origin. The twin city of Sekondi-Takoradi[1] cradled my early days, its culture and vibrancy deeply ingrained in my being. As I ventured into the Ashanti, Greater Accra, Central, and Eastern Regions, I discovered the rich diversity that defines our nation. Each region, with its unique traditions, festivals, and historical sites, became a vivid chapter in my evolving story. From the vibrant kente cloth of the Ashanti to the majestic castles of the Central Region, these experiences have woven together to create the intricate tapestry of my identity, forever rooted in Ghana's enchanting heartland.

The discourse of decolonising methodologies[2] within the African academic landscape emerges as a pivotal dialogue in the annals of African historiography. Embarking on this voyage required a sojourn into the places and spaces that framed my upbringing, a reflective journey through the corridors of my past. This inward voyage gained a deeper resonance against the backdrop of my scholarly endeavours in Australia—a land afar, its terrain unfamiliar, made more distant by the unyielding tide of a global pandemic that stretched the miles between me and the warm embrace of my homeland.

The scholastic environs of Australia presented a tableau of nuanced challenges. The academic fabric there sculpted a part of my scholarly identity, yet the echo of my African heritage was a persistent whisper, a reminder of the distinctive lens I bore. The endeavour to meld postcolonial theoretical scaffolds with the pragmatics of mixed methods research unveiled a dance between diverging paradigms. The quantitative data, nurtured in the womb of positivist tradition, seemed entrenched in the very colonising academic edifices I sought to critique. It strayed from the path of authentic African representation I aspired to traverse. A moment of epiphany beckoned the realisation that to authentically decolonise my research, a pilgrimage to the African traditions of storytelling and poetic discourse was essential. It was a summons to transcend the boundaries of conventional Western-style elucidation and to embrace a methodology that resonated with the rhythmic cadence of African epistemology.

This book is a result of an extensive refining process where the rigors of academic inquiry meet the storytelling essence of the African narrative tradition. It aims to transcend the formal boundaries of scholarly discourse, rendering the insights and dialogues accessible, engaging, and resonant with a diverse readership. The endeavour to decolonise design education, as explored in this narrative, traverses beyond mere theoretical discussions. It delves into the heart of lived experiences, cultural heritage, and the potential for design education to serve as a conduit for reclaiming and celebrating Indigenous knowledge systems. As we transition from the structured pathways of the thesis to the expansive landscape of this book, the core remains steadfast—the quest to unearth, understand, and articulate the nuances of decolonising design education in Ghana and the broader African context. This narrative offers an opportunity to delve into the rich array of stories, reflections, and insights interlaced throughout the chapters, each contributing to a deeper comprehension of the decolonization journey within design education. I entitled my doctoral thesis *'Sankofa: Stories of a Postcolonial Space, African Philosophy, Decolonisation, and Practice in Design Education in Ghana.'* The use of *Sankofa*, itself a term from the Akan tribe in Ghana, embodies the spirit of this narrative.[3] It signifies the importance of reaching back to our roots, to glean wisdom from our past as we stride forward into a future filled with promise and potential. This principle has been the compass guiding the narrative from its thesis origin to its current embodiment as a book, urging a continual return to Indigenous knowledge and cultural heritage to foster a more authentic, responsive, and decolonised design education. As you delve into the ensuing chapters, you will find that the journey from thesis to book has allowed for a richer, more layered exploration. It has provided space for deeper engagement with the lived experiences, cultural narratives, and pedagogical dialogues that form the backbone of this inquiry into decolonising African design education. Through this book, the discourse around decolonisation, African philosophy, and design education seeks to reverberate through classrooms, design studios, and academic halls, igniting conversations and actions towards a decolonised design pedagogy that is reflexive of and responsive to the African ethos.

Welcome, Dear Reader, to a narrative where each page is a stride on the path of decolonisation, where every chapter is an invitation to engage with the pulsing heart of African design education, and where the journey from thesis to book symbolises a broader, collective quest for a decolonised narrative in African design discourse. Your engagement with this narrative is more than just a scholarly endeavour; it's a joining of minds and hearts towards envisioning and actualising a decolonised space where African design education can thrive, resonate, and contribute to the global design narrative.

Definition of Design

The word *design* has long been a subject of fascination, scrutiny, and even contestation. It is a term often conjured in the sparsely furnished rooms of high-tech companies, in the polished floors of art galleries, or in the cerebral halls of academia. Yet, can this singular term adequately capture the rich spectrum of creativity, as well as the diverse human needs and sociocultural identities that it encompasses? Is design a universal language or does it carry the dialect of its historical roots? In its traditional Western-centric conception, design is often understood as the marriage of form and function. It is the meticulous process of transforming imagination into tangible reality, the conversion of scientific principles into usable products, the artful crafting of experiences that transcend the ordinary. This view, however well intentioned, is laden with assumptions that can be limiting, even imperialistic. It suggests a linear process with a fixed start and end point, which is more reflective of the Enlightenment ideals of progress and rationality than the circular, relational worldviews prevalent in many non-Western cultures.

The design philosophies of many Indigenous and non-Western communities can feel starkly different. Take, for example, the African concept of "Ubuntu," which emphasizes communal life and interconnectedness. Here, design is not just about the individual user's experience but also about the collective wellbeing. The Indigenous Maori in New Zealand employ "Whakapapa," focusing on the genealogical descent of an object or idea, adding layers of spiritual and historical dimensions to the design process. In these frameworks, design does not merely solve a problem; it narrates a story, maintains a tradition, and honours a shared identity. Thus, the very act of defining *design* forces us into a precarious balancing act. On one hand, a definition can offer clarity, direction, and shared understanding. On the other, it can constrain, exclude, and even subjugate. The word itself, laden with Eurocentric undertones, can inadvertently become an act of intellectual colonisation, glossing over the rich mosaic of global design traditions to highlight a singular, often Western, viewpoint.

So, is the word *design* limiting and colonial? It can be if we let it. Yet words, like design itself, are ever-evolving artifacts of human culture. They carry the power to both divide and unite, to marginalise and to emancipate. As we journey through this book, we will delve into the complex terrain of design, not just as a technical discipline but as a social, ethical, and deeply political act. We will traverse geographical boundaries and time zones to interrogate, critique, and reimagine design as a decolonised space, one that is as multidimensional, as diverse, and as beautifully complex as the people it seeks to serve. In the African context, design transcends mere functionality or aesthetics; it becomes a nexus where tradition, storytelling, communal ethos, and Indigenous knowledge converge. In Africa, the act of "designing" is often not segregated as a stand-alone practice but interwoven into the broader context of community life. From the patterns inscribed on mud huts to the intricate beadwork in traditional attire, design is not merely about making; it's a dialogue with ancestry, environment, and future generations.

However, is the term *design*, as we know it, capable of encompassing this complex, community-oriented, ancestral dialogue? The challenge lies not so much in the term itself, but in the frameworks, education, and paradigms that surround it. Western design pedagogy has often been rooted in individualistic, capitalist systems that value product over process, the end over the means, the individual creator over the collective inheritance and contribution. The risk, then, is that the term *design*—when viewed solely through this Western lens—becomes a tool of exclusion rather than inclusion, limiting rather than expansive, colonial rather than emancipatory. However, words are not static; they are dynamic constructs subject to redefinition and recontextualization. By critically engaging with and expanding upon traditional design vocabularies and frameworks, we can decolonise the term *design* itself, infusing it with values and nuances that reflect Africa's rich social and cultural landscapes. It involves deconstructing predefined notions and biases, questioning the status quo, and most importantly, creating space for voices that have been historically side-lined.

Thus, the term *design* can indeed be reclaimed and transformed into an inclusive, multidimensional concept that serves not just markets but also communities, not just individual users but collective identities. By doing so, we engage in a radical act of redefinition, one that aligns the scope and purpose of design with Africa's unique historical, social, and cultural exigencies. So, yes, the term *design* can be limiting and colonial if we allow it to be. But if we actively engage in this process of intellectual and practical reclamation, we can turn it into a powerful tool for social justice, communal wellbeing, and cultural preservation. As this book aims to show, *design* in Africa can be—must be—a liberating force that reflects the continent's vast diversity and its unyielding aspiration for a brighter future.

Let us begin.

Design Education

The halls of design education are echoing, resonating with voices that have long been considered peripheral. As you hold this book, you are joining a chorus of inquiry, critique, and reimagination—a chorus that questions the very foundations of design education. Is design education a Western practice? Can it be universal, transcending geographical and cultural boundaries? These are questions not just of academic interest but of existential significance, especially in the context of Africa, a continent marked by both diversity and commonality, both tradition and modernity. The historical narrative often attributes design education to the West. With Bauhaus in Germany, Parsons in the United States, and the Royal College of Art in the United Kingdom, the Western world has indeed been a crucible of influential design philosophies. Yet, to argue that design education is solely a Western construct would be to disregard the abundant array of creative pedagogies that have flourished across Africa and other parts of the world for centuries.

African design is not just an afterthought, an imitation, or an appendage to Western paradigms. It is an intrinsic practice steeped in local materials, communal values, and Indigenous technologies. The intricacies of Moroccan sellige tiles, the mathematical genius in African fractal architecture, and the symbolic depth in Adinkra and Nsibidi scripts are all testament to a long-standing, vibrant tradition of design. These practices have been passed down generations not just as skills but as philosophies, interwoven with spirituality, social ethics, and communal welfare. Education has always been more than the mere transmission of knowledge; it has been a tool for social engineering. In Africa, as elsewhere, the arts have been an integral part of education, serving various ends from cultural preservation to social cohesion and even resistance against oppression. Dance, storytelling, sculpture, and design have been channels through which Africans have engaged with, critiqued, and transformed their worlds. These arts, design education included, have been vehicles for propagating political ideologies, whether of liberation or, unfortunately at times, of colonisation.

As we peel back the layers of history, we find that design education has been used as a tool—sometimes for oppression but also for liberation. Its universality does not lie in a one-size-fits-all curriculum but in its capacity to serve the immediate, specific needs of a community, reflecting its aspirations, challenges, and ethics. This book challenges the notion that Africa is merely a recipient of Western design education and asserts its role as an active contributor to the global design dialogue. This is more than just a book; it is a rallying cry for a reimagined, decolonised design education that honours the universality of human creativity. In the ensuing chapters, we will break down the walls that have limited design education to Western classrooms, and we will venture into the bustling markets, the vibrant festivals, and the quiet, sacred spaces across Africa where design education has been practiced, in some form, for centuries.

So let us embark on this intellectual odyssey, not as passive readers but as active questioners, challengers, and most importantly, as designers of a new educational landscape.

As we stand on the threshold of a new era, Africa finds itself at an inflection point, teetering between historical impositions and future possibilities. The narrative of Africa, often crafted from an external vantage point, has been one of passivity, of silence, of echoes rather than voices. But times have changed. The tectonic plates of global culture, technology, and politics are shifting, and Africa is not just witnessing this seismic change; it is an active, throbbing epicentre. It is time for Africa to change its narrative from within, to speak up, and to show the world not just who it is but who it can be.

In this zeitgeist, the African drumbeat is resonating across global stages, transcending linguistic and geopolitical borders. Music from the continent—whether it be Afrobeats, Highlife, or Kwaito—has become a pulsating force in global pop culture. Artists like Burna Boy, Angelique Kidjo, and Wizkid are not just African musicians; they are global icons who have carved out spaces in the international arena, spaces that reverberate with African rhythms and sensibilities. It is not just in the realm of music that Africa is making its influence felt. African designers, from fashion to architecture, are receiving international acclaim, bridging the gap between traditional African aesthetics and contemporary design languages. Names like Laduma Ngxokolo in fashion and Kunlé Adeyemi in architecture are testament to this. They represent a new wave of thinkers who defy simplistic labels and instead bring a complex, nuanced African narrative to the global stage.

Culture, an omnipresent yet elusive term, has been Africa's unspoken language, its silent yet roaring advocate. The world is slowly waking up to the richness of African art, the depth of its oral traditions, the complexity of its social fabrics, and the spirituality of its native religions. From the global spread of African culinary staples like jollof rice to the international recognition of Nollywood, the impact of African culture is a story that is unfolding in real time, and it is a narrative being written from within Africa, by Africans. This book, therefore, is not just a solitary endeavour but part of a larger, bubbling conversation—a dialogic renaissance, if you will—that is redefining what it means to be African in today's interconnected world. We are questioning established norms, breaking down preconceived barriers, and above all, we are declaring that our stories, our songs, and our designs are not just footnotes in a Western-dominated narrative. They are chapters in a sprawling, complex anthology of human experience.

It is time for Africa to take the pen and write its own narrative. And as you turn these pages, you are not just reading a book; you are participating in a revolution, one that is not coming soon—it is already here. Welcome to the conversation. Welcome to the future. Welcome to a new Africa.

Roots and Wings: Embracing Sankofa in African Education

As the African proverb says, "Wisdom is like a baobab tree; no one individual can embrace it." This sentiment underpins our journey into the heart of decolonising education in Africa, a voyage as complex and deeply rooted as the baobab itself. Decolonisation, in its broadest sense, refers to the undoing of colonialism, the process where nations emerge from the shadow of imperialism to forge their own identity, policies, and educational systems. Historically, this process has been tumultuous, marked by struggles for independence and the reclamation of cultural and intellectual sovereignty.

In the context of African education, decolonisation is not merely a shift from Western pedagogies but a profound transformation that seeks to centre African experiences, values, and knowledge systems. It is akin to the Ghanaian concept of "Sankofa"—going back to our roots to move forward. This philosophy underlines the importance of reconnecting with our Indigenous knowledge and cultural heritage, not as an act of nostalgia, but as a foundation for a future where African perspectives are not just included but are central. Yet, the counterargument posits that globalisation necessitates a cosmopolitan approach to education, where Western and African educational paradigms coexist and complement each other. Advocates of this view argue for a synthesis of educational models, where Western scientific rigor and African traditional knowledge converge, preparing students for a globalised world.

My personal journey mirrors this dichotomy. I recall, during my education in Ghana, how the curriculum oscillated between extolling Western advancements and tentatively acknowledging African contributions. In Australia, this contrast became even starker, as I navigated an education system that seemed worlds apart from my African roots. These experiences highlight the complexity of decolonising education—it's not about discarding Western knowledge but repositioning African knowledge within the global educational landscape. The proverb "It takes a village to raise a child" resonates profoundly with the African approach to education. It underscores the importance of community and collective wisdom—a stark contrast to the individualism often espoused in Western education. This communal aspect of African education, where learning is interwoven with social and cultural life, is vital in decolonising efforts. It is about creating an education system that is not just about imparting knowledge but nurturing well-rounded individuals rooted in their culture and capable of global interaction.

Decolonising education in Africa thus presents an opportunity to redefine what education means. It's a chance to create a system that celebrates diversity, fosters critical thinking, and respects the myriad ways of knowing and being in the world. As we embark on this journey, we hold the conviction that African design education can be a beacon of hope and transformation, not just for Africa, but for the world.

Notes

1 The city of Sekondi-Takoradi, often referred to as the Twin City, is situated in the Western Region of Ghana, along the Gulf of Guinea. It is the region's largest city and serves as its administrative and economic centre. Sekondi-Takoradi is known for its harbour, which plays a crucial role in Ghana's economy, facilitating the export and import of goods. The city is an amalgamation of two distinct cities, Sekondi and Takoradi, each with its unique historical and cultural identity, yet unified in administrative purpose. Sekondi-Takoradi's historical significance is often traced back to the precolonial and colonial eras. It was a focal point of interaction between European traders and local communities, particularly during the trans-Atlantic slave trade. The construction of the railway and harbour during the colonial era significantly impacted the city's development, transforming it into a vital economic hub. In contemporary times, Sekondi-Takoradi has witnessed growth and diversification in its economy, with the discovery of oil in the region further boosting its economic relevance. The city is also rich in cultural heritage, with numerous festivals and traditional celebrations showcasing the vibrant cultural tapestry of the region. Moreover, Sekondi-Takoradi's natural beauty, marked by its picturesque beaches and lush greenery, makes it a compelling destination for both locals and tourists. Furthermore, Sekondi-Takoradi has been a base for discussions and initiatives centred around urban planning and sustainable development, reflecting the broader national discourse on these critical issues. The city's evolving narrative embodies a blend of historical resonance, economic vitality, and cultural richness, making it a significant locale within the Ghanaian national fabric.
2 The journey into decolonising methodologies was akin to venturing into an uncharted territory, confronting the entrenched neocolonial educational paradigms that had shaped my academic trajectory hitherto. My initial foray was rooted in a pragmatic approach, leveraging mixed methods in educational research, reflecting a conditioning by a system that often prised quantitative over qualitative inquiry. However, the exploration of the controversy surrounding positivist and interpretative methodological perspectives, as highlighted by Carey (1993). Linking qualitative and quantitative methods, and integrating cultural factors into public health, served as a catalyst, nudging me towards a deeper engagement with decolonising methodologies. The process unfolded in phases, beginning with a quantitative inquiry employing Technacy Genre Theory (TGT) to garner insights into the teaching of design, while concurrently identifying inhibitory factors concerning the integration of Ghanaian cultural nuances within it. The evolution of my methodological lens was significantly informed by readings on decolonising research, which envisioned a protracted process of reimagining co-existence between colonisers and Indigenous peoples (Adjei [2007]; Keikelame, M. J., & Swartz, L. [2019]; Phillips, L. G., & Bunda, T. [2018]). This theoretical engagement resonated with my quest to understand and interpret educational phenomena through a lens that acknowledged and celebrated Indigenous epistemologies. Delving into the phases of decolonisation as outlined by Laenui, P. (2000), I found parallels between the experiential contours of Indigenous peoples and the personal and collective epistemological

journeys of those entrenched in colonial educational paradigms. The reflection on these phases not only enriched my understanding but also provided a scaffold upon which I could structure my engagement with decolonising methodologies. The immersive reconnection with my culture, epitomised by the reminiscence of late-night storytelling, singing, and poems shared by my grandmother, unlocked a realm of Indigenous knowledge and epistemological richness. These experiences were mirrored in the creative endeavours of artisans, designers, and carpenters in Ghana, whose narratives and songs enlivened their craft, embodying a rich tapestry of Indigenous knowledge and creativity. As I delved deeper into decolonised methodological approaches, the imperative to encapsulate my epistemological journey as a Ghanaian seeking authenticity became evident. This process evolved into a storied-ethnography methodological research paradigm, enabling a nuanced exploration of the epistemological decolonisation of design education. The encapsulation of this journey now finds its expression in the current book, serving not only as a reflection of my personal and academic evolution but also as an exemplar of the profound transformative potential inherent in the engagement with decolonising methodologies. The unfolding of this methodological narrative, encapsulated in the ensuing chapters, serves as a testament to the profound epistemological and methodological shifts that are possible when one engages earnestly with the principles and practices of decolonising methodologies.

3 *Sankofa*, a quintessential Ghanaian concept, serves as a rich metaphorical backdrop against which the journey of decolonising design education in Ghana is envisaged. Literally translating to "go back and get it," *Sankofa* is emblematically represented by a bird looking backward, while cradling an egg in its beak. This profound imagery underscores the essence of drawing from the past to foster progressive forward movement. In the context of my thesis and subsequently this book, *Sankofa* impelled a reflective journey back to the Indigenous cultural and traditional ethos of Ghana, serving as a catalyst to question and re-evaluate the dominant Western paradigms that have pervasively shaped design education. This journey was not merely a nostalgic trip down memory lane, but a critical endeavour to reclaim and revalorise the Indigenous design principles and practices intrinsic to Ghanaian cultural heritage. Employing *Sankofa* as a theoretical lens allowed for a critical examination of prevalent design education narratives, challenging the overshadowing Western perspectives, and engendering a space for dialogic engagement with Indigenous design paradigms. The essence of looking back to the rich traditions and cultural practices of Ghanaian communities was not a mere romanticisation of the past, but a pragmatic approach to garnering a more holistic understanding of community-centric principles that could inform contemporary design education and practice in a culturally resonant manner. The Sankofa-inspired approach transcended mere critique, evolving into a constructive paradigm that championed diversity and inclusivity in design education. By weaving the tapestry of Ghanaian community perspectives and experiences into the fabric of design education, a more contextualised, responsive, and participatory design pedagogy was envisaged. This symbiotic engagement between the design education realm and the community not only enriched the design process but also fostered a sense of ownership and engagement among community members, propelling the journey towards more sustainable and culturally congruent design solutions. This book epitomises the evolution of this Sankofa-inspired journey from the thesis stage to a broader scholarly and practical discourse. It extends an invitation to delve into a deeper understanding of how the principles of Sankofa can catalyse a decolonial ethos in design education in Ghana. By challenging the hegemonic narratives and fostering a culture of inclusivity and equity, Sankofa emerges as a potent decolonising research theory. It beckons a transformation towards a design education milieu that is not only respectful and responsive but also integrally connected to the needs, aspirations, and cultural tapestry of Ghanaian

communities. In essence, the Sankofa-driven narrative encapsulated in this book underscores a paradigmatic shift towards a more holistic, community-engaged, and culturally resonant design education in Ghana. It is a clarion call to rekindle a dialogic engagement between the past and the present, between the global and the local, and between the academy and the community, thus embarking on a transformative journey towards a decolonised design education landscape.

References

Adjei, P. B. (2007). Decolonising knowledge production: The pedagogic relevance of Gandhian satyagraha to schooling and education in Ghana. *Canadian Journal of Education / Revue canadienne de l'éducation*, *30*(4), 1046–1067. https://doi.org/10.2307/20466678

Carey, J. W. (1993). Linking qualitative and quantitative methods: Integrating cultural factors into public health. *Qualitative Health Research*, *3*(3), 298–318.

Keikelame, M. J., & Swartz, L. (2019). Decolonising research methodologies: lessons from a qualitative research project, Cape Town, South Africa. *Global Health Action*, *12*(1). 1561175. https://doi.org/10.1080/16549716.2018.1561175

Laenui, P. (2000). Processes of decolonization. In M. Battiste (Ed.), *Reclaiming Indigenous voice and vision*, 150–160. https://doi.org/10.17953/aicr.17.1.v520565l30116036

Phillips, L. G., & Bunda, T. (2018). *Research through, with and as storying*. Routledge. https://doi.org/10.4324/9781315109190

1
CULTIVATING THE FOUNDATIONS

The Role of Design Education in Transforming the Legacy of African Education

The opening chapter sets the stage for an exploration that goes far beyond pedagogical theories and classroom practices. It probes into design education as a potent catalyst for disrupting entrenched narratives and legacies that have long shaped African education. Rooted in a colonial past, many educational systems across the continent have perpetuated a Eurocentric world view, often side-lining Indigenous knowledge, cultures, and practices. Design education, inherently problem-solving and multidisciplinary, holds the promise to be a transformative force in recalibrating these imbalances. This chapter argues for the importance of framing design education within the context of Africa's rich cultural diversity and complex social fabrics. It proposes that design education should not be an isolated endeavour of skill acquisition but a comprehensive approach to problem-solving, deeply entrenched in the socio-political realities of African societies. It should serve as a vehicle to explore issues ranging from the preservation of Indigenous knowledge to the development of sustainable, locally relevant solutions for pressing social problems.

Here, we will investigate the historical legacy of African education, the limitations imposed by colonial mindsets, and the need for a radical departure towards more inclusive, Indigenous, and context-specific educational models. We will then delve into concrete examples and case studies that demonstrate the transformative power of design thinking and practice in this context. By the end of this chapter, the aim is to equip the reader not just with academic insights but with a call to action. The transformation of education in Africa is not just an institutional responsibility but a collective one, involving educators, policymakers, students, and communities at large. With design education as a focal point,

DOI: 10.4324/9781032692647-1

2 Cultivating the Foundations

we can start to imagine—and work towards—a more inclusive, equitable, and uniquely African educational paradigm.

Introduction: Tales Woven in Kente—A Journey Back to Roots

As the sun rises over the remote Ghanaian village of Kumawu, young Akosua adjusts her kente cloth school uniform, woven in a kaleidoscopic array of reds, yellows, and greens that mirror the vivacious spirit of the Ashanti Region. Her fingers tremble ever so slightly as she fastens the last button of her uniform; today is her first day at a new school, and a blend of apprehension and excitement courses through her veins like the Volta River. Her thoughts turn to the stories her grandmother, Efia, used to recount—stories of colonial schools, austere edifices where the medium of instruction was English, and the richness of her Ashanti culture was dismissed, overwritten as a colonial footnote. In those schools, the walls seemed to close in like a cage, severing the children from the roots of their heritage.

Akosua grabs her handmade satchel, stitched together by her mother, Abena, with Adinkra symbols that whisper tales of ancient wisdom and valour. The "Gye Nyame" symbol, signifying the omnipotence of God, adorns the bag's flap, a silent prayer and blessing for her educational journey. As she steps into the sunlight, the atmosphere embraces her; she inhales the unique aroma of rain-soaked soil mixed with shea butter, as the essence of home fills her senses. Planting her feet on the native earth, she feels the nurturing pulse of the land that has sustained generations before her.

Taking her first steps toward the new school, she consciously leaves behind the oppressive shadows of colonial institutions that once loomed over her ancestors. This school is different. Named "Nkrumah Educational Centre," after the great Kwame Nkrumah, it is built and managed by her own community, individuals who know the significance of an education that honours the wisdom and contributions of the Ashanti people.

As she walks, children from neighbouring compounds join her. Together, they create a procession—a lively caravan of hopes, aspirations, and a unified anticipation for an education that validates their identity. The children talk in a lively mix of Twi[1] and English, sharing stories of the famed Ashanti kings and queens, like Yaa Asantewaa, comparing them to modern-day Ghanaian heroes like Kofi Annan. Their conversation reveals a seamless blend of traditional folklore and current events, embodying the very essence of what the Nkrumah Educational Centre aims to instil: a symbiotic relationship between their cultural heritage and the broader world.

Finally, the rustic yet dignified structure of the school comes into view. The walls are decorated with murals of Ananse, the clever spider, outwitting foes in stories passed down for generations. Akosua's eyes widen at the sight of the computer lab, made possible through community funding and international partnerships. She envisions herself navigating the world through keystrokes and clicks, accessing knowledge both ancient and new—perhaps even contributing to it someday.

The children are welcomed by their headmaster, Mr. Ofori, a stout man with a gentle smile who encourages them to excel, not just as students but as custodians of their rich cultural legacy. The teachers, all from various regions of Ghana, prepare lessons that are deeply interwoven with Ashanti folklore, history, and ethical values, making education a panoramic view of their collective identity.

As Akosua sits in her classroom listening to the Twi proverbs infused in her first lesson, she feels an indescribable connection—a golden thread linking her to her ancestors, to her community, and even to the generations yet unborn. Each proverb, each lesson, feels like a conversation with her lineage, echoing Efia's words, "Sɛ wo werɛ fi na wosan kofa a, yɛnkyi"—"If you know where you come from, then you're never lost."

The day's horizon stretches before her, a vast expanse of infinite possibilities. For Akosua, the Nkrumah Educational Centre is not merely a building; it is a living promise. A promise that her education will be a harmonious melody composed of her ancestral wisdom and the opportunities of an ever-evolving world. With each lecture, each shared laugh, and even each challenge, she senses the metamorphosis of her initial nervousness into burgeoning optimism—an optimism that whispers in her ear that her education is not just an academic endeavour, but a soulful pilgrimage back to herself, a conscious claiming of her identity, and a lifelong tribute to her roots.

The Systems of Colonial Education

As we traverse the complex landscape of colonial influences on African education, it is critical to examine the structural changes that reshaped Indigenous systems. The inception of formal educational institutions was more than a mere infrastructural adjustment; it was an ideological upheaval. Pre-colonial Africa had its education grounded in an ecosystem of community learning, where knowledge transfer occurred in the fields, at home, or in community settings like the "Mud Schools" of Ghana. It was in stark contrast to the strictly defined walls and Eurocentric curricula that came to characterise the formal educational institutions set up by colonial powers.

Quoting Nana Kwame, a Ghanaian teacher who lived through the initial phase of this transformation, "The schools before were rooted in who we were. Suddenly, it felt like the education was happening to us, rather than something we were a part of." The new institutional models were designed, intentionally or unintentionally, to align with the requirements of the colonial workforce, marginalising Indigenous ways of knowing. Even architectural design—usually a reflection of community values—was replaced by buildings that resembled European models, thereby evoking a feeling of displacement among students and teachers alike. In a design education perspective, reimagining these spaces is a seminal step in the reclamation process. With a focus on participatory design involving community members, educators, and students, the walls of the formal institution can be transformed into canvases where cultural narratives are shared and celebrated. Design elements can incorporate traditional motifs, materials, and technologies to create educational environments that foster a sense of belonging and cultural pride. This is not merely an aesthetic adjustment but a structural reformation that echoes into the learning experience itself, making it more relatable and holistic. Language policies under colonial rule further accentuated this feeling of alienation. The forced adoption of European languages, like English and French, was not just a superficial alteration; it had deep-rooted psychological implications. In his memoir, Ayi Kwei Armah,[2] a Ghanaian writer and former student under the colonial education system, stated, "In those classrooms, our names became twisted, and our souls seemed tied to a tongue that felt too heavy to speak" (Armah, 1988) It is a powerful illustration of how language policies were instruments of disconnection, severing generations from their heritage.

Design education offers a robust platform to reintegrate linguistic diversity into the educational landscape. It can facilitate the creation of educational materials that are bilingual or multilingual, fostering cognitive development while maintaining cultural connections. Moreover, design thinking[3]/decolonising methodologies can be employed to adapt teaching methods, ensuring that they are culturally sensitive and linguistically inclusive, bridging gaps that have existed for decades. From a design education perspective, the potential for reclamation and transformation is significant. Community participatory design offers an avenue for incorporating traditional motifs and Indigenous technologies into the learning environment. Chinua Achebe, another renowned African scholar, echoed similar sentiments about the need for Indigenous languages and histories to occupy a significant place in African education. The curriculum itself underwent a transformation that had far-reaching consequences. African histories were rewritten or entirely left out, and Indigenous knowledge systems were undermined. This skewed presentation is something Frantz Fanon discussed extensively, pointing out the detrimental effects on the psyche of colonised peoples. The academic content delivered was tailored to portray the colonisers as saviours, fostering a mindset of subjugation among the educated African elite. A review of the educational materials from the colonial era reveals, for example, that the Ashanti Empire's resistance against colonial rule was often depicted as mere rebellions, undermining their organised, calculated efforts to maintain sovereignty.

In applying a Meadows-inspired[4] design approach to educational transformation, the emphasis is on revealing the systemic structures and feedback loops that perpetuate existing problems. Meadows, an environmental scientist and systems thinker, identified "leverage points" in a system—places where a small change could lead to significant, enduring improvements. In the context of education, this could mean identifying the aspects of curricula that disproportionately serve the colonial narrative, then reengineering them to provide more balanced, locally relevant content.

When it comes to curriculum development, visual narratives and mental models could take the form of infographics, interactive multimedia presentations, or experiential learning activities that explicitly map out the historical and systemic forces that shaped current educational content. These representations serve multiple purposes. First, they provide an accessible way for educators, students, and the broader community to grasp the complex systems that perpetuate colonial legacies in education. Second, they serve as tools for participatory discussion, facilitating community engagement in co-creating more accurate and authentic narratives. For example, a design education class might construct a timeline comparing traditional African scientific knowledge with the scientific ideas introduced through colonial education. By juxtaposing these, the class could identify gaps, inaccuracies, or points of bias in the current curriculum. This exercise could act as a starting point for a broader community dialogue around what a more equitable, accurate science curriculum might look like.

By involving the community in the design process, we align with Meadows' principle of democratising systems. In this case, the community is empowered to be part of both problem identification and solution formulation, thereby sharing ownership of the educational transformation. Furthermore, mental models—a key feature in systems thinking—can be explicitly integrated into the educational experience. For example, students could be taught to recognise how certain narratives (like the portrayal of colonisers as saviours) act as self-reinforcing loops that perpetuate a colonial mindset. Understanding this systemic structure provides the tools to dismantle it, an essential step toward creating a curriculum that is rooted in African histories, philosophies, and ways of knowing.

In Africa, there is a growing desire to shake off old, colonial influences in education. The scrutiny of Sabelo J. Ndlovu-Gatsheni (2013) illuminates this colonial inertia that anchors the hierarchy of educational systems to Eurocentric content, thus shadowing what is taught and how students' knowledge is assessed. Although postcolonial reforms have swept across the continent, the ghost of epistemicide continues to haunt these systems, devaluing the richness of Indigenous knowledge and learning methodologies.

Design education can significantly contribute to transformative change, serving as a bridge across divides and fostering collaborative engagement among educators, students, and community stakeholders. This vision aims to cultivate educational experiences that resonate with cultural rhythms and contextual realities, challenging the remnants of colonial legacies within curricula and pedagogies. This mission transcends superficial modifications, reaching for a structural metamorphosis that aligns educational outcomes with local needs and Indigenous epistemologies, thus nurturing a globally informed yet locally rooted educational ecosystem. The resonance of secondary school teacher Adwoa Agyeiwaa's[5] observations with the critiques from Chika Eseanya-Esiobu (2019) ushers in a chorus calling for the valorisation of Indigenous knowledge and histories within African educational landscapes. Eseanya-Esiobu's advocacy extends an invitation for a deeper pedagogical transformation—one that does not merely append a chapter on Ashanti history but reconfigures the educational compass to centre African experiences, languages, and cultural practices.

The narrative now intertwines with the intellectual threads of the Kenyan literary and academic icon, Ngũgĩ wa Thiong'o (1992), who for decades has championed the cause of decolonising the mind as a fundamental stride towards broader decolonisation. Here, design-oriented thinking emerges as a methodology for this mental liberation, offering a multidimensional approach to curricular metamorphosis. This vision sees educational spaces, materials, and teaching methodologies reborn in a cultural milieu that is both local and global, enabling students to traverse the terrains of ancient wisdom and modern innovation.

The multidisciplinary nature of design education conjures a confluence where historians, educators, and policymakers converge to redesign curricula. Borrowing the lens of Paulo Freire (1970; cf. Garavan, 2010), who heralded problem-posing education, a new vista opens for the development of educational materials that embrace local art forms, oral traditions, and storytelling methods deeply rooted in African cultures. As we navigate the linguistic landscape, the words of Boubacar Boris Diop (2000) echo through the corridors of discourse, emphasising the interplay between language, power, and education. The lingering dominance of English in official and educational realms, despite the aspirations for Indigenous languages like Twi or Ga[6] to serve as mediums of instruction, unveils a saga of cultural hegemony extending beyond the colonial epoch. Kofi Agyekum's (2018) nostalgia for a postindependence era where Indigenous languages would flourish in educational arenas embodies this linguistic lament.

Design education, echoing the ethos of Ngũgĩ wa Thiong'o, unveils the potential to weave Indigenous languages not merely into curricula but into the physical and digital complexities of the educational environment. Through multilingual signage and digital platforms offering multilingual content, design education transcends academic growth, morphing into a catalyst for social metamorphosis. The journey towards systemic transformation meanders into the realm of assessment methods. Kwame Akyeampong's exploration of educational reform unveils the colonial relics within evaluation systems that prioritise rote learning and standardisation, thus stifling the flames of creativity and critical thinking. Contrarily, a design-focused educational paradigm accentuates problem solving, collaboration, and innovation—values resonating with both modern educational theories and traditional African pedagogies rooted in experiential learning and community engagement.

Francis Opoku, a seasoned educator from Accra, reminisces about a traditional setup where one's worth was gauged by the effectiveness of applying knowledge to solve real-world community challenges. This sentiment mirrors the teachings of both Ngũgĩ wa Thiong'o and Cheikh Anta Diop and Cook (2012), who stressed the criticality of knowledge application within an African context. By infusing design principles into assessments, educational institutions can foster a learner-centric milieu, evaluating not just knowledge retention but its contextual application. This educational odyssey, honouring both the individual and the collective, reflects the deeply entrenched African values, heralding an era where education morphs into a fabric intricately woven with the threads of ancestral wisdom, contemporary insights, and a forward-looking vision.

The imperatives for transforming education in Africa require acknowledging and dismantling the structures that colonial legacies have left behind. Supported by decolonial theorists like Walter Mignolo (2012), who explores the concept of "decoloniality" in depth, the focus shifts towards questioning existing norms and hierarchies. Through the lens of design education, the possibilities for creating meaningful change are multifold. In this context, scholars such as Audrey Bennett have discussed the importance of decolonising design education. Bennett suggests that design education should not only be inclusive but also critical and reflective, interrogating the structures that uphold systemic inequities. It enables a multidimensional approach that considers the complexities of language, curriculum, and assessment mechanisms.

The aim is to provide a nuanced perspective that recognises the unique challenges and opportunities present in reclaiming the inherent richness of African educational systems. In expanding the narrative on redefining educational systems in Africa, consideration of global initiatives and standards that are evolving in parallel becomes pertinent. The United Nations' Sustainable Development Goal 4 aims to "ensure inclusive and equitable quality education and promote lifelong learning opportunities for all" (Carlsen and Bruggemann, 2022). While this is a global mandate, its localisation is critical, especially in postcolonial contexts like Ghana.

A student from Takoradi, Daniel Kwame, said, "[l]earning becomes more relevant when we can see its direct impact on our community. Design projects that tackle local problems like waste management or local history make me feel more connected to my studies." This perspective echoes a broader sentiment supported by scholar Freire (2021),[7] who championed the concept of "problem-posing" education that is rooted in the realities of the learners. Education must be useful, accessible, and directly beneficial to the community to be genuinely impactful. Global educational initiatives often champion ideas like STEM (Science, Technology, Engineering, and Mathematics), but applying STEM in an African context could be more effective if local problems and resources are taken into consideration. Arturo Escobar (2018), a critic of one-size-fits-all development models, argues that design thinking can risk being another form of cultural imperialism if not adapted to local contexts. Here, a design education framework offers a tailored approach to STEM, where the *T* for Technology could incorporate Indigenous technologies, and *E* for Engineering might focus on sustainable practices that are already rooted in local traditions. "Mathematics and science have been part of our history long before the colonial period," reflects Ama Serwaa, a Ghanaian educator specialising in curriculum development. She echoes scholars like Audrey Bennett (2006), who asserts that design education should actively interrogate and transform existing norms: "Design education allows us to introduce these subjects in a way that speaks to that history, using local examples and methodologies." (Bennett, 2006 p. 43). Translating global standards into local practices also demands a review of assessment metrics. If standardised testing cannot accurately measure capacities like creativity, problem solving, and critical thinking, then alternate forms of evaluation need to be devised. Design education, backed by the research of Else Hamayan (1995), who speaks to the importance of alternative assessment forms, offers templates that could be adapted to local needs and global standards alike. Yet, there are challenges in achieving this synthesis. The funding required for such sweeping changes is a significant concern, as are the requisite shifts in teacher training, resource allocation, and infrastructure development. Design thinking, endorsed by thinkers like Tim Brown (2008), but critiqued for its Western bias by scholars like Dori Tunstall, helps here by offering a systematic approach to problem solving, enabling stakeholders to identify priorities, allocate resources more efficiently, and measure impact more accurately.

The conversation about reshaping the educational landscape in Africa often omits a crucial element: the teachers who bring these concepts to life in the classroom. As we ponder the structural shifts and innovative approaches, it is vital to understand the educators' perspectives, a point highlighted in the work of bell hooks, who emphasizes the role of educators in transformative education. "In my years of teaching, I have seen curricula come and go," says Kwabena Owusu, a seasoned educator from Kumasi. "However, the key to a successful educational system is not just what is taught but how it is taught" (personal communication, March 6, 2021). Owusu's observation highlights the need for extensive teacher training that goes beyond updating lesson plans to include design thinking concepts. Teacher training needs to equip educators with a mindset—a new way to approach pedagogy that emphasizes active learning, critical thinking, and most importantly, cultural relevance.

In essence, the focus of training should shift from teaching to learn to facilitating learning, a notion supported by scholars like John Dewey (1916). This shift is not insignificant; it requires an overhaul of existing pedagogical models and perhaps even the roles teachers play. Instead of being mere disseminators of predetermined information, teachers would become facilitators who guide students through a process of discovery, contextualisation, and application, a point also articulated by scholars like Seymour Papert (1993). This approach is inherently more challenging but also more rewarding as it engages both the teacher and the student in a meaningful educational experience.

Samira Mensah's—a seasoned educator from Tamale, Ghana—voice adds fresh notes to the discourse, backed by Paolo Freire's call for education that resonates with one's cultural reality. For Samira, the battle is against a curriculum shackled by colonial legacies. She fights this by promoting a design education that highlights Africa's own ingenuity. As we traverse into the classroom, the narrative takes a curious turn. Here, the echoes of a scholarly vision reverberate through the halls, advocating for a shift towards a more integrated, multidisciplinary learning environment. The outline of an urban planning project morphs into a cocktail of history, science, and social studies, smashing the academic silos that have long stood unyielding. Yet, the path to a seismic shift in education is laden with inertia. Budgets, bureaucracy, and the old guard loom as towering roadblocks to progress. Despite the hurdles, the spirit of transformation is undeterred. The focus pivots towards changing the angle of approach, rather than awaiting a full arsenal of resources. It is a blueprint for change that seeks to understand the mechanics—the *how* that accompanies the *what* and the *why*.

The narrative then ventures into the realm of global paradigms, emphasising the importance of adapting them to resonate locally. The vision is not to strive for a uniform educational model, but to craft a quilt of many colours and patterns—a system robust yet flexible, globally informed yet locally rooted. As the discourse on systemic change in education unfolds, the conversation inevitably steers towards financial allocation. The intricate dance of fund distribution is a pragmatic concern that policymakers grapple with daily. "Should money go into teacher training or curriculum development?" echoes through the chambers of decision making. Systems-thinking theorists offer a lens to view this dilemma, suggesting an interlinked approach. Money poured into teacher training could nurture educators capable of making lemonade out of financial lemons, possibly reducing the urgency for top-dollar infrastructure.

In Sekondi-Takoradi, Ghana, a crowdfunding initiative is reimagining resource mobilisation for curriculum development. The program's power to engage the community unveils a new horizon of collective action and new forms of organising without organisations, reminiscent of modern theories on collaborative action. As I delve deeper into the role of technology in this educational system, a tension surfaces. Is technology a catalyst for equalising opportunities, or does it lay down another layer of inequality? The digital divide emerges as a poignant concern, urging a meticulous examination of technology's implementation in the educational realm.

The application of design education can be particularly impactful in this sociocultural dimension. Its emphasis on problem solving, creativity, and critical thinking offers a framework that can resonate with communal and collaborative aspects inherent in many African societies. Design education does not just teach students to create; it teaches them to understand context, to be sensitive to cultural elements, and to innovate within those constraints. However, implementing this in an environment where rote memorisation and exam-focused learning are the norms is not trivial. Esi Atta, a current student in Accra, highlights this tension. "It's hard to be creative when you're constantly worried about exams and what's going to be on the test," she says. The stress related to performance metrics, often based on outdated colonial systems, suppresses the creative and collaborative potential that design education could unleash. Yet, sociocultural change is slow and often met with resistance. Traditions, even if they stem from colonial imposition, take on lives of their own and create new forms of social capital and networks of influence. To disrupt this, design education must be introduced thoughtfully, taking into consideration the potential backlash from various stakeholders, including parents, educators, and even policymakers.

An example of this comes from a participatory approach undertaken in Tamale, Ghana, where local educators, parents, and students were involved in codesigning a new curriculum focused on sustainable agriculture. By involving the community in decision-making processes, the initiative managed to circumvent much of the resistance that often accompanies top-down changes. However, despite these initiatives and the optimism they generate, the elephant in the room remains: How do we measure success? Traditional metrics like exams and standardised tests are ill-suited to capture the nuanced outcomes of a design education-based curriculum. Existing metrics, rooted in colonial frameworks and serving those agendas, prove inadequate for gauging the nuanced, multifaceted development fostered by a design education approach. Moreover, given the strong sociocultural factors at play, including the historical burden of colonial education, the need for locally relevant and culturally sensitive assessment methods becomes ever more critical. Yaa Gyasi, an educator in Takoradi, articulates this dilemma: "I see students blossoming in ways that cannot be quantified by a standardised test. Their ability to connect with their community, to solve problems, to empathise—these are not things that can be easily measured, yet they are essential." Her voice echoes a growing sentiment that academic evaluations should not be monolithic but rather adaptive, sensitive to the specificities of local educational landscapes.

In this vein, initiatives like performance-based assessments and portfolio reviews are promising. These methods shift the focus from rote memorisation to the acquisition of skills and competencies, thereby aligning more closely with the objectives of design education. However, replacing entrenched assessment methods is a logistical and political undertaking that requires careful negotiation across various educational stakeholders. A pilot project in Cape Coast employed a hybrid evaluation model, blending traditional exams with project-based assessments. Though initially met with scepticism, early results indicate a positive impact not just on academic performance but also on student engagement and wellbeing. "You could feel the atmosphere in the classrooms change," remarks Kojo Antwi, a participating teacher. "Students were no longer passive recipients of knowledge but active contributors to their learning journey." Yet, even as we celebrate these incremental victories, a larger question persists: Are these adaptations sufficient for a complete overhaul of an educational system still weighed down by its colonial legacy? As we ponder this, the road ahead is a long one. Reclaiming the richness of African educational systems is not merely a task of policy redesign but a profound cultural realignment, a decolonisation of the mind that goes hand in hand with changes in institutional structures.

Psychological Effects

Amara sat in her classroom, surrounded by the sterile white walls that seemed to close in on her like an unyielding cocoon. Her history textbook lay open in front of her, its pages filled with tales of far-off lands and towering figures who looked nothing like her—people from a world where she felt like an unwelcome visitor. The weight of that book seemed to echo the heaviness in her heart, each chapter an added stone to a mounting pile that threatened to crush her youthful curiosity.

The teacher, Mr. Johnson, was tracing the roots of the Renaissance, his voice filled with the kind of fervour that one reserves for cherished love stories. But to Amara, each word was like a drop of ink in clear water, muddying her sense of belonging. Leonardo da Vinci, Michelangelo—names celebrated as beacons of human achievement, yet they deepened her feelings of invisibility.

It was as if she were a fading painting in a grand museum filled with vibrant masterpieces. Her culture, her history, her identity—all seemed to be erased, like pencil markings easily rubbed away to make room for a more dominant narrative. In this academic arena, her ancestral heroes were side-lined, their stories submerged in the abyss of footnotes and optional reading lists.

During lunch, she found herself staring at the school's bulletin board, its surface adorned with flyers heralding Model UN conferences and STEM innovation fairs. Her eyes settled on a poster for an upcoming performance of Shakespeare's Hamlet. *The line "To be, or not to be" seemed to pierce her soul. She pondered her own existential struggle: To be herself in a world that subconsciously yet relentlessly tried to mould her into something else, or not to be true to her heritage and surrender to the undertow of cultural erasure?*

Her dilemma was not merely a knot of intellectual musings but an aching void, a gnawing hunger for recognition and validation. She craved to see herself in her education, to find her reflection in the stories told and values celebrated. The absence of that mirror felt like a shroud, suffocating the embers of her identity until they were nothing but cold ashes.

That evening, she sat down with her grandmother, who noticed her subdued demeanour and asked what was troubling her. As Amara spilled the contents of her heavy heart, her grandmother listened intently, her eyes soft but intense—windows to decades of untold stories and unwritten histories.

"My child, you are the living embodiment of our ancestors," her grandmother said softly, her voice tinged with a blend of sorrow and resilience. "Don't let anyone unravel the threads of your identity. Stitch your own story; weave your own legacy."

Amara felt the weight lift slightly. Her grandmother's words were like the first rays of dawn breaking through a long, dark night, illuminating the path to a day where she could be an artist in her own right, sketching lines that celebrated her heritage, while daring to colour outside the outlines drawn by a world still learning to see her.

Psychological Effects of Colonisation

Drawing from Frantz Fanon's seminal analysis of colonialism's psychological impacts, we begin our exploration by acknowledging the profound identity crisis induced by the established educational systems in Africa (Dei, 2010; Fanon, 1961, 2008). This crisis manifests as a cognitive dissonance that tortures young minds. Students find themselves wedged between the heritage they inherit and the foreign doctrines imposed upon them in educational settings. Psychologist Leon Festinger, known for formalising the theory of cognitive dissonance, posits that the conflict between these opposing systems of belief results in a psychological discomfort, pushing individuals to seek reconciliation (Morvan & O'Connor, 2017).

The palpable emotional strain is best exemplified through the experience of a student like Amara, who attends a school where the curriculum emphasizes histories and philosophies foreign to her ancestral roots. She sits in a classroom adorned with images of foreign heroes, absorbing lessons that marginalise her own culture. This fosters a sense of alienation and confusion, leaving her questioning her place in her own history and the broader world. This dissonance is not an isolated psychological hiccup but a symptom of a larger issue that can have a profound impact on both individual and collective identities. Design education offers a potential balm for these psychic wounds. Gloria Ladson-Billings, an expert in educational theory, emphasizes the importance of a "culturally relevant pedagogy." (Ladson-Billings, 1995 p. 466). Such an approach could serve to mitigate the cognitive dissonance experienced by students like Amara, by integrating elements of their own culture into the educational framework. This creates a sense of belonging and affirmation, which is crucial for psychological well-being (Ladson-Billings, 2022).

Thus, as we consider the deeply embedded issues within the educational systems in Africa, particularly through the lens of design education, it becomes imperative to address this cognitive dissonance as a starting point for any meaningful transformation. In subsequent sections, we will explore further dimensions of this complex issue, such as cultural alienation and the birth of elitism, and delve into how design education can offer innovative solutions. In the context of cultural alienation—another psychological dimension of the educational dilemma—students like Amara face a forced detachment from their heritage, a form of loss rarely spoken about in pedagogical circles. Edward Said's work on orientalism delves into how the West tends to interpret the East through its own cultural lens (Said, 1978). The same dynamics apply here, where the educational system in many African countries, inherited from colonial powers, positions Western knowledge and culture as universally applicable standards. This creates a psychological chasm in students, who begin to view their own cultural heritage as inferior or irrelevant.

Consider a classroom environment where Amara is exposed to literature, art, and history that rarely, if ever, references her own culture. A constant diet of such foreign intellectual fare becomes internalised, making her feel as if her own heritage is something exotic, something othered. This experience can be likened to a mirror that reflects a distorted image. When you stare at it long enough, you begin to mistake the distortion for reality. Renowned educational theorist bell hooks talks about the alienation that ensues when education is an exercise in domination (hooks, 1996). A student like Amara might feel dislocated in her own skin, as if her identity is a puzzle missing several pieces. This is where the transformative power of design education steps in. Nin (2012 p. 45) once wrote about the role of the writer to "taste life twice." In the same vein, decolonised design education allows students to taste their own culture twice, first through experience and then through a decolonised designed reflection of that experience. By incorporating local art forms, Indigenous technologies, and community-based problem solving into the curriculum, decolonised design education not only provides a more rounded skill set but also acts as a bridge between the student and their often-ignored cultural heritage. Scholars like Gayatri Spivak emphasize the need to reclaim voices that have been subdued or erased by dominant narratives (Spivak, 2003). Decolonised design education can serve as a tool to precisely do that. Through projects that encourage community engagement or exploring local problems, students can develop a newfound appreciation for their culture and traditions, shifting from alienation to a sort of reorientation. Thus, tackling the issue of cultural alienation is not just about modifying curricular content; it is about reframing the entire educational experience as an act of cultural reaffirmation. As I transition into examining the genesis of elitism within the educational landscape, it is crucial to recognise that the emotional and psychological toll of education extends beyond the walls of the classroom. The impact reverberates through society, as the sense of alienation and inferiority is not merely an individual experience but a collective one. Paulo Freire's seminal work, *Pedagogy of the Oppressed*, argues that the educational system can become a tool for social control, cementing the existing hierarchies and power dynamics (Freire, 1970).

Let us look at the case of Kwame, a bright young student from a modest background. He was fortunate enough to receive a scholarship to a prestigious school, but upon entering, he felt like an outsider. His schoolmates, hailing mostly from affluent backgrounds, seemed to navigate the educational environment with ease, as if born into it. They effortlessly engaged in classroom discussions about European philosophy, Western political theories, and abstract art, topics alien to Kwame's upbringing. Despite his academic prowess, he felt as if he had entered a walled garden, beautiful but foreign, where he did not quite belong. This experience is analogous to entering a labyrinth with multiple exits but no signs, causing him to question his own worth and identity in a system seemingly designed for another class. The scenario Kwame finds himself in is symptomatic of what Pierre Bourdieu described as "cultural capital"—the nonfinancial social assets that empower individuals to move freely within social hierarchies (Bourdieu, 1986). In educational settings, this form of capital is often predefined by existing norms and biases, effectively promoting a form of elitism that favours certain cultural backgrounds and socioeconomic statuses. Decolonised design education presents an opportunity to flatten this deeply hierarchical structure. By introducing a curriculum that values problem solving, creativity, and local knowledge, students from varied backgrounds find themselves on a more equal footing. It encourages them to leverage their unique perspectives, whether those are rooted in rural traditions or urban sensibilities. When students like Kwame are empowered to incorporate their own lived experiences into their education, they are no longer navigating a labyrinth but are rather walking in a landscape filled with landmarks they recognise. One may argue, drawing from Carol Dweck's research on "growth mindset," that such an inclusive approach can foster a more holistic form of intelligence, one that values adaptability and resilience as much as it does analytical prowess (Claro et al., 2016). This shift does not only benefit the marginalised; it enriches the entire educational ecosystem by introducing diversity of thought, thereby mitigating the formation of elitist attitudes. As we continue, it is fitting to address how the practicalities of implementing systemic change intersect with the philosophical and psychological discussions. In concrete terms, addressing the endemic issues of cultural alienation and elitism requires not just a theoretical understanding but also actionable strategies. Here, Marginson and Sawir (2011) work on real-world educational constraints is enlightening, reminding us that lofty ideals often come up against the brick wall of financial and bureaucratic limitations. Consider the case of Ama, a progressive educator in a rural school. Fuelled by enthusiasm and equipped with a curriculum that integrates design thinking and local knowledge, she is nonetheless hampered by a lack of resources. The school lacks even a basic computer lab, and her students have minimal exposure to technological tools that could amplify their learning experience. Ama's story epitomises the harsh realities many educators face when trying to translate educational theories into practice. Decolonised design education, although resource-intensive on the surface, offers a nuanced solution. Scholars like Tony Wagner have pointed out that meaningful changes can often be accomplished with minimal resources (Wagner, 2010). As Wagner argues, critical thinking, collaboration, and adaptability can be taught without expensive infrastructure. Activities designed to foster these skills can include group problem-solving tasks, community projects, or even role-playing exercises. These activities not only enrich the student's educational experience but also help to mitigate the detrimental effects of a culturally insensitive curriculum (Wagner, 2010).

Moreover, the role of public-private partnerships and alternative funding mechanisms like crowdfunding, as demonstrated in the Sekondi-Takoradi pilot program, reveal promising avenues for overcoming resource constraints. However, these solutions come with their own ethical dimensions. Who gets to dictate the curriculum in a privately funded education system? How do we ensure that the voices of marginalised communities are heard when decisions are being made? The challenge then is to reconcile financial realities with ethical imperatives, a point echoed in Heugh (2011)'s advocacy for nuanced decision making in resource allocation. On a larger scale, strategic planning that targets key areas for small, yet impactful changes can prove revolutionary. By identifying and focusing on these pressure points, schools can adapt and evolve without necessitating a complete overhaul of the existing system. This incremental approach aligns well with a Meadows-inspired systems-thinking perspective, which advocates for small changes that can ripple through the system, affecting broader transformation.

In a world increasingly defined by digital interactions, the technological divide exacerbates existing inequalities, creating a new form of digital elitism. Warschauer and Matuchniak (2010) elucidates this point, arguing that the mere presence of technology does not equate to equal access or utility. Indeed, how technology is integrated into the classroom can either foster inclusion or deepen divisions. Even in environments where technological resources are available, there is a lingering question: Do these tools serve to amplify the cultural alienation and cognitive dissonance we have discussed earlier? In his work on media ecology, Neil Postman argues that technology is never neutral; it has its own biases and can shape cognition and cultural perceptions in subtle ways (Postman, 2011). For example, an English-only software program for learning mathematics could further alienate students who are already struggling with language barriers. Yet, technology also offers the promise of customised, adaptive learning experiences that can cater to diverse learning styles and paces, potentially mitigating some of the elitism traditionally associated with educational systems. Researchers like Audrey Watters are optimistic about the capacity of "ed tech" to radically democratise learning, even as they caution against uncritical adoption of technology (Watters, 2023). So how can decolonised design education navigate these choppy waters? One solution is by adopting what Davidson and Goldberg (2009 p. 23) calls "collaborative pedagogy," which focuses on fostering teamwork and interdisciplinary learning. For instance, a decolonised design education curriculum could integrate traditional storytelling methods with digital media, allowing students to explore their heritage while also acquiring new-age skills. Such integration not only makes the education more culturally sensitive but also prepares students for the multidimensional challenges they will face in their careers.

Furthermore, the utilisation of open-source platforms and resources can democratise access to quality educational materials. Benkler et al. (2015) highlight the importance of shared knowledge in modern society, suggesting that community-driven platforms could be a powerful tool for social change. Such platforms would enable educators to share best practices, curriculum resources, and even technological tools designed to minimise cultural alienation and the negative psychological impacts discussed earlier. As I delve deeper into the practical aspects of implementing a transformative decolonised design education within existing systems. These are the nuts and bolts that can make or break a reform initiative, and they are often ignored in academic discussions about the lofty goals of decolonising education or bridging cultural divides. As pointed out by Datnow and Stringfield (2014), successful implementation often hinges on several factors, such as teacher buy in, adaptability of curriculum, and sustained resource allocation. The reality is that grassroots-level educators often find themselves in a tug-of-war between bureaucratic constraints and the aspirational objectives of education reform. Cuban (1990) notes that changes in educational practices typically require changes in organisational structures and policies. This means rethinking teacher training programs to include modules on design thinking and cultural sensitivity. It also involves revisiting assessment methods to reflect a more holistic understanding of student achievement, as argued by scholar Yong Shao (Zhao, 2012). But change is rarely linear or smooth. Educational change is a deeply complex process, fraught with resistance and setbacks (Fullan, 2007). Fullan advocates for what he calls "change management," an incremental approach that anticipates roadblocks and employs contingency plans (Fullan, 2007 p. 53). This kind of pragmatic focus does not lose sight of the larger goals but understands that reaching them involves navigating a labyrinth of real-world challenges, such as securing ongoing funding, addressing the concerns of sceptical stakeholders, and updating antiquated systems and procedures.

The influence of political currents on educational policies cannot be overstated. The narrative of reform is often entangled with political agendas, which can either propel the cause forward or stymie progress. For instance, initiatives that aim for a more inclusive and representative curriculum can be politicised and thus face resistance at various bureaucratic levels. Hess (2009 p. 6) emphasizes the need for educators and policymakers to engage in what she calls "deliberative dialogues," where differing viewpoints are discussed openly, and compromises are sought (Hess, 2009). In this complex landscape, partnerships play a crucial role. Whether It is collaborations between educational institutions and NGOs, or alliances with industry partners to provide hands-on experience to students, these collaborations can offer both material and intellectual resources. Levin (2006 p. 28) discusses the concept of "educational entrepreneurship" as a mechanism for sourcing and implementing innovative solutions (Levin, 2006). This involves not only resource mobilisation but also crafting synergies between different stakeholders, thus enriching the educational ecosystem as a whole (Belfield & Levin, 2007).

In wrapping up this exploration, the essence of what we are grappling with crystalises: it is not just about a curriculum overhaul or injecting new pedagogical ideas. The objective is systemic, aiming to shift the very fulcrum around which education revolves. Schein's (1996) work on organisational culture, deep-seated assumptions and beliefs that underlie educational systems need re-examination and, where needed, reinvention. With that understanding, practicality takes centre stage. Pioneering efforts do not just require vision; they demand a roadmap. Hatch et al. (2005 p. 21) underscores the value of "implementation science" in educational transformation, advising that scalable success is often born from small-scale, carefully evaluated pilots. The key is to be agile, iteratively adapt, and scale efforts based on what has been empirically shown to work. Then there is the looming question of sustainability. How do you make sure that once the spotlight dims, the hard-fought changes do not unravel? Elaine Unterhalter offers a compelling viewpoint here, suggesting that educational change must be institutionalised, with systemic checks and feedback loops (Unterhalter, 2019). Sustainability is not a passive outcome; it is an active, ongoing process. And while the focus here is on Africa, the implications are far reaching. As Mundy and Verger (2016) suggests, the continent's experience with design education could offer global insights on the interplay of culture, identity, and pedagogy. Mundy's work reveals that the local is never just local; it contributes to a global conversation about the purposes and possibilities of education (Mundy & Verger, 2016). We should not forget, the point is not just to produce citizens who can merely survive in a global economy but to cultivate individuals who thrive, who can ponder the deep questions, challenge prevailing norms, and contribute meaningfully to society. In that sense, design education becomes not just a tool but a lens, a way to view the world that empowers students to reshape it actively.

In sum, steering educational systems towards this paradigm-shifting direction is no small feat. It is a mountainous task that is as ambitious as it is necessary. By integrating the theoretical with the practical, pondering ethical considerations

18 Cultivating the Foundations

and staying attuned to the socio-political context, the quest becomes not just about education but civilisation-building at its core. It is a journey, one that is not just for the brave but for all of us. Because, in the end, we are not just teaching subjects; we are shaping futures.

Philosophical Perspectives

As we pivot to a philosophical examination, we find solace in the words of African poet Chinua Achebe, who wrote, "When we gather, the gods throw a feast." This line reflects the communal nature of African societies, where the collective is as important as the individual. This concept challenges the conventional, often Western-centric, educational paradigms that prioritise individual achievement over collective wellbeing.

The African philosophical concept of Ubuntu, encapsulated in the saying, "I am because we are," holds a mirror to our discourse. This principle, strongly advocated by philosophers like Ifeanyi Menkiti, calls into question the individualistic orientation of much contemporary education. Menkiti's writings insist that a communal ethos should form the basis for not just social relations but also for educational systems. Through this lens, we can see how design education could bring Ubuntu to life in the classroom, emphasising cooperation, empathy, and shared experiences.

In this section, we also bring forth the words of Senegalese poet Leopold Senghor, who said, "I feel the other, I dance the other, therefore I am." This captures the essence of what we are proposing for design education—creating a pedagogy that allows students not only to understand but also to feel and dance multiple perspectives, be they cultural, historical, or scientific. Such an education does not just prepare students to meet workforce demands but enriches their inner lives, respecting and embracing their multiple identities.

The philosophical work of Ghanaian scholar Kwame Gyekye offers another avenue for exploration. His concept of personhood, steeped in Akan philosophy, challenges Western notions of individualism. Gyekye argues that personhood is attained through moral and intellectual development and community participation (Gyekye, 1997). His arguments find resonance in a design-based educational framework that values ethical, cognitive, and communal development.

And how could we ignore the potent words of Nigerian writer Ben Okri who mused, "The most authentic thing about us is our capacity to create, to overcome, to endure, to transform, to love, and to be greater than our suffering." (Okri, 1997 p. 12). These words encapsulate the transformative power of education, reiterating our earlier discussions about the potential for design education to heal historical wounds, resolve identity crises, and unite fragmented communities.

Fanon on the Coloniality of Design Education: Stories from a New Independent Colony

I begin this story having returned from a visit to Ghana after a painful three-year absence due to the global COVID-19 pandemic preventing international travel for two years. Now I was home. I had left home in my late twenties, full of ambition and drive, and frustrated with the political and economic system. I look back now, as a thirty-one-year-old man, surprised at my age. I never thought thirty years would come so fast.

I am sure my sixty-nine-year-old father looks a tad older than when I left, and also older is a woman I now spot, who is carrying a big bowl of assorted fruits, bananas, oranges, and pineapples. She saunters, wearing a folded cloth whilst balancing a big plastic bowl perfectly on her head. I call out to her. She skips the incoming car traffic; her feet are dusty. She wipes the sweat on her face with the extra cloth she has tied around her waist. She dashes towards me as I help her place the bowl on a cement stone we both find, next to where we stand. She unties a small knot on her cloth, in which she keeps her money, bringing out different currency denominations. I point to the fruits I like as she handpicks them. She picks them up, placing them in a black polythene bag.

Her clothes are a bit faded; they are green, you can tell they have had a long life. The patterns and lines are deep and curvy, and some circles meet the lines. Each circle has a yellow square in the middle. Her hair is tied behind her back, her skin is dry, and she has puffy, tired eyes. We begin to talk as I help her lift the bowl back onto her head.

"Please, how are you doing?" she asks. "Madam, I'm doing fine," I mumble, avoiding eye contact. At this point, my whole body is sweaty. The armpits of my t-shirt are saturated with sweat. I change my mind and decide to buy more fruit. This time I point to a blue kiosk about 20 metres away. She agrees, and we begin to walk there to avoid the hot 2 p.m. tropical African sun.

She tells me about her son, who is my age. She narrates how the son had to leave technical school to work as a labourer at a Chinese illegal mining site. "It's been three years!" she cries out, breathing heavily. She says softly, "Kwaku was a fine designer, but I could not save enough money to take him to school." My heart is filled with guilt and sadness; Kwaku could have been me. The deep sadness in her voice echoes through my heart and fills my eyes with tears. She picks more fruits for me, this time promising to pick the best ones. She hands them over to me. Then she looks at me one more time and yells, "God bless you!," as I hand over the money to her.

Our encounter was short, but it gave me so much to be grateful for. It illuminated the current state of the country's access to education, social life, and the economy. Opportunities are few and far. The reality of most youth in my country is that the education system needs to fit the cultural, social, and economic context of Ghana.

20 Cultivating the Foundations

I flip-flop through the dust on my way back home. My feet are now coated with dust too. I begin to think about the three years I have been away. My parents look older, my friends have new partners, but my country mostly looks the same.

I am eager to meet old friends and schoolmates and enjoy the Ghanaian hospitality. There is a need to reconnect with my culture and traditions. Importantly, I want to visit the museum, cultural centres, and art and design market. I want to compare the writings of a returning Black man to Africa, as documented by Frantz Fanon in his writings. In the contradicting realities of living in the West and returning to Africa, I am judging my language, my notions, and my knowledge, to determine whether I have changed, and if so, how. These ideas strengthen my resolve to pursue critical theoretical questions in design education, such as Educational free will or educational determinism? or Why does the Black man have no design history?

These theoretical questions have plagued my mind for three years, and I am in search of answers. My resolve to link colonisation, racism, education, politics, socioeconomic factors, and the pedagogy of design education has brought to itself fundamental questions that seek to disrupt the Western imperial neo-colonial programming in the Ghanaian education system. I wanted to do a deep dive into the theoretical and psychological aspects of every aspect of African society and history, to conceptualise a framework that unearths a unique pedagogical tool in the teaching and learning of design.

Back at home, I pick up my Dad's old watch. On the back of the watch is an inscription: "Ghana, the land of freedom, 1960." I remember when Frantz Fanon was the Algerian Ambassador to Ghana in 1960. If I could go back in time, I'd be able to talk to him over coffee at the famous Labone coffee shop. I have always wanted to feel the atmosphere and spirit of the country during the time of independence, and I felt this was my chance to refer to articles, books, and writings to create a simulacrum of 1960 Ghana.

The Walk to Freedom: Past, Present and Future

As I stand here, transported back in time, I am overwhelmed by the passion and determination that fills the air. I am witness to a time of great change and upheaval, as Africa rises to claim its independence and shake off the shackles of centuries of oppression and exploitation. The struggle for freedom is palpable, and it evokes deep emotions within me. I feel a sense of pride and hope as I see leaders like Kwame Nkrumah, with his socialist positive action, inspiring a new generation of independent political leaders, scholars, and social activists to fight for their rights and their future.

But the fight is not without its challenges. I feel a sense of tension and unease as I see the colonial powers and Western countries exerting their power through economic and military means, often resorting to bullying tactics to maintain control. The tragic example of Congo's first prime minister, Patrice LuMumba, assassinated for daring to challenge the colonial attempts to control Congo, is a stark reminder of the high stakes and sacrifices made in the quest for freedom (Gerard & Kuklick, 2015). Despite the challenges and the sacrifices, there is also a sense of happiness and triumph in the air. I can feel the energy and determination of the people, united in their fight for independence and a better future. I am honoured to be a witness to this pivotal moment in history, and I am filled with hope for the future of Africa.

I am transported back in time. I walk past posters announcing the first ever All African People's Conference in Accra, 1960. The streets are clean; the police wear black uniforms with shorts and no boots, they walk barefoot. The buildings are Stalinist style architecture. They have an exterior of different Adinkra symbols. The car that passes has messages written on the back in gothic and sans serif typeface. The number plates are plain black and white, with the Ghana flag at the right top corner. The road kerb is painted black and white. The street poles are draped with red, yellow, and green silk wraps. The men wear huge, afro hair, slim-fitting, single-breasted suits, and skinny, stove-pipe trousers. Some wear the more traditional Ghanaian dress, of brightly coloured cloths wrapped around their shoulders and waist. The women wear kaba and slit, an eclectic buffet that includes many styles, from bold and bright to more laid back and casual. In a period of political and social freedom, fashion is a powerful medium for conveying messages. And though many wear afro hairstyles, most have traditional pattern wave hair.

Delegates for the conference walk past me, speaking French, Portuguese, English, and various native languages. There is excitement in the air, there is hope, and you can feel it in the way people walk freely and talk. The doorbell rings as I enter, bringing both the cold sea breeze of the southern Atlantic Ocean and the dry, hazy air of the northern Sahara Desert —the December harmattan. A soft voice greets me. "Hi, you are welcome." While turning to see who it is, my arm accidentally knocks a cup of water off the table. I sit near the window for the view of the sea. The café is a popular meeting spot for academics, bureaucrats, and political leaders who come to have discussions and meetings. Traditional highlife music by E. T. Mensah fills the room with music: "Ghana, the land of freedom (freedom) Ghana, the country of freedom Paaah paaaph, the toil and sweat of courage."

My fingertips feel the warmth of the coffee when it arrives at my table. The vapour from the cup fills my nose with the thick aroma of freshly roasted coffee beans. I go around in circles with my finger each time I touch the cup, whilst enjoying the music. For a moment, I am lost in my thoughts and the vibrant colours of red, yellow, and green. The strings of the guitar feel heavy in the highlife music being played, and the aroma of freshly roasted coffee beans engulfs my mind. I pick up my bag, bringing out a copy of the newly published *Black Masks,*

White Faces by Frantz Fanon. My plan for today is to finish reading the book while enjoying a cup of coffee and the view of the Atlantic Ocean.

I have a sense of someone looking directly in my direction. I try to hide behind the book as I bring out my left eye to see if my senses are picking up the proper signal. On the corner of the other side of the café is a tall man, about 180 cm, who is looking directly at the cover of my book. He is wearing the usual 1960s fashion of slim-fit trousers and a patterned sport coat. His left eye is somewhat brighter than his right. I am at a distance, so I am unsure, but I assume that is the case. Quickly avoiding eye contact, I hide behind my book. I hear footsteps clip-clop, approaching my table. As the clattering noise comes to a halt, I am curious to see who is approaching my table. I place the book down and look directly at him. He looks at me, pointing to the back of the book cover.

"Bonjour," he says softly, making himself comfortable in the chair in front of mine. "Hello," I say, looking him in the eyes, trying to figure out why he is sitting down. He brings forward his hand, offering a handshake. He looks stern, but he smiles as we exchange handshakes. "Are you enjoying the book?" He looks at me with a smile on his face and his eyes wide open. "I think so." I was trying not to give too much attention to this stranger. He can tell I am lying. The waiter comes over to ask if we need anything before I can say more. "A-a-are you sure?" He seems surprised by my answer. "I heard from a friend that it is a bestseller." I want to burst out laughing, but the stern looks on his face tells me he is serious about what he is saying. "Mm . . . uh . . . it is an excellent book." I grab the book, and I look back, thinking I am going to read out the blurb, to help answer the question about how good the book is. Without even thinking about it, I keep glancing at the picture I see on the back cover and the person sitting right next to me. I cannot help but think, how on earth did I just meet the book's author? I am now staring at him instead of him staring at me. The table has turned. "Hello, sir." He smirks at me as the waiter hands him his coffee.

Every now and then, as he holds the cup closer to his mouth, his gaze falls upon me, but I pay little attention as I am in shock. I venture tentatively, leaning on the table, ignoring that he is drinking hot coffee, Monsieur Fanon, with the loudest voice I could conjure: "H—HELLO! It is my pleasure to be sitting next to you! "Forgive me for not introducing myself. I'm Yaw, from Ghana," I begin the conversation. I make a mental note whilst sipping on my coffee. "I see myself as an educator attempting to bring together and highlight difficult knowledge." My concern has been the over theorisation of Fanon's writings as an academic excuse to link education, politics, and design. I see our discussion as an opportunity for me to continue the decolonial/ anticolonial intellectual path in ways inspired by his writings and those of early anticolonial theorists, and I am excited about the prospect of doing so.

His reply is immediately reassuring. He says, "I am pleased to pass the time with you, Yaw." And so, I tell him. "Frantz, as a graphic design teacher, I have been heavily influenced by your concepts of decolonisation and the erosion of societal conventions in my approach to teaching. My goal is to help my students in Ghana understand and shape their experience of cultural symbols and elements, to develop unique and meaningful works that celebrate their Blackness and Africanity. However, I have noticed that the long-standing colonial education system still poses a challenge in this endeavour," I say, noticing that I am drinking my coffee faster than I had planned, a sign of my nervousness.

"In my research, I have been exploring the history of Ghana and Africa, as well as the literature on art and design in Ghana. I am challenging Western hegemonic perceptions and assumptions that are ingrained in the Ghanaian design curriculum, and the issues of technical and vocational design student training that arise from this," I continue, feeling breathless with excitement. "Your work on decolonisation has been a guiding force for me in this journey, and I am eager to discuss further with you how these concepts can be applied to the field of design education in Ghana."

"Certainly, Yaw," Monsieur Fanon replies. "The belief is that a Black man, in his drive to eradicate racism, can himself be racist. And that the Black man suffers from an 'inadequacy syndrome' in part because of his 'economic inferiority' in comparison to the white man. Additionally, he asserts that the Black man must demonstrate his intelligence and existence in the presence of whites. "In your case, Yaw, fooling himself into feeling he is closer to the white man." "Oh, that's normal; believe me, I was one of the bumbling fools that have misread you!" I thought with a mental eye roll. I have this horrible tendency to excessively flush at the first hint of humiliation. Monsieur Fanon pauses and looks seriously at me before continuing.

"The difference between the coloured lady and the white guy is noted. A Black woman will never be valued highly enough by a White man, even if the white guy loves her, and a Black woman will never appreciate herself due to her skin colour. African women feel that becoming white provides them with redemption and hope."

"The privileging of white skin over Black in media is evident in the desire for Black women to marry white men," as stated by Frantz Fanon. He explains that there is a dichotomy between Black men and white women, where Black men desire to be loved by white women to gain respect in white society. "This is not only for recognition, but also as a form of retribution against the white man for the injustices inflicted upon him. However, this desire is problematic as it requires Black men to deny their own identity and swear devotion to white culture." He continued. "This is the so-called dependence complex of colonised people that employs not only historical objectives but also human attitudes towards those situations." He added. "However," Monsieur Fanon continues, "'The Fact of Blackness' states that if a Black man remains at home, he will not labour for anybody else. The Black man adores his home and has no sense of inferiority there. Additionally, he is a guy who is implicitly aware that even when the white man humiliates him, he takes pride in his stature."

"I believe fragments of it," I mumble incoherently. I am worried he will take me to areas my mind cannot handle. While reading his writing has been engaging, I found it difficult to follow the first time I read the book. I was not yet a philosopher the first time I read it, and I had to go back and reread it several times before I finally understood what he was saying.

"Monsieur Fanon, in my research, I am trying to understand racialisation processes in graphic design education and have been wondering about decolonising the classroom space," I said.

"I would be happy to discuss this with you," replies Fanon. "In my view, decolonising design education in Africa is crucial for breaking free from the legacy of colonialism and for promoting the development of a truly Indigenous design tradition." For a few seconds, he remains silent. His chin is tucked into the hollow of his neck, and he pulls his head down so that his lips are cupped by his right hand. His index finger is placed over his top lip, and his thumb is placed under his chin. "In my book, *Black Skin, White Masks* I wrote how colonialism and whiteness affect Black people who live in colonies, arguing that the link between investigating how colonisation's effects may be seen in language and, more controversially, in creative design works and interracial relationships." Naturally, the first three chapters investigate how colonisation's effects may be seen in language and, more controversially, in the arts and interracial relationships. These chapters, in my opinion, are very important because they look at how postcolonial Black people internalise and reproduce whiteness."

I agree, but how do we go about decolonising design education in Africa? "One important step is to recognise the ways in which colonial powers have imposed their own design traditions on Africa, and to reject these traditions in favour of a more authentic and Indigenous approach. This means embracing the unique cultural and historical traditions of Africa and using these traditions as the basis for a new design aesthetic," Fanon replied. Fanon beams a smile, revealing his gleaming white teeth.

"Educators must pose novel questions to their students in order for them to contribute to the body of knowledge about how to resist colonialism, racism, exploitation, and alienation." He continues, "It is the pursuit of critical education, which occurs most frequently when we examine the colonial encounter and the colonised experience. Educators should provide concrete examples to pupils interested in modifying their education to fit the requirements of various populations." Monsieur Fanon explains how the symbolic, material, interpersonal, and sociopsychological dimensions develop a "psychopathological and philosophical description of the situation of being a Black person."

That makes sense, but what about the influence of Western design traditions on Africa? Frantz Fanon said, "we must be careful not to simply reject Western design traditions outright. Instead, we must seek to critically engage with these traditions and to use them in a way that is respectful of African culture and history. This means recognising the value of Western design traditions, but also challenging and subverting them to create a truly African design aesthetics" (Fanon, 2008 p. 32)

In my brain, I reflect, and I spend some time thinking through what Monsieur Fanon has said. Yes, I am gaining a deeper grasp of why curricular reform and adjustments might benefit students. Nevertheless, my brain is almost straining to keep up with everything that is going on, and I think I am starting to get a migraine as a result. My mind is whirling with different thoughts and possibilities at this point, and I need time to process his comments and evaluate how they relate to my concepts. It is rather thrilling because everything makes perfect sense, even though it seems dense. I believe that this will be the first time that I will be able to understand why colonisation had such a significant effect on the psychology of Ghanaians and how it altered the structure of our education system.

"I see, so decolonising design education in Africa is about creating a new, Indigenous design tradition that is rooted in African culture and history, but also engages with the broader design world."

"Exactly, by decolonising design education in Africa, we can create a new design tradition that is truly authentic and reflective of the unique culture and history of Africa" replied Fanon. He continued, "This will not only benefit the design community in Africa, but it will also enrich the global design world by bringing new perspectives and ideas to the table."

By now, the sunset can be seen through the window. The sun's glare is shining over Monsieur Fanon's right shoulder and chest. It makes the dust motes in the air around him appear to float and dance. The late afternoon hum of the bone shaker engines lulls cars driving down the dusty road and customers entering and exiting the cafe in a soothing rhythm.

While I am muddling through what we have discussed, I see that Monsieur Fanon is checking his watch. We have lost track of time and I sense we have come to the end of our conversation. He is preparing to get up and is signalling to the waiter to bring the bill. He begins to rise from his chair. "Thank you so much, Monsieur, for taking the time to speak with me and assisting me in better understanding my students' experiences and, by extension, my own experiences as a teacher, as a Black man, and as a human. You have introduced me to a slew of new concepts."

"You are most welcome, Yaw," he says. "I also enjoyed our conversation. The educated elite's unpreparedness, their lack of practical ties to the masses, their lethargy, and, should we say, their cowardice at the vital moment of the conflict will result in fatal catastrophes. I'm delighted to have been of help to you in answering some of your questions." And with that, he makes his departure.

Reading *Black Skin, White Masks* has been an emotional and instructive experience for me as a Black guy whose contradictions in a white world have blinded me to the truths of the book and its link to the everyday lives of Black people. Fanon's book, in my opinion, remains an essential complement to the Black African lived experience. Fanon emphasized the importance of confronting the significant ways in which institutional racism affects the ideas, relationships, and everyday politics of People of Colour and white people in a society that is unequal and harsh in terms of racial dynamics.

As I watch Monsieur Fanon wave goodbye as he opens the café door, I feel that, by considering these new perspectives, I have found myself moving in the correct direction. They may be able to point me in the direction of the things that are contributing to my vision of laying the groundwork for the creation of new knowledge and genuine Indigenous epistemological and ontological practices. I view our conversation as a chance for me to continue the decolonial/anticolonial intellectual path in ways inspired by the writings of Frantz Fanon and those of early anticolonial theorists, and I am very excited about the prospect of doing so.

Frantz Fanon was a key figure in the field of postcolonial theory, and his work has had a profound impact on our understanding of the effects of colonialism on individuals and societies. Fanon's theory of postcolonialism focuses on the psychological and social effects of colonialism on colonised peoples, and the ways in which they resist and challenge colonial power. Examining schooling and how teachers' pedagogical, instructional, and communicative practices contribute to decolonising education requires a comprehensive understanding of Fanon's perspective on decolonisation. Working on the minds and intellects of those being educated and those being taught is necessary for decolonisation.

One of the central ideas in Fanon's postcolonial theory is the concept of "internalised colonialism." This refers to the ways in which colonialism penetrates the minds and consciousness of colonised peoples, shaping their perceptions, values, and beliefs. As a result, colonised people often internalise the dominant values and beliefs of the colonisers, leading to feelings of self-hatred and inferiority.

There are different ways from which we might approach the subject of decolonisation and education. First, there is the issue of decolonising our classrooms and other learning environments, always working towards creating a teaching setting that is free of colonial influences. A decolonised place is not merely available for anybody to use at their leisure; we put up a fight, we battle, and we create these places. The idea of "decolonised space" originates in the battles and contestations fought to claim a voice, experience, history, and body of knowledge, much like the concept of community.

Considering this, decolonisation, which may be seen as the fight for an anticolonial space, calls for collaborative efforts between educators and students to address issues about power, history, knowledge, identity, and representation.

Another important concept in Fanon's postcolonial theory is the idea of "the wretched of the earth." This term refers to the oppressed and marginalised people who are most deeply affected by the ravages of colonialism. For Fanon, the plight of the wretched of the earth is a result of the violence and exploitation of colonialism, and the ways in which it dehumanises and impoverishes those it conquers.

The practice of encouraging (rather than punishing) resistance is fundamental to decolonising a learning environment. The process starts with asking new crucial questions that recognise varying degrees of identities and intellectual skills, required for different types of students. It is a process that involves asserting multiple knowledges (based on experience and emotional interactions) and fostering in learners a sense of ownership and responsibility for their own learning by having them come to claim this emotion. This sense of ownership and accountability is a product of the process. It is about bringing to the forefront the voices, narratives, and experiences of those who have been oppressed. It is about establishing legitimacy for practice and experience as the foundation of knowledge in their own contexts.

Learners and teachers alike need to be able to see the connection between their identities, the education system, and the creation of knowledge for decolonising a classroom environment to be successful. It is about negotiating around power and the unequal power relations that govern educational processes. Specifically, this refers to the power dynamic. It is crucial to bring up issues of accountability and complicity so that we can have a conversation about how each of us is involved in creating an environment that is favourable to learning for everyone.

Furthermore, Fanon's postcolonial theory also emphasizes the role of resistance and rebellion in challenging colonial power. For Fanon, violence is a necessary and inevitable aspect of the struggle against colonialism, as it is the only language that the colonisers understand and respect. This idea of revolutionary violence as a means of liberation is a key aspect of Fanon's postcolonial thought and has been highly influential in shaping subsequent theories of postcolonialism.

Through the lens of psychoanalysis, Fanon tells me about the relationship between the Black and White worlds. The Black man, the arts, education, and language are inextricably linked, as these enable the Black man to exist in a social context. He will, however, act differently in the presence of the White man than in the presence of the Black man. These are the ways of adopting a culture and becoming a part of it. Fanon goes on to tell me that colonialism has induced in the Black man a desire to flee his Blackness, which would end in a desire to acquire Whiteness. When he speaks the White man's language and education to his fellow Black men, he will correct improper usage of the language.

Overall, Frantz Fanon's postcolonial theory provides a powerful and insightful analysis of the psychological and social effects of colonialism on colonised peoples. By focusing on the ways in which colonialism shapes the minds and consciousness of the colonised, and on the role of resistance and rebellion in challenging colonial power, Fanon's theory offers a profound and provocative critique of the legacy of colonialism. Frantz Fanon's postcolonial theory provides a valuable framework for understanding the impact of colonialism on the field.

By focusing on the ways in which colonial power shapes the minds and consciousness of colonised peoples, Fanon's theory highlights the ways in which colonial education systems and curriculums often perpetuate the cultural and ideological values of the colonisers. This is particularly relevant to design education in Ghana, where the field is still heavily influenced by Western design principles and practices.

One key aspect of Fanon's theory is the idea of internalised colonialism, which refers to the ways in which colonised peoples internalise the values and attitudes of the colonisers, leading to a sense of inferiority and alienation. This can be seen in the ways in which design education in Ghana is often geared towards mimicking Western design styles and approaches, rather than fostering a sense of local identity and cultural relevance.

Another important aspect of Fanon's theory is the role of resistance and rebellion in challenging colonial power. This can be applied to the efforts to decolonise design education in Ghana, which involve reclaiming and re-centring Indigenous knowledge and perspectives in the curriculum and design practice. This can include incorporating traditional design techniques and materials, as well as highlighting the contributions of local designers and design movements.

Overall, Fanon's postcolonial theory provides a powerful and insightful analysis of the psychological and social effects of colonialism on colonised peoples and offers a valuable framework for understanding the impact of colonialism on design education in Ghana. By focusing on the ways in which colonialism shapes the minds and consciousness of the colonised, and on the role of resistance and rebellion in challenging colonial power, Fanon's theory can inform efforts to decolonise design education in Ghana and promote a sense of local identity and cultural relevance in the field.

Conclusion

In the year 2050, let us imagine a young student named Amina, walking into her classroom in Accra, Ghana. The walls are adorned with Indigenous art forms, and interactive holographic systems bring to life not only the theories of Newton and Einstein but also the scientific insights of ancient African scholars like Imhotep and Ahmed Baba. Amina feels seen and heard; her identity validated at every corner of her educational experience.

Her curriculum is an exemplification of what Kwame Anthony Appiah envisioned as "rooted cosmopolitanism." She learns computer coding and artificial intelligence alongside traditional storytelling and drumming. Her ethics class is not just a peripheral subject but is woven into the fabric of her education. Philosophical debates based on the works of Socrates and Aristotle happen side by side with explorations into the African concept of Ubuntu and its ethics of communalism and collective responsibility.

This education system does not just pay lip service to cultural inclusion but embeds it in its essence. Amina is taught in English, but also in her mother tongue, Twi, and she learns other African languages like Swahili and Yoruba as part of her language arts program. The aim here is not merely linguistic but ethical, reinforcing the idea that her own culture and those of her continental neighbours are valuable.

By the time Amina graduates, she is a rooted cosmopolitan. Her education has equipped her with the hard skills to compete in a global market, but it has also instilled in her a strong ethical framework. Amina has a sense of self-worth, fortified by an educational system that validated her cultural identity while broadening her horizons.

The holographic interface in her classroom was constructed using Meadows' systems thinking principles, portraying the interconnectedness of ecology, society, and individual wellbeing. It serves as a constant reminder that one cannot flourish at the expense of others, echoing the essence of Ubuntu.

And so, as Amina steps into the world, she is the embodiment of an education system reimagined and realised, a testament to the power of integrating ethical and cultural considerations into the very DNA of educational structures. She is a beacon of what African education has achieved—unity in diversity, ethical grounding, and an unwavering sense of identity. In Amina, we see the future, not just of Africa, but of a world that has learned to educate its children as whole beings, deeply rooted yet cosmopolitan, ethical yet open. Overall, the integration of academic discourse with narrative elements, cultural works, and systems visuals creates a multi-layered, enriching mosaic that engages readers on multiple fronts. This multimodal approach serves to link abstract philosophical and ethical concepts to the lived experiences and cultural realities that shape human perspectives.

Contemporary Efforts: Decolonising Education

The landscape of African education is undergoing a transformative shift, marked by critical dialogues and actions aimed at decolonising the educational system. At the forefront of these contemporary efforts are thinkers like Ngũgĩ wa Thiong'o, whose advocacy for linguistic decolonisation reverberates through academic corridors, challenging the supremacy of colonial languages (Wa Thiong'o, 1992). This development is far from isolated; it is a nexus in a broader movement that aims to dismantle various facets of colonial influence in African educational systems. This momentum towards decolonisation is catalysed further by the increasing use of technology as an educational tool. Projects such as the African Virtual University, backed by the African Union, strive to harness the digital medium to offer quality education while keeping the curriculum deeply rooted in African contexts. It is a blending of global technological advancements with local knowledge systems, creating a pathway that could lead to the ideal of "rooted cosmopolitanism" as proposed by Kwame Anthony Appiah (Appiah, 1991).

A sharp turn in policy directives complements these intellectual and technological developments. Governments across the continent are slowly but surely revising their educational systems. Take, for instance, South Africa's Curriculum 2005, which aimed to infuse the educational process with African perspectives (Higgs, 2016). Although not without its critiques, it serves as a stepping stone for future policy formulations, providing a template that acknowledges the need for an Afrocentric educational paradigm. The palpable change is not merely a top-down approach dictated by policy and academia. Grassroots organisations and community-driven initiatives also play a critical role. These entities often collaborate with scholars and policymakers, creating a symbiotic relationship that enriches both theory and practice. An example would be the "Each One Teach One" literacy programs, inspired by the philosophies of Paulo Freire, which have found resonance in various African countries (Freire, 1970). Such programs challenge the conventional dynamics of education, aiming for a more participatory and community-based learning experience.

These currents of change are not just disparate events; they are threads in an ever-changing ideological and practical shift. They signify the collective endeavour of an entire continent to reclaim its educational heritage, spurred by a new generation of scholars, policymakers, and activists. They bear witness to Africa's undying spirit to navigate its destiny, a commitment to transforming the educational landscape into a fertile ground for cultivating not just intellect but also a robust sense of cultural identity and ethical grounding. The revitalisation of African education is a multipronged effort, characterised by both sweeping changes and nuanced shifts, aimed at reconfiguring the underlying structures that shape the way generations of Africans think and feel. These endeavours, driven by an array of stakeholders, from individual educators to governmental bodies, mark an epoch of change, resonating with the same urgency and complexity that our previous discussions of colonial education systems and their critique have presented.

This wave of decolonisation goes beyond superficial amendments to curricula or the integration of local dialects. It digs deeper, addressing the latent epistemologies that are often the vestiges of colonial mindsets. Cognisant of these multilayered complexities, scholars like Sabelo Ndlovu-Gatsheni argue for the necessity of decoloniality as an ongoing process, rather than a single event, with emphasis on intellectual decolonisation (Ndlovu-Gatsheni, 2018). It is not just about undoing what has been done but also about reimagining what education could and should be. There is a discernible shift towards research methodologies that are inherently African, as seen in works such as "Indigenous Methodologies" by Smith (2021). These methodologies provide a necessary counterpoint to traditional Western research methods, often imposed as the norm, and offer insights that are more attuned to the lived experiences of African communities. This intellectual move is not merely academic; it is highly political, challenging the global hegemony of Western epistemology.

Concurrently, there's a growing recognition of Indigenous knowledge systems, not just as folklore but as valid frameworks for understanding and engaging with the world. Researchers like Odora Hoppers (2001) have been advocating for the integration of these systems into the academic fabric, making education more contextually relevant and culturally affirming. Transcending the realm of theoretical discussion, recent years have witnessed the burgeoning of local initiatives to implement these ideas. For instance, in Nigeria, the Teach for Nigeria program, modelled after global "Teach For All" networks, takes a culturally tailored approach, working to equip teachers with the necessary tools to promote a localised yet comprehensive education (Teach For Nigeria, 2021). Technology continues to be an enabler in this transformation. Platforms like the African Storybook Project work to provide open access to stories in various African languages, enabling a younger generation to engage with their culture and language actively (African Storybook Project, 2021). It is a bottom-up approach that empowers communities to participate in the reclamation of their educational spaces.

Taken together, these developments delineate a multifaceted movement towards educational decolonisation in Africa. Driven by a consortium of stakeholders, from theorists to practitioners to policymakers, it marks a concerted effort to redefine what education means in an African context, to remove the scars left by colonial influence, and to build anew. This evolution is far from complete, but the directionality is clear: towards a system that pays more than mere lip service to the idea of African identity and heritage, moving steadily towards a future where the education of an African child is rooted in the richness of their own culture and context. In shifting gears, we should not overlook the power dynamics at play, both in the global educational dialogue and in the steps taken to reform the system locally. In works like *Decolonising the Mind*, Wa Thiong'o (1992) gives us a searing critique of language as a tool of cultural domination. His insights have resonated strongly with policymakers pushing for educational frameworks that are not merely imported but grown from native soil.

In similar spirit, the resurgence of interest in Afrocentric pedagogy shows a promising path ahead. For instance, Molefi Kete Asante's works have gained traction among educators intent on bringing an African worldview into the classroom (Asante, 1991). His scholarship suggests a shift in focus—from education about Africa to education from an African perspective. Local governments are also stepping up. Legislative measures in countries like Ghana have been enacted to decentralise educational governance, making room for regional adaptability (Republic of Ghana, 2008). It is not just about standardisation anymore; it is about contextual relevance. And this represents a radical departure from a past filled with prescribed, often irrelevant, educational goals.

Activism also finds its way into this new educational landscape. Grassroots initiatives are proactively tackling issues that often get swept under the rug—like gender disparities in education. Organisations such as CAMFED (Campaign for Female Education) make it their mission to break down these barriers, emphasising the need for an inclusive decolonisation process (CAMFED, 2020). Another ingredient in this complex recipe is the role of international partnerships. While the colonial past involved a one-way street of cultural and educational imposition, today's alliances are increasingly characterised by reciprocity. Programs funded by agencies like USAID now more often include local educational experts in the decision-making process (USAID, 2020). It is a more democratic arrangement, echoing the global push towards a more egalitarian international dynamic. The mosaic we are describing here is rich and variegated. It involves academic discourse, legislative action, grassroots initiatives, and international cooperation. These multidimensional efforts show a common thrust: a concerted move towards not just altering, but essentially transforming, how education is conceptualised and delivered in Africa. Each thread, while unique in its texture, contributes to a fabric that promises warmth and shelter for future generations, cocooning them in an educational experience that speaks their language, respects their heritage, and prepares them for a future that is wide open with possibility.

Unveiling New Horizons: Decolonising African Design Education

In the quest to redefine and reclaim authentic narratives, the act of decolonising education, particularly within the domain of design, has emerged as a pivotal endeavour in African academic and professional landscapes. The historical imprints of colonialism have often led to a Eurocentric hegemony over design pedagogies, consequently marginalising Indigenous knowledge systems and aesthetic paradigms. As we navigate the contours of decolonising African design education, we tread the path towards a more inclusive and contextually resonant educational milieu. The first step on this path involves a thorough critique and understanding of the inherited colonial educational frameworks. These frameworks have traditionally prioritised Western design principles, often side-lining African design aesthetics and Indigenous knowledge. The ramifications extend beyond the classroom, influencing how communities perceive design and its role in societal development.

In challenging these colonial legacies, the discourse then shifts to the recognition and reintegration of Indigenous design philosophies and practices. Africa, with its richness of cultures, offers a vast reservoir of design knowledge rooted in traditional practices and local materials. These Indigenous design paradigms embody a deep understanding of local contexts, sustainable practices, and community engagement. They offer not only a source of inspiration but a critical lens through which to evaluate and evolve contemporary design education. A crucial aspect of this decolonisation process is the development of curricula that are reflective of African contexts and global trends. This involves fostering a dialogical space where Indigenous and global design principles converse and inform each other. It is about creating a pedagogical ecosystem that values and integrates diverse design narratives, promoting a cross-pollination of ideas and methodologies. The emphasis on community engagement and real-world problem solving within the decolonising agenda aligns with the broader global shift towards more socially responsive design education. Here, design is perceived not merely as an aesthetic effort but as a potent tool for social innovation and community development. Engaging with local communities, understanding their needs, and co-creating solutions are fundamental aspects of this educational paradigm shift.

Moreover, the language of instruction and communication within the educational space plays a significant role in this decolonial journey. Ensuring that the languages through which design education is delivered are inclusive and accessible is paramount. This not only democratises education but also fosters a deeper understanding and appreciation of local design narratives. Additionally, creating platforms for dialogue, research, and publication that celebrate and disseminate African design knowledge contributes to the broader global recognition of the value and uniqueness of African design philosophies. This not only challenges the existing hierarchies of knowledge but also enriches the global design discourse. The journey of decolonising African design education is a complex yet rewarding venture. It holds the promise of nurturing a generation of designers who are deeply rooted in their cultural contexts, yet adept at engaging with the global design landscape. Through this lens, the act of decolonising design education transcends geographical and cultural boundaries, contributing to a more inclusive, diverse, and socially responsive global design narrative.

Teacher Training and Pedagogical Innovations

In this section, we turn our attention to one of the most pivotal facets of educational transformation in Africa: Teacher Training and Pedagogical Innovations. This shift represents a considerable departure from traditional teaching methods that prioritised rote learning and mere transmission of information. Teachers are evolving into agents of change, navigating the complex academic and sociocultural terrains with agility and foresight, bridging the gap between traditional wisdom and modern pedagogy. As we delve further, one cannot help but notice the sweeping changes in classroom dynamics. No longer are students' passive recipients of knowledge; they are active participants in an educative process that is participatory, engaging, and notably inclusive. The landscape of pedagogy has been enriched with approaches that emphasize experiential learning, thereby shifting the focus from instruction to experience.

What is catalysing this transformation? An assortment of specialised training programs is equipping teachers not only with subject matter expertise but also with the ability to be culturally responsive. These programs integrate traditional African knowledge systems with contemporary teaching methods, offering a syncretic form of education that echoes the diversity and dynamism of the continent. The results are classrooms that are as vibrant and eclectic as Africa itself. Visual and pedagogical elements blend seamlessly, drawing on both Indigenous art forms and universal themes in science and literature. Teachers now have the aptitude to connect with students from diverse backgrounds, rendering classical texts and modern theories relevant across cultural contexts. As we navigate this transformative terrain, we will examine various strategies, tools, and conceptual frameworks that underpin this educational renaissance. Voices from academia lend credence to the argument that the regeneration of African education is inextricably tied to the capabilities of its teachers, whom we may aptly describe as the architects of future intellectual landscapes. What we are observing is nothing short of a radical reconfiguration of educational norms and practices. This is not merely an alteration but a transformation, one that benefits not just the individual learners but also contributes to the broader aspects of African society. The vision is clear: a holistic educational system that acknowledges each voice, respects every cultural nuance, and embodies the spirit of Ubuntu in its ethos. With this, the promise of the future appears not only hopeful but also tangibly attainable. Continuing our journey through this transformative educational landscape, it is time to look at the fuel driving this engine of change: cutting-edge pedagogical frameworks. We are not just talking about digital integration, although that is part of the picture. We are speaking of frameworks that are comprehensive, that consider cognitive, social, and cultural factors, ensuring an inclusive learning environment for all.

Now, how are these frameworks being implemented? A plethora of training workshops, seminars, and e-learning modules provide ongoing professional development for teachers. The content is not just abstract theory; it is rooted in field-tested methods and insights derived from educational psychology, as well as Indigenous wisdom. In terms of implementation, some countries are setting the pace. South Africa, for example, has seen the rise of various government and NGO-led initiatives aimed at curriculum localisation and teacher training.

Their impact is not just quantifiable in academic performance metrics but is visible in the increasing sociocultural harmony in educational settings. This contextual localisation is not confined within national borders. It is part of a broader Pan-African dialogue about education, with regional consortia and academic partnerships playing a key role. Sharing of best practices across borders has accelerated due to digital platforms, allowing real-time collaboration between educators in different countries. Even global educational bodies like UNESCO are recalibrating their focus. Funding allocations increasingly prioritise Indigenous pedagogical methods and seek to combine them with universally recognised best practices. This approach is a departure from the erstwhile top-down imposition of curricula and serves as a model for how international organisations can facilitate rather than dictate educational transformations.

It is also crucial to highlight the innovative methodologies that are gaining traction. Take problem-based learning (PBL), which replaces the teacher-as-the-centre model with a more student-focused approach. Or the increasing prevalence of STEAM—Science, Technology, Engineering, Arts, and Mathematics—curricula that move beyond the linear, compartmentalised learning to interdisciplinary explorations. So, what we have here is a multilayered, highly collaborative, and organically evolving system that positions teachers as both beneficiaries and drivers of change. And the ripple effects are wide-ranging. Improved teacher training is not merely a means to an end. It is part of a broader sociocultural renaissance that is gradually undoing the vestiges of colonialism while celebrating African identity. Thus, the narrative is not only about pedagogical innovations; it is also about sociocultural renewal, both of which are interdependent and mutually reinforcing.

Alright, folks, as we near the end of this exhilarating rollercoaster of educational transformation, let us take a moment to visualise the cascading impact of all these innovations. Teachers, re-energised and reskilled, aren't just influencing classrooms; they are moulding entire communities! Their reach extends beyond the four walls of a school, and their influence permeates every facet of society. Think of them as the catalysts in a chain reaction of positive change. But let us not get too comfortable patting ourselves on the back just yet. As the old African proverb says, "It takes a village to raise a child." This transformation is not just about teacher development; it is a communal effort. Parents, administrators, policymakers—they are all part of this incredible mosaic, and each plays a pivotal role in taking these ground-breaking ideas from the seminar room to the classroom and beyond. The narrative we have been unravelling does not end here; it is an ever-expanding saga. The next steps involve integrating these advancements into broader educational policies and societal structures. Think inclusive curricula, community-based educational projects, and public-private partnerships that amplify the effectiveness of these pedagogical innovations. These are not pie-in-the-sky concepts; they are the next chapters in this unfolding story.

Even as we bask in the glow of progress, challenges do remain. Resource limitations, cultural conservatism, and systemic inertia can act as roadblocks. However, the momentum generated by this reimagining of teacher training and pedagogical practice is unstoppable. It is not a question of *if* but *when* these changes will become the norm rather than the exception. So, as we wrap up this segment, let us take a collective deep breath and relish the promise of what lies ahead. A new dawn is breaking over the educational landscape in Africa, and it is painting the sky with hues of inclusivity, innovation, and sheer brilliance. Teachers are at the helm, guiding us toward a future where learning is not just an act but an experience, not just a mandate, but a celebration. With the spirit of Ubuntu guiding every lesson plan and every classroom interaction, we are not just constructing better schools; we are building a more harmonious, equitable, and vibrant society. So let us keep the conversation going, the collaboration flowing, and the innovation glowing. The best is yet to come, and the future is as bright as the minds we are nurturing. Onward and upward!

Conclusion

In tying together the myriad threads of our exploration into the decolonisation of African education, we find ourselves confronted with a landscape of both promising possibility and daunting challenges. We have dissected the historical underpinnings of colonial education, examined the ethical frameworks that underlie educational change, and highlighted the wave of contemporary efforts aimed at reclaiming educational sovereignty. At its core, this chapter serves as both an autopsy and a blueprint. We have dissected the cadaver of colonial education, laid bare its pernicious impacts—cultural alienation, ethical distortion, and sociopolitical subjugation. At the same time, we have spotlighted the seeds of regeneration—cultural resurgence, ethical recalibration, and systemic reform, planted by scholars, policymakers, and educators across the continent. Kwame Anthony Appiah's discourses on ethics and identity have served as guideposts in understanding how education can be a tool for ethical empowerment as much as it has been for ethical subversion. Contemporary efforts—ranging from legislative reforms to Afrocentric pedagogies—are reshaping not just the form but the very essence of education in Africa.

The Way Forward: A Vision for African Education

In projecting the road ahead, the vision that emerges is one of inclusive, culturally rooted, and ethically enriched education. This is not a mere romanticisation, but an attainable reality rooted in the efforts we have observed. Imagine a classroom in 2050 where an African child learns computational thinking through the lens of traditional African logic systems, where stories of Sundiata Keita stand proudly beside those of Isaac Newton, providing a multiperspectival approach to knowledge. Envision an educational ethos where community engagement is the norm, where local languages flourish in academic discussions, and where the virtues of communal living are embedded in the curriculum. As we conclude, the urgency of this moment cannot be overstated. While the scaffolds of colonial education are eroding, the building blocks of a new educational edifice are being laid down. We stand at the cusp of what could be a transformative epoch in African history, an era where education serves as a catalyst for the broader decolonisation of African societies. What is required now is a collective, committed engagement from every stakeholder in this grand project.

It is a call to action for governments, an invitation for scholars, an inspiration for educators, and a beacon of hope for students. As we engage in this monumental task, we must remember that we are not merely shaping an educational system; we are shaping the intellectual, cultural, and ethical heritage of a continent. The project of decolonising African education is not just an academic endeavour; it is a form of social justice, a tribute to cultural dignity, and most of all, a commitment to the generations yet unborn. We invite you, the reader, to become a co-author of this unfolding story, to contribute your insights, energies, and actions towards a future where every African child can partake in an education that is empowering, enlightening, and enriching. This is not the end, but the beginning of a new chapter in the annals of African education.

Notes

1 Twi, often referred to as Akan Twi, is one of the principal and most widely spoken languages of Ghana, originating from the Akan ethnic group, which is the largest ethnic community in the country. The Twi language is divided into three main dialects: Asante Twi, Akuapem Twi, and Fante Twi, each representing distinct regions and cultures within the Akan populace. Asante and Akuapem Twi dialects are more commonly grouped together due to their similar linguistic features, whereas Fante Twi holds a slightly varied structure and pronunciation. Twi is not merely a medium of communication, but a rich tapestry of cultural expression, embodying the historical, social, and philosophical ethos of the Akan people. The language is a repository of the community's wisdom, often encapsulated in proverbs, adages, and folktales that have been handed down through generations. These linguistic nuggets of wisdom serve as moral and ethical compasses, guiding individual and communal behaviour. Twi's significance transcends the borders of Ghana, as it serves as a linguistic bridge connecting the Ghanaian diaspora to their roots. The language has also found a place in academic and cultural discourse outside Ghana, contributing to African Studies programs worldwide. Moreover, Twi has been instrumental in the global appreciation and understanding of Ghana's rich cultural heritage, as it provides an authentic narrative lens through which the world can engage with and appreciate the nation's history and traditions. In contemporary Ghana, Twi continues to play a critical role in educational, social, and media platforms, often being used alongside English, the official language, to ensure broader comprehension and cultural resonance. The language remains a vital part of Ghana's identity, serving as a living testament to the nation's rich cultural legacy and its ongoing journey of self-definition and global engagement.
2 Ayi Kwei Armah, born in 1939 in Takoradi, Ghana, is a distinguished Ghanaian novelist known for his poignant exploration of the socio-cultural and psychological struggles faced by Africa post-colonisation. His seminal work, "The Beautyful Ones Are Not Yet

Born" (1968), is a critical examination of corruption and decay in Ghana following its independence from British colonial rule. Through his writings, Armah delves deep into the African psyche, revealing the complexities of identity, heritage, and the lasting impacts of colonialism.
3 Design thinking is a human-centred approach to problem-solving that emphasizes empathy, experimentation, and iteration. Rooted in the fields of industrial design and architecture, this methodology is characterised by a systematic process typically consisting of five stages: Empathise, Define, Ideate, Prototype, and Test. Central to design thinking is the belief in understanding users' needs, rapidly prototyping solutions, and refining based on feedback, allowing for innovative solutions that are both user-centric and feasible.
4 The mention of Meadows-inspired design invokes the seminal work of Donella Meadows, an environmental scientist and a pioneering systems thinker. Meadows was acclaimed for her insights into systemic structures and the identification of "leverage points" within those systems—spots where a small shift could generate substantial and lasting changes. Her work, although primarily focused on environmental and economic systems, extends a valuable framework for analysing and transforming other structured setups, including educational systems.
5 Adwoa Agyeiwaa, a dedicated art and design educator at a secondary school in Ghana, advocates for the integration of Indigenous knowledge systems into the curriculum. Through personal dialogues and pedagogical practices, she champions the idea that design education in Africa should not only reference global standards but also deeply engage with local histories, traditions, and narratives. Her perspective underscores the broader movement towards decolonising educational frameworks across the continent.
6 The Ga language is a significant linguistic element within the cultural tapestry of Ghana, particularly concentrated in the southeastern parts of the country, including and around the capital city, Accra. As a member of the broader Niger-Congo language family, specifically within the Kwa branch, it underscores a linguistic lineage shared with numerous other African languages. The Ga-speaking populace is predominantly associated with the Ga people of Ghana, whose linguistic and cultural practices are integral to the broader sociocultural narrative of the nation. The language is spoken by a notable segment of the Ghanaian population, with estimates ranging from around 600,000 to about 1.5 million speakers, mainly residing in the Greater Accra Region. Historically, the Ga-speaking communities were organised around six distinct towns: Accra, Osu, Labadi, Teshi, Nungua, and Tema. Each of these towns had a central stool, a symbol of sociopolitical authority and cultural significance, which played a crucial role in the Ga traditions. The central stool, in many African cultures, often symbolises the unity, authority, and cultural heritage of a community, thereby playing a central role in traditional governance and cultural practices. The Ga language, being a key aspect of the Ga people's identity, encompasses not only a mode of communication but also a vessel through which cultural norms, values, and historical narratives are transmitted across generations. Moreover, as with many Indigenous languages, Ga contributes to the rich linguistic diversity of Ghana, which is home to numerous ethnic groups each with its own unique language and cultural practices. While the Ga language represents a crucial element of Ghanaian cultural heritage, it, like many other Indigenous African languages, faces challenges posed by globalisation, modernisation, and the predominance of official languages like English. These factors potentially threaten the survival and vitality of Indigenous languages, making efforts towards their preservation and revitalisation, both within educational systems and broader societal contexts, a matter of cultural sustainability and identity preservation.
7 Di Carlo, P. (2018). Towards an understanding of African endogenous multilingualism: Ethnography, language ideologies, and the supernatural. *International Journal of the Sociology of Language, 2018*(254), 139–163.

References

African Storybook Project. (2021). Home page. http://www.africanstorybook.org

Agyekum, K. (2018). Linguistic imperialism and language decolonisation in Africa through documentation and preservation. In J. Kandybowicz, T. Major, H. Torrence, & P. T. Duncan (Eds.), *African linguistics on the prairie*, 87–104. https://doi.org/10.5281/zenodo.1251718

Appiah, K. A. (1991). Is the post-in postmodernism the post-in postcolonial? In D. Brydon (Ed.), *Postcolonialism*. 85–104. Routledge. https://doi.org/10.18533/journal.v3i9.552

Armah, A. K. (1988). *The beautyful ones are not yet born*. Heinemann.

Asante, M. K. (1991). The Afrocentric idea in education. *The Journal of Negro Education*, *60*(2), 170–180. https://doi.org/10.2307/2295608

Belfield, C. R., & Levin, H. M. (2007). *The price we pay: Economic and social consequences of inadequate education*. Brookings Institution Press.

Benkler, Y., Shaw, A., & Hill, B. M. (2015). Peer production: A form of collective intelligence. In T. W. Malone & M. S. Bernstein (Eds.), *Handbook of collective intelligence*, 175–204. MIT Presss.

Bennett, A. (2006). *Design studies*. Princeton Architectural Press.

Bourdieu, P. (1986). The force of law: Toward a sociology of the juridical field. *Hastings Law Journal*, *38(5)*: 805–813.

Brown, T. (2008). Design thinking. *Harvard business review*, *86*(6). https://hbr.org/2008/06/design-thinking

CAMFED. (2020). Homepage. https://www.camfed.org

Carlsen, L. & Bruggemann, R. (2022). The 17 United Nations' sustainable development goals: A status by 2020. *International Journal of Sustainable Development & World Ecology*, *29*(3): 219–229.

Claro, S., Paunesku, D., & Dweck, C. S. (2016). Growth mindset tempers the effects of poverty on academic achievement. *Proceedings of the National Academy of Sciences*, *113*(31): 8664–8668.

Cuban, L. (1990). Reforming again, again, and again. *Educational researcher*, *19*(1), 3–13.

Datnow, A., & Stringfield, S. (2014). Working together for reliable school reform. In A. W. Boykin & R. E. Slavin (Eds.), *Crespar Findings (1994–1999)*, 183–204. Psychology Press.

Davidson, C. N., & Goldberg, D. T. (2009). *The future of learning institutions in a digital age*. The MIT press.

Dei, G. J. S. (2010). CHAPTER ONE: Rereading Fanon for His Pedagogy and Implications for Schooling and Education. *Counterpoints*, *368*: 1–27. https://doi.org/10.1163/9789460910449

Dewey, J. (1916). Nationalizing education. *Journal of Education*, *84*(16): 425–428. https://doi.org/10.1177/002205741608401602

Di Carlo, P. (2018). Towards an understanding of African endogenous multilingualism: Ethnography, language ideologies, and the supernatural. *International Journal of the Sociology of Language*, *2018*(254): 139–163.

Diop, B. B. (2000). *Murambi, le livre des ossements*. Stock Paris.

Diop, C. A., & Cook, M. (2012). *The African origin of civilization: Myth or reality*. Chicago Review Press.

Escobar, A. (2018). *Designs for the pluriverse: Radical interdependence, autonomy, and the making of worlds*. Duke University Press.

Ezeanya-Esiobu, C. (2019). Africa's indigenous knowledge: From Education to Practice. In C. Ezeanya-Esiobu, *Indigenous Knowledge and Education in Africa*, 55–80. Springer.

Fanon, F. (1961). The wretched of the earth. Grove Press.

Fanon, F. (2008). *Black skin, white masks*. Grove Press. https://doi.org/10.1093/obo/9780190221911-0001

Freire, P. (1970). *Cultural action for freedom. Harvard Educational Review*, 68(4): 476–522.
Freire, P. (2021). *Pedagogy of hope: Reliving pedagogy of the oppressed*. Bloomsbury Publishing.
Fullan, M. (2007). *Leading in a culture of change*. John Wiley & Sons.
Garavan, M. (2010). Paulo Freire's Pedagogy of the Oppressed. In F. Dukelow & O. O'Donovan (Eds.), *Mobilising classics—Reading radical writing in Ireland*. 123–139. Manchester University Press. https://doi.org/10.2307/30023905
Gerard, E., & Kuklick, B. (2015). *Death in the Congo: Murdering Patrice Lumumba*. Harvard University Press. https://doi.org/10.4159/harvard.9780674735729
Gyekye, K. (1997). *Tradition and modernity: Philosophical reflections on the African experience*. Oxford University Press. https://doi.org/10.2307/2585497
Hamayan, E. V. (1995). Approaches to alternative assessment. *Annual review of applied linguistics*, 15: 212–226.
Hatch, T., White, M. E., & Faigenbaum, D. (2005). Expertise, credibility, and influence: How teachers can influence policy, advance research, and improve performance. *Teachers College Record*, 107(5): 1004–1035.
Hess, D. E. (2009). *Controversy in the classroom: The democratic power of discussion*. Routledge.
Heugh, K. (2011). *Theory and practice-language education models in Africa: Research, design, decision-making and outcomes*. UNESCO.
Higgs, P. (2016). The African renaissance and the transformation of the higher education curriculum in South Africa. *Africa Education Review*, 13(1): 87–101.
hooks, b. (1996). *Teaching to transgress: Education as the practice of freedom*. https://doi.org/10.4324/9780203700280
Ladson-Billings, G. (1995). Toward a theory of culturally relevant pedagogy. *American Educational Research Journal*, 32(3): 465–491. https://doi.org/10.3102/00028312032003465
Ladson-Billings, G. (2022). *The dreamkeepers: Successful teachers of African American children*. John wiley & Sons. https://doi.org/10.2307/2077209
Levin, H. M. (2006). Why is educational entrepreneurship so difficult. In F. Hess (Ed.), *Educational entrepreneurship*, 28–42. Harvard Education Press.
Marginson, S., & Sawir, E. (2011). I*deas for intercultural education*. Palgrave.
Mignolo, W. (2012). *Local histories/global designs: Coloniality, subaltern knowledges, and border thinking*. Princeton University Press. https://doi.org/10.4000/nuevomundo.
Morvan, C., & O'Connor, A. (2017). *An analysis of Leon Festinger's a theory of cognitive dissonance*. Macat Library.
Mundy, K., & Verger, A. (2016). The World Bank and the global governance of education in a changing world order. In K. Mundy, A. Green, B. Lingard, A. Verger (Eds.), *The handbook of global education policy*, 335–356. John Wiley & Sons.
Ndlovu-Gatsheni, S. J. (2013). *Coloniality of power in postcolonial Africa*. African Books Collective.
Ndlovu-Gatsheni, S. J. (2018). *Epistemic freedom in Africa: Deprovincialization and decolonization*. Routledge.
Nin, A. (2012). *The Diary of Anaïs Nin, 1955–1966*. HMH.
Odora Hoppers, C. A. (2001). Poverty Power and Partnerships in Educational Development: A post-victimology perspective. *Compare: A Journal of Comparative and International Education*, 31(1): 21–38. https://doi.org/10.1080/03057920020030144
Okri, B. (1997). Whisperings of the gods. *Island*, (71): 43–51.
Papert, S. (1993). *The children's machine: Rethinking school in the age of the computer*. Basic Books.
Postman, N. (2011). *Technopoly: The surrender of culture to technology*. Vintage.
Republic of Ghana. (1992). Constitution of the Republic of Ghana. Accra, Ghana.

Said, E. (1978). *Orientalism*. Routledge. https://doi.org/10.1002/9781119118589.ch2

Schein, E. H. (1996). Three cultures of management: The key to organizational learning. *MIT Sloan Management Review*, October 15.

Smith, L. T. (2021). *Decolonizing methodologies: Research and indigenous peoples*. Bloomsbury Publishing. https://doi.org/10.2307/j.ctv19m61z3.10

Spivak, G. C. (2003). Can the subaltern speak? *Die Philosophin*, *14*(27): 42–58. https://doi.org/10.5840/philosophin200314275

Teach For Nigeria. (2021). About the Teach for Nigeria program. https://www.teachfornigeria.org/about

Unterhalter, E. (2019). The many meanings of quality education: Politics of targets and indicators in SDG 4. *Global Policy*, *10*: 39–51.

USAID. (2020). Education Programs. https://www.usaid.gov/education

Wa Thiong'o, N. (1992). *Decolonising the mind: The politics of language in African literature*. East African Publishers. https://doi.org/10.2307/524049

Wagner, T. (2010). *The global achievement gap: Why even our best schools don't teach the new survival skills our children need-and what we can do about it*. ReadHowYouWant.com.

Warschauer, M., & Matuchniak, T. (2010). New technology and digital worlds: Analyzing evidence of equity in access, use, and outcomes. *Review of research in education*, *34*(1): 179–225.

Watters, A. (2023). *Teaching machines: The history of personalized learning*. MIT Press.

Zhao, Y. (2012). *World class learners: Educating creative and entrepreneurial students*. Corwin Press.

2
BRIDGING THE DIVIDE

Culturally Relevant Pedagogy and Curriculum Development

In chapter 1, we examined the complex layers of colonial influence that have shaped African education, setting the stage for understanding the deeply embedded issues it presents. As we move into chapter 2, our perspective shifts from identifying the problem to exploring solutions, specifically through the integration of rich African heritage into current educational frameworks. The purpose of this chapter is not merely to condemn the past, but to illuminate the future, and in doing so, find means by which education can be a transformative force that empowers the individual and uplifts the community. Our investigation takes an interdisciplinary approach, incorporating systems thinking, psychological critique, and philosophical discourse, as we delve into the possibility of using design education to rejuvenate and reshape the African educational landscape.

Several focal points constitute our exploration. Firstly, we scrutinise the role of educational institutions that, in the colonial past, served as conduits for Eurocentric ideas and ways of learning. We then explore how these spaces can be redesigned to echo the rich diversity and dynamism that once characterised African education. Secondly, we discuss language policies. The imposition of foreign languages was not merely a syntactical shift, but an alteration that had profound cultural implications. We examine how design education can help in re-embracing the linguistic diversity native to Africa, thereby re-establishing a deeply rooted cultural connection. Lastly, we dissect curriculum shifts engineered to entrench colonial power and erase Indigenous knowledge. Through systems thinking, we aim to unveil the deeply ingrained patterns that have perpetuated educational inequality and cultural erosion.

Drawing upon psychological and philosophical insights, particularly from thinkers like Frantz Fanon and Kwame Anthony Appiah, we intend to go deeper

DOI: 10.4324/9781032692647-2

into understanding the psychological scars and ethical dilemmas created by the colonial educational systems. We assess how education led to identity crises and cultural alienation, and how modern pedagogical design can be used to heal and reclaim these fractured identities.

Towards the end, we also turn our attention to contemporary efforts aimed at decolonising African education. Here we spotlight curriculum reforms and innovations in teacher training, acknowledging the challenges and opportunities that lie ahead. In summary, chapter 2 serves as an avenue to think constructively about the future, utilising our rich past as both a guide and a resource. We aim to move beyond the constraints of history, advocating for an educational landscape that is as complex, diverse, and rich as Africa itself. By doing so, we hope to set a course for an education system that not only transmits knowledge but also serves as a catalyst for personal and collective empowerment.

Opening Narrative Profile: Meet Mrs. Akosua Mensah, a Pioneer in the Classroom

In a bustling classroom in Kumasi, Ghana, Mrs. Akosua Mensah, a thirty-five-year-old science teacher, is revolutionising education. Her room is a vivid display of Ghanaian culture; kente cloths are proudly draped on the walls, interspersed with quotes from African scholars like Chinua Achebe and Wole Soyinka adorning the space. However, what truly distinguishes her classroom is not merely its aesthetics, but the radical transformation in teaching and learning that it houses.

The day's lesson begins uniquely. Mrs. Mensah unfolds an Indigenous Asante folktale to explain the water cycle. Rather than rely on abstract diagrams or dry textbooks, she brings in the tale of Ananse, the cunning spider, who navigates through challenges involving rain, rivers, and the ocean. Her students, who often seemed disengaged, are today wide eyed and attentive, riveted by how she weaves scientific concepts of evaporation, condensation, and precipitation through the twists and turns of Ananse's journey.

Transitioning from storytelling, Mrs. Mensah divides the students into groups, assigning them local landmarks such as the Volta River and Lake Bosomtwe. They are tasked with explaining how the water cycle interacts with these landmarks, incorporating their own experiences—family outings, community stories, and local rituals.

"Your own experiences and observations are forms of knowledge," she emphasizes. "They are as legitimate and educational as what the textbooks tell you."

The classroom dynamic transforms. Even the usually reticent students become vocal. Kwabena, a boy who seldom participated, excitedly discusses the changing water levels in Lake Bosomtwe, connecting it with the water cycle. His newfound confidence radiates, and his classmates listen, visibly intrigued and more invested in the lesson.

What Mrs. Mensah is doing transcends traditional teaching. She is empowering her students with a renewed sense of identity and cultural pride, impressing upon them that their cultural heritage is a resource that enriches their learning. The outcomes are remarkable: students are not just more knowledgeable but also more engaged and self-assured.

Yet, implementing such a teaching methodology comes with its set of challenges—scepticism from a traditional education system, the scarcity of culturally relevant resources, and sometimes, resistance from colleagues questioning her unorthodox techniques. Despite this, the evidence is clear: her students are transformed, a testament to the potential efficacy of culturally relevant pedagogy in African classrooms.

Mrs. Akosua Mensah's classroom is not just an educational setting but also a ground that nurtures culturally grounded, intellectually engaged future African leaders. Her pedagogical approach offers an embodied example of culturally relevant pedagogy in action. It also sets the stage for the ensuing discussion on how this form of education is essential for bridging the gaps created by colonial educational legacies and modern African realities.

As we journey through this chapter, guided by the inspiring work of educators like Mrs. Akosua Mensah, we will explore in detail the principles, practices, and potentials of culturally relevant pedagogy in Africa.

Principles and Concepts: Reframing Pedagogy through a Culturally Relevant Lens

In recognising the historical evolution of education within Africa, particularly the enduring effects of colonial pedagogical practices, there is a compelling case to explore the promise of what Ladson-Billings (2022) termed "Culturally Relevant Pedagogy." Before examining its intricacies, consider a narrative juxtaposition. A colonial-era textbook in Kenya, for instance, might have perpetuated Eurocentric views, depicting Africans as "savage" or "inferior," in need of civilisational upliftment. Compare this with a modern-day Kenyan classroom, where curriculum developers work to reinvigorate Indigenous languages and histories. The change in perspective is not just a cultural correction but an epistemological shift, better reflecting the lived experiences of the student body.

In design education, the transformation from a Eurocentric to a more locally centred perspective can be seen as parallel to the epistemological shift described above. Just as history textbooks can be insidiously influential in shaping a person's understanding of themselves and their culture, so too can design education curate a specific view of what is aesthetically valuable, functionally efficient, or socially responsible. And just like a colonial-era history textbook in Kenya, traditional design education has often perpetuated a narrow worldview. For instance, a curriculum steeped in the Bauhaus tradition or the principles of Swiss design—while undoubtedly rich and worthy of study—may implicitly suggest that these Eurocentric paradigms are universally applicable. In doing so, it risks marginalising or completely ignoring other design languages and philosophies that are equally rich but rooted in different cultural experiences. A Kenyan student learning about typography solely through the lens of Helvetica is akin to learning history only from a coloniser's point of view; the story is incomplete and potentially distorting. Let us delve further into the importance of context in design, specifically how design solutions are often most effective when they draw on a deep understanding of local conditions, needs, and aspirations. For example, in architecture, a Eurocentric design education may emphasize energy-intensive solutions that are suitable for colder climates but utterly inappropriate for much of Africa. By contrast, Indigenous building techniques often incorporate an intuitive understanding of local materials and climate conditions, offering solutions that are both sustainable and culturally resonant. When design education integrates these Indigenous insights—when it recognises them as valuable forms of knowledge and expertise—it broadens the student's design vocabulary and offers a more complex, nuanced toolset for problem solving.

Or consider the field of User Experience (UX) Design, where understanding the cultural context is crucial for designing interfaces that people find intuitive and easy to use. In a multicultural, multilingual continent like Africa, the "universal" principles of UX Design may require significant adaptation or even rethinking. Students trained in a culturally relevant framework would be well-equipped to develop tech solutions that resonate with local users, perhaps using Indigenous storytelling methods as navigational aids, for example. In a sense, what we are advocating for is not just the inclusion of African culture in design education but the positioning of this knowledge as a central pillar that informs all other aspects of the design process—from conceptualisation to execution. This is the essence of Culturally Relevant Pedagogy as applied to design education. It is not about compartmentalising "African design" into a niche corner but allowing it to inform and permeate the entire educational experience.

This narrative juxtaposition—from colonial-era textbooks to modern-day classrooms that honour and integrate local culture—is a move from an extractive to a more participative form of education. In the realm of design, it is a shift from a pedagogy that, knowingly or not, prepares students to design for the "Global North," to one that empowers them to shape and influence their immediate environment. It is an evolution from learning how to fit into a pre-existing design world to actively contributing to the making of a world—a design, a solution, a narrative—that better reflects the richness of Africa's diverse cultures and histories. For a moment, let us hear it in the words of those who are living this change. A student notes, "When my teacher started incorporating stories from Kikuyu folklore into our history lessons, I felt seen for the first time." A teacher echoes this sentiment, indicating that the incorporation of culturally grounded elements into teaching has translated into better academic engagement and outcomes. Such voices stand as real-world testimony to the shift towards a more culturally relevant pedagogy. In the context of design education, this move toward culturally relevant pedagogy is equally transformative and resonant, both emotionally and intellectually, for students and educators alike. Imagine a graphic design student stating, "When we started studying the patterns of Kitenge fabric and their meanings, I finally felt like design could speak my language." Or consider an educator in an industrial design course reflecting, "I never saw my students so engaged as when we were redesigning everyday objects to better suit local ergonomics and cultural practices."

The emotional aspect—feeling seen or represented—does not merely fulfil an affective function; it also has cognitive and practical implications. In fields like graphic, industrial, or UX design, cultural elements often carry nuanced messages that are critical for effective communication. Understanding these elements is not just "nice to have" but essential for success in these fields. For example, colour choices in graphic design can carry different cultural meanings. While white might be associated with purity or peace in one context, it could signify mourning or death in another. Similarly, a UX designer ought to know that certain navigation patterns might be intuitive in one culture but confusing in another. These intricacies can only be understood fully if the cultural context is a central part of the curriculum. Furthermore, the integration of culturally grounded elements is not just about adding a layer of "local flavour" but about fundamentally rethinking how design problems are defined and solved. For instance, if an industrial design student learns how to make ergonomic furniture based on global standards, they might miss the opportunity to innovate in ways that consider the local habits, postures, and cultural practices. Designing a chair based on Western dining habits, for instance, may be irrelevant for communities who traditionally sit on the floor during meals.

Now, let us extend this to the realm of academic outcomes. Pedagogically, the integration of culturally relevant content can translate into better problem-solving skills, more effective critical thinking, and heightened creativity. Why? Because students learn to approach problems from multiple perspectives, drawing upon a richer, more diverse set of resources. By incorporating culturally relevant elements—be it the patterns of Kitenge fabric, the philosophy behind traditional architectural styles, or the user behaviours specific to local digital ecosystems—design education can become a more robust field. It not only equips students with a toolset that is immediately relevant to their local context but also prepares them to enter the global design arena with a unique, culturally rich perspective that stands out among more generic approaches. Therefore, when we talk about incorporating culturally relevant pedagogy into design education, we are talking about a change that impacts the affective, cognitive, and operational dimensions of learning. The first-hand testimonials of students and teachers highlight not just an emotional resonance but also point towards the ripple effects this pedagogical approach can have on academic engagement, creative output, and, ultimately, real-world problem solving.

At the core of this pedagogy lie three foundational principles: cultural competence, cultural capital, and critical consciousness. "Wisdom is like a baobab tree; no one individual can embrace it." This African proverb fits well here as cultural competence is not a checkbox but a deeply rooted pedagogical orientation. It moves beyond mere cultural acknowledgment to active cultural inclusion. Within this context, cultural competence evolves into a tool to challenge and dismantle pre-existing stereotypes laid out by Edward Said's work *Orientalism*, which discusses the West's skewed portrayal of "Eastern" cultures. Within this context, cultural competence evolves into a tool to challenge and dismantle such pre-existing stereotypes. In design education, cultural competence becomes an essential skill set, particularly given design's broad influence on how cultures are represented and understood. When students are taught to be culturally competent, they learn to challenge the conventional wisdom and stereotypical portrayals that often permeate design work. They learn to ask questions like: Whose perspective does this design represent? or Could this design unintentionally marginalise or stereotype a certain group?" This is vital in today's world where design intersects with various sectors such as technology, healthcare, and even politics. For instance, a culturally competent UX designer would not merely translate an app into different languages but would consider the cultural norms and taboos around user interaction and visual communication in different settings.

The second foundational principle, cultural capital, elevates this idea by considering the specific knowledge, skills, education, and other cultural assets that students bring into the classroom. Gloria Ladson-Billings' work stresses the need to recognise and utilise these unique forms of capital as educational resources. In a design classroom, this means acknowledging that students come from varied backgrounds, each rich in specific traditions, aesthetic sensibilities, and problem-solving approaches. These can be harnessed as valuable inputs into design thinking and process. For example, a student from a community with a rich textile heritage could bring in unique patterns and weaving techniques that can be incorporated into fabric design courses. Another with a background in sustainable living could provide insights into eco-friendly design solutions. In the realm of design education, the concept of cultural capital can be expanded to include not just traditional forms of knowledge, but also aesthetic traditions, craft skills, and local modes of problem solving. These intrinsic cultural assets are too often overlooked or marginalised in design curriculums that have historically leaned toward Western aesthetics and methodologies. However, when these diverse forms of cultural capital are integrated into the learning environment, it enriches the design process and leads to more nuanced and inclusive outcomes.

Let us take, for instance, a design course focused on urban planning. A typical curriculum might emphasize models and strategies developed in Western contexts. Students, particularly those from other parts of the world, might find these models somewhat detached from their lived experiences. Now, consider a curriculum that encourages students to tap into their cultural capital by integrating local urban planning strategies, Indigenous architectural styles, or even community social dynamics into their projects. Such an approach would not just make the content more relatable; it would also drive home the point that effective design solutions are often grounded in the specific cultural and social ecosystems they are meant to serve. This idea can be even more impactful in specialised design sectors like biophilic design, which focuses on integrating natural elements into architectural environments. A student from a coastal community could bring unique insights into utilising oceanic elements in building designs, while another from a forest community could incorporate woodland features. These are practical manifestations of cultural capital that have the potential to make designs more sustainable and rooted in local ecology.

Furthermore, embracing cultural capital fosters a deeper engagement with the subject matter. In a graphic design class, for instance, students might be encouraged to explore typography that is rooted in their cultural histories, leading to an appreciation of design elements that go beyond the commonly used Latin alphabet. Or in a fashion design course, traditional garments and Indigenous fabrics could be studied and integrated into contemporary designs, giving students a broader aesthetic palette to work from. Overall, the integration of cultural capital into design education not only acknowledges but celebrates the diverse array of skills, knowledge, and perspectives that students bring to the table. It pushes educational boundaries and challenges the status quo, leading to a more equitable and enriched learning environment. This inclusivity does not just benefit students from diverse backgrounds; it enriches the learning experience for everyone involved, ultimately contributing to a design industry that is more reflective of the world's complex cultural landscape.

Lastly, critical consciousness serves as the mechanism through which cultural competence and cultural capital can be channelled into meaningful action. Drawing upon the ideas of Frantz Fanon and Ngũgĩ wa Thiong'o, students and educators alike must become aware of the power dynamics and systemic inequalities that affect educational contexts. In design education, this translates to a critical examination of whose needs are being met by existing design solutions and who is being excluded. Students are taught to not just design but to question for whom they are designing and why. Consider a class tasked with designing a public transportation app. A critically conscious approach would necessitate a look at who uses public transport, how accessible current design solutions are for people with disabilities, or those who are not tech-savvy. It pushes students to consider the broader socio-political landscape, perhaps leading them to design features that make it easier for marginalised communities to access essential services through public transport.

The second pillar, cultural capital, builds on the work of Pierre Bourdieu and speaks to the importance of recognising the intrinsic cultural assets every student brings into the classroom. "It takes a village to raise a child." This proverb emphasizes how such relatable contexts, like a math problem situated in a local marketplace rather than an abstract store in a faraway land, allow students to tap into their existing cultural knowledge. This makes the learning process more accessible and meaningful. In the context of design education, the principle of cultural capital takes on nuanced dimensions that extend beyond the classroom into the world of professional practice. Consider a course in urban planning design: students who can draw on their lived experiences of informal urban settlements may offer innovative solutions that differ markedly from conventional, textbook models of urban planning. Their cultural capital—their firsthand experience and knowledge of the social dynamics, needs, and constraints of these spaces—becomes an invaluable asset, challenging traditional theories and sparking fresh thinking.

Moreover, there is an untapped potential in aligning design education with Indigenous knowledge systems. For example, traditional African textiles often carry intricate patterns embedded with symbolic meanings. A fashion design student familiar with the cultural capital of these patterns could incorporate them into modern apparel, marrying traditional motifs with contemporary style. This type of contextual design not only pays homage to tradition but also helps to keep it alive, creating a form of cultural continuity that is deeply meaningful. Similarly, in graphic design, students who can integrate elements of Indigenous art into digital mediums can bridge historical gaps. They not only express creativity but also reflect their unique cultural capital in their projects. This has a dual benefit: first, it allows a deeper, more nuanced narrative to enter design spaces typically dominated by Western aesthetics; and second, it provides an avenue for the celebration and commercialisation of Indigenous art forms, which can catalyse economic benefits for local communities.

But the impacts of leveraging cultural capital in design education can go beyond aesthetics or representation; they can foster social innovation. Consider students in a product design course tasked with creating household water purification systems. Those with cultural capital stemming from regions where water scarcity is a grave issue might draw upon local practices of water purification in their designs. They could integrate natural filtering methods involving native plants, for instance, turning their cultural capital into a problem-solving tool. Thus, recognising and validating the cultural capital that each student brings can enrich the educational experience in profoundly impactful ways. It disrupts the status quo, encouraging a fertile cross-pollination of ideas that elevates the educational experience while also preparing students to be better, more inclusive designers. It pushes design education to be more than a monolithic curriculum; it transforms it into a dynamic, cocreated space. This is not just educational theory; this is pedagogical practice at its most transformative, harmonising the individual, the community, and the ever-globalising world of design.

Taking this forward, one cannot ignore the third foundational pillar of culturally relevant pedagogy: critical consciousness. Just as design education must expand to incorporate the broad cultural capital students bring into the classroom, so too must it nurture an environment where students can critically interrogate not only their designs but the very frameworks and contexts within which those designs operate. This is where critical consciousness becomes pivotal. For instance, a curriculum on sustainable design should extend beyond the technicalities of eco-friendly materials and energy-efficient systems to include an investigation into the ethical considerations around sustainability. Who benefits from these designs? Who bears the brunt of unsustainable practices? How do issues of social justice intersect with design choices? Let us look at a real-world application in design education—a course focused on technology design in healthcare. In many Western contexts, the emphasis might be on cutting-edge technologies like machine learning algorithms for diagnostics or virtual reality modules for medical training. But when the lens is widened to consider healthcare in regions with limited resources or differing cultural beliefs about health, the design challenges multiply. Here, critical consciousness pushes students to consider the availability of power sources, internet connectivity, and local receptivity to certain technological solutions. Such a shift in focus can lead to more inclusive designs—like mobile-based health monitoring systems that do not rely on continuous power supply, or the use of Indigenous symbols and languages in user interfaces to improve usability and acceptance.

But critical consciousness should not stop at the borders of the classroom or the design lab. Students should be encouraged to carry this critical lens into their professional lives, examining the design briefs they receive and the projects they undertake for implicit biases or colonial legacies. They must feel empowered to ask difficult questions: Whose voices are included or excluded in this design? What power dynamics are at play in the decision-making processes? Does the project perpetuate stereotypes or contribute to cultural erosion? Drawing inspiration from African philosophers like Wa Thiong'o (1992), one can envision a form of design education that not only equips students with skills but also fosters an awakening—a realisation of their potential role as architects of a more equitable society. By interweaving the principles of cultural competence, cultural capital, and critical consciousness into the fabric of design education, there is a compelling opportunity to counteract the residual impacts of colonial mindsets. Through this approach, design becomes not just a technical discipline but a transformative force, driving changes that resonate deeply with the diverse and rich cultural mosaic that is Africa. This is not just education; this is empowerment. And in this empowerment lies the future of design education in Africa, standing at the intersection of tradition and modernity, anchored by respect for the past and an unwavering commitment to a more equitable future.

The third and perhaps most transformative principle is fostering critical consciousness. In classrooms nurturing this attribute, students transcend from being mere absorbers of information to becoming critical interrogators of content. "Until the lion learns how to write, every story will glorify the hunter." This proverb aligns here as students learn to question, challenge, and dissect societal norms, including those which might be residues of colonial imprints. Psychological theories like the dual process theory further enrich this approach by delineating between intuitive and analytical thinking, thereby promoting deliberate, logical, and conscious dissection of design choices and their broader implications. They learn to question, challenge, and dissect societal norms, including those which might be a residue of colonial imprints. Consequently, the education becomes not merely a process of learning but a vehicle for social transformation. The notion of fostering critical consciousness in educational settings is an essential dimension that reaches back to the writings of Paulo Freire and forward into modern discussions on neuroeducation and the psychology of learning. In Freire's *Pedagogy of the Oppressed*, he articulates the idea that education can be a tool for liberation, allowing students to recognise systemic societal issues and then actively work to transform them. In this context, critical consciousness serves as a mechanism for decolonising thought, promoting self-awareness, and challenging systemic imbalances.

When we delve into the realms of psychology and neuroscience, the concept of critical consciousness resonates strongly with theories on metacognition—the understanding of one's own thought processes. The act of reflecting upon and understanding our cognitive biases is foundational to the development of a critical consciousness. From a design education standpoint, this becomes increasingly vital. For example, when studying the design of built environments, students might question why spaces often exclude certain user groups, reflecting biases and prejudices ingrained in society. Such questioning not only pertains to the overt but also to the covert or unconscious biases that influence human behaviour. Incorporating psychological perspectives into the realm of critical consciousness deepens its richness and applicability, especially when thinking about design education.

One of the key theories that come into play here is the dual process theory, a psychological framework that classifies human thought into two categories: system 1, which is intuitive, quick, and sometimes emotional; and system 2, which is slower, analytical, and more deliberate. Here is where it gets fascinating: What if we consider design education as a metaprocess that can be calibrated

52 Bridging the Divide

to encourage a specific type of thinking? By integrating the dual process theory into the curriculum, educators could design activities or environments that stimulate system 2 thinking, pushing students to engage deeply with their projects. For example, a design brief might be constructed to include ethical or sustainability constraints that demand more than cursory thought, pushing the students to scrutinise the full spectrum of their design's impact. This essentially trains them to toggle more frequently into system 2 thinking, ensuring that their design decisions are intentional, ethical, and well considered. To add another layer of complexity, let us sprinkle in a bit of game theory and neuroplasticity. Game theory can offer insights into how design choices can influence human behaviour. Suppose a student's project involves designing a public space. Game theory would urge them to consider how different design elements could incentivise or discourage certain behaviours among users, such as littering or social interaction. Meanwhile, neuroplasticity, the brain's ability to reorganise itself, suggests that prolonged engagement with system 2 thinking can, over time, become a learned behaviour, effectively rewiring the brain to engage with problems in a more analytical and conscious manner.

Breaking it down more simply: the idea is to use what we know from psychology to make the educational process in design not just a skill-building exercise but also a form of mental training. Just like a musician practices scales to improve, a design student engaging in system 2 thinking frequently can cultivate a habit of deeper analytical thought. The inclusion of game theory adds a layer of strategic understanding, teaching students to anticipate how their designs could influence human behaviour. And the concept of neuroplasticity gives hope that these skills, once developed, are not just passing phases but lasting changes, shaping not only better designers but also more conscious and critical thinkers. The philosophy of mind also intersects this discussion by exploring the nature of consciousness and its manifestation in the cognitive and material world. Phenomenological philosophy can offer students a nuanced understanding of how objects and spaces are experienced, providing a grounding for ethical and inclusive design. Think, for instance, of a product design student contemplating the ethical implications of creating a device that collects user data. The student is not just considering the design's usability but is critically evaluating the ethical ramifications of data collection and potential privacy infringements.

Furthermore, it is worth noting that in contemporary psychology and neuroscience, there is growing interest in the phenomena of "blindsight" and "implicit cognition," which explore how people can respond to stimuli they report not consciously seeing. The insights from these studies challenge traditional pedagogical concepts that rely heavily on conscious awareness and overt articulation. Design students informed by this knowledge could thus be more attuned to subtle, unconscious influences on behaviour and choice, from colour psychology in visual design to spatial arrangements in architectural layouts. In essence, the fostering of critical consciousness in design education becomes an intricate weave of psychology, philosophy, and even neuroscience. It encourages a multidimensional, deeply introspective pedagogical paradigm that values the unearthing of subconscious biases, the interrogation of systemic norms, and the continual questioning of the ethical and social implications of design choices. This approach nurtures not just skilled professionals but enlightened individuals committed to leveraging design for equitable, meaningful, and transformative societal impact. And the journey towards fostering critical consciousness does not stop at the classroom—it is a lifelong commitment to introspection, improvement, and, inevitably, social transformation.

Thus, in integrating the principles of cultural competence, cultural capital, and critical consciousness, a new form of education is emerging. It is an education that not only acknowledges the diverse tapestry of its learners but also employs this diversity as a pedagogical tool, making the education process a powerful counter-narrative to historical marginalisation. Far from being theoretical constructs, these principles are finding real-world applicability, leading to tangible benefits in both academic and sociocultural domains. They offer a way to transform the educational landscape into a space that is not just inclusive but empowering, and they represent a significant departure from education as a tool for assimilation to education as a platform for meaningful cultural dialogue and societal change.

In sum, these three principles—cultural competence, cultural capital, and critical consciousness—act synergistically in the context of design education. They encourage a multifaceted, culturally inclusive approach to problem solving. They ask students and educators to challenge preconceived notions and power structures, both in the design world and in broader society. And most importantly, they validate the varied cultural legacies that students bring with them, transforming these into powerful resources for learning and innovation. This framework not only offers an emotionally and intellectually enriching educational experience but also prepares students to be ethically and socially responsible designers. In the crucible of design education, the symbiotic relationship among cultural competence, cultural capital, and critical consciousness becomes not just a theoretical premise but a pedagogical necessity. The interplay between these elements catalyses a unique educational experience that is both intellectually rigorous and culturally nuanced.

Take the example of a design student working on sustainable housing solutions. With cultural competence as a guiding principle, the student will not just look at best practices from Western architectural paradigms but will also consider Indigenous building methods that are more sustainable and contextually relevant. Here, the student's cultural capital—whether it is understanding of local materials, climate, or aesthetic preferences—becomes a vital asset. For instance, if the student understands of the traditional "mud huts," they can innovate within that framework, incorporating modern engineering principles for durability while maintaining the ecological advantages of the original design. At the same time, fostering critical consciousness pushes the student to question underlying assumptions. They might probe why certain sustainable methods are undervalued or stigmatised, revealing hidden biases or systemic inequalities that might be perpetuating unsustainable practices. A critical consciousness, enriched by insights from psychology and philosophy, would encourage the student to dissect not just the design problem but also the sociocultural and economic systems that define the problem's parameters. The potential outcomes are multifold. On one level, the student produces a design solution that is technically sound and culturally sensitive. On another, they emerge as a designer grounded in ethical imperatives and social awareness, capable of navigating the complexities of global design challenges that are inherently tied to local contexts. Moreover, this student is better prepared for the moral ambiguities and ethical dilemmas that will invariably come their way in their professional journey. In essence, the integration of these principles not only enriches the individual experiences of the students but also has the potential to redefine the design field as a whole. It creates a cadre of designers who are not just problem-solvers but problem-questioners, individuals who do not just seek to fulfil the needs of a brief but look to question the brief itself. This offers an emotionally rich and intellectually stimulating educational journey while preparing students to enter the professional world as designers who are not just technically proficient but also ethically and socially insightful.

Case Study Reflections

As we embark on this journey to understand the decolonisation of education in Africa, it is crucial to ground our discussion in real-world applications. This section brings to light case studies from Kenya, Nigeria, and South Africa, which serve as living proof of the transformative impact of culturally relevant pedagogy. Each case study presents compelling evidence of increased student engagement and improved academic performance, offering not just isolated success stories, but potential blueprints for educational reform across the continent.[1]

Case Study 1: Re-introduction of Indigenous Languages in Kenya's Schools

Language is the bedrock of any culture, embodying its history, values, and worldview. In Kenya, a policy change has reintroduced Indigenous languages such as Kikuyu and Luo into the school curriculum, which had previously been dominated by English and Kiswahili. This case study focuses on the transformation witnessed in a primary school in Nairobi following the policy's implementation.

Bridging the Divide 55

In the case of Mukuru Primary School, teachers reported that introducing local languages led to heightened engagement among students, particularly in early grades. It was observed that comprehension levels increased, and students began participating more actively in classroom activities. An empirical study conducted by the Kenyan Institute of Curriculum Development supported these anecdotal observations, revealing a 15% improvement in overall academic performance in schools that adopted Indigenous languages in their teaching.[2] The case of Mukuru Primary School in Nairobi is not an isolated one. Across Kenya, schools are experiencing a similar surge in academic performance and student engagement. This seems to indicate that the inclusion of Indigenous languages is not a step back into the past but a stride into a more inclusive and effective educational future.

Case Study 2: Incorporation of Local History and Folklore in Nigerian Classrooms

Nigeria, a nation steeped in diverse cultures and traditions, provides an exciting landscape for the integration of culturally relevant pedagogy. At the Adeola Odutola College in Lagos, teachers have started to infuse local folklore, myths, and historical events into subjects like Literature and Social Studies. An immediate impact of this shift has been an increase in students' engagement with the subject matter. Previously abstract concepts in history and social studies now take on local and recognisable forms. For instance, in teaching the concept of heroism, teachers utilise stories of Nigerian heroes like Funmilayo Ransome-Kuti or Queen Amina, alongside international figures like Martin Luther King Jr. A survey conducted at the school revealed a 22% increase in students stating they find their coursework "meaningful and engaging."[3] The adoption of local history and folklore is not merely a surface-level change but a paradigm shift. By teaching students through the lens of their own culture, the educational system becomes a tool for empowerment rather than subjugation. Such pedagogical strategies could serve as a blueprint for other African countries grappling with the colonial legacy in their educational systems.

Case Study 3: Integration of Indigenous Mathematics Concepts in South Africa

South Africa offers an intriguing case for the incorporation of culturally relevant pedagogy in education. A school in Cape Town has pioneered the integration of Indigenous mathematical concepts into their curriculum, a notable stride in the quest for cultural relevancy in education. The traditional counting system of the San people, which employs base 12 instead of base 10, has been integrated into elementary math lessons. This not only acknowledges the culture but also introduces students to alternative numerical systems. Postintervention testing revealed a 16% increase in students' mathematical problem-solving skills.[4] This South African initiative suggests that the realm of culturally relevant pedagogy need not be confined to the arts and social sciences. The impact in terms of student engagement and performance, and the acknowledgment of a culturally diverse mathematical system, creates a multifaceted win. The journey toward decolonising education in Africa is fraught with challenges but laden with opportunities. Schools across the continent can learn from these cases, forging their path towards a more equitable and culturally resonant educational landscape. In the sections to follow, we will delve deeper into quantifiable benefits and the long-term implications of these transformative educational models.

Challenges on the Road Ahead

As promising as the journey toward culturally relevant pedagogy is, it comes with an array of challenges that educators, policymakers, and communities must grapple with. To appreciate these challenges is to arm ourselves with the tools required for effective reform. This section focuses on two primary categories of challenges: resource constraints and cultural and institutional resistance. In advancing toward a more inclusive and culturally relevant educational landscape, there exists a multitude of impediments, spanning from financial limitations to ingrained institutional ideologies. Understanding these challenges not only illuminates the hurdles we must overcome but also equips us with the insights needed for transformative action. Starting with resource constraints, the issue is not merely monetary, although funding is indeed a significant concern. Financial support is essential for designing new curricula, facilitating teacher training, and obtaining culturally diverse educational materials. Additionally, the technical infrastructure needed for empirical research to gauge the effectiveness of new pedagogical methods often falls by the wayside in schools that are already struggling with underfunding. Here, Paulo Freire's seminal work, *Pedagogy of the Oppressed*, offers a pertinent lens. Freire elucidated that education should be a "practice of freedom" that liberates individuals from various forms of oppression. However, this idealistic vision of education cannot be realised without adequate resources, aligning with Nelson Mandela's notion that education is the most potent tool for societal transformation.

Yet, even when resources are available, the second category of challenges comes into play—cultural and institutional resistance. Schools and educational institutions are, by their nature, highly resistant to change. Factors contributing to this rigidity include established curricula, pressure to perform well on standardised tests, and sometimes even political and nationalistic agendas. To make room for diverse cultural material, it is not enough to simply replace a few textbooks; an entire shift in institutional culture is required. At this point, Freire's critique of the "banking model of education" becomes highly relevant. This model views students as passive vessels waiting to be filled with standardised knowledge, leaving no room for contextual or critical thinking. In a way, the banking model serves to perpetuate existing systems of inequality and cultural erasure, echoing academic Henry Giroux's views on how educational institutions can unwittingly serve as instruments of ideological perpetuation.

In the quest for culturally relevant pedagogy, the role of design and design education often goes underexplored, yet they can be integral to reframing and enacting educational reform. Design, in its most fundamental form, is about problem solving and creating solutions that are both functional and aesthetically pleasing. When applied to education, design thinking encourages an interdisciplinary approach, inviting us to consider multiple perspectives, including those typically marginalised or excluded. Design education specifically challenges the traditional "banking model" critiqued by Paulo Freire by promoting a participatory learning environment. Students are not just passive recipients of prepackaged knowledge; they are encouraged to co-create, iterate, and adapt—activities that align well with the principles of culturally relevant pedagogy. It extends Freire's "practice of freedom" by actively involving students in the learning process, allowing them to incorporate their cultural backgrounds into their projects and problem-solving approaches. Design as a discipline also has its own set of cultural competencies. The history of design is rich and diverse, with deep-rooted influences from multiple cultures worldwide. Thus, a design education that incorporates these various cultural elements not only enriches the learning experience but also serves as a counternarrative to the Eurocentric focus that often prevails in educational settings.

However, implementing design-focused, culturally relevant pedagogy comes with its unique set of challenges. Resource constraints become even more complex when one considers the materials and software often required for effective design education. On the flip side, the highly interactive and project-based nature of design classes can sometimes clash with established curricula that emphasize theoretical knowledge and rote learning. Moreover, there is the challenge of preparing educators who are proficient in both design and the specific cultural contexts of their students, a challenge that demands a rethinking of teacher training programs. Contextualising these insights within the broader struggle for culturally relevant pedagogy brings a nuanced layer to our understanding of what educational reform entails. It is not merely a matter of updating reading lists or bringing in guest speakers from diverse backgrounds. The goal is a more radical rethinking of what education could look like, a rethinking that design and design education can significantly inform and shape.

Bringing these considerations together, it is evident that the path toward implementing culturally relevant pedagogy is riddled with obstacles, both tangible and ideological. Even so, understanding these challenges provides a stepping stone for constructing strategies that engage both policy and grassroots actions, aimed at dismantling these barriers. This sets the stage for the recommendations and strategies explored in the subsequent sections, guiding us in the concerted effort to foster an educational environment that is as diverse and inclusive as the world it seeks to represent.

Resource Constraints

Resource constraints serve as a significant hurdle to the meaningful implementation of culturally relevant pedagogy, especially in design and design education.[5] The issue is multifaceted, affecting not just the availability of tangible assets like design software, studio space, or art supplies, but also intellectual resources like qualified teachers, updated curricula, and access to research. Here, we encounter a fundamental tension between the need for quality education that reflects cultural diversity and the scarcity of resources to make this a reality. In a well-resourced environment, design education can serve as an especially powerful tool for such empowerment. However, the lack of adequate resources can greatly restrict the scope of Freirean education, reducing it to a mere transactional activity devoid of its liberatory potential. The ideas of John Dewey also offer valuable insights here. Dewey, in his progressive educational philosophy, emphasized the importance of experiential learning, which is a cornerstone of design education (Dewey, 1916). Learning by doing, he argued, enriches educational experience and makes it more engaging and effective. However, this approach inherently requires resources—be it materials for a design project, software for digital designs, or even trained professionals who can guide experiential learning. In underfunded settings, the absence of these resources can cause the educational experience to revert to passive learning modes, thereby defeating Dewey's ideal of an active, engaged educational process.[6]

From a philosophical standpoint, the discussion of resource constraints raises larger questions about the nature and purpose of education. Is it merely to prepare students for gainful employment, or is it a broader endeavour aimed at equipping them with the intellectual tools to critique and shape the world around them? The limitations posed by resource constraints often force this question to the forefront, as they can make the latter objective seem like a luxury rather than a right. When applied to design education, the question becomes even more pressing, given the discipline's potential for fostering both professional skills and critical thinking. In summary, the issue of resource constraints is not merely logistical but also profoundly philosophical and ethical. It touches upon the most basic questions about what education should accomplish and for whom. The insights of scholars like Freire and Dewey, when applied to the realm of design and design education, serve to deepen our understanding of these challenges, pushing us to consider not just the practical but also the ideological impediments to educational equity and empowerment.

Cultural and Institutional Resistance

Cultural and institutional resistance in educational reform manifests in a variety of nuanced ways, becoming a complex battleground of ideologies, traditions, and power dynamics. It is not merely an issue of unwillingness to adapt; rather, it is a multifaceted resistance rooted in deep-seated beliefs and systemic structures. To dig deeper into institutional reluctance, we can consider Foucault's (2016) views on the relationship between knowledge and power. In his work *Discipline and Punish*, Foucault argues that institutions like schools serve as mechanisms of social control, normalising certain behaviours and ideologies. In this context, an educational system that adheres to traditional or nationalistic curricula serves not just an educational function, but a political one, reinforcing the existing power structures and cultural norms. Therefore, the resistance to culturally relevant pedagogy is not simply about maintaining academic status quo; it is a struggle to retain social and political control.

Judith Butler's concept of "performativity" can also offer an angle for understanding institutional resistance (Butler, 2009). Butler's notion that identity is socially constructed through repeated performances could be applied to educational institutions, which perform their own sort of institutional identity through the repetition of established curricula and teaching methods (Butler, 2009). Altering this performance is not merely an administrative adjustment; it represents a profound identity shift, one that schools and educators may be loath to undertake. Goodson (2005) work on the politics of curriculum adds another layer to this discussion. Goodson emphasizes the complexity behind curriculum choices, which are often the result of political, social, and even economic factors (Goodson, 2005). For example, subjects that are perceived to contribute more directly to economic productivity may be favoured in the curriculum, at the expense of subjects that promote critical or cultural awareness. This economic motivation can add an additional layer of resistance to the implementation of culturally relevant pedagogy, particularly in disciplines that are not traditionally viewed as directly contributing to economic growth. This makes the challenge of cultural and institutional resistance to pedagogical change not just a logistical hurdle but an ideological and existential one. It is a resistance deeply entwined with issues of identity, power, and the nature of education itself. Understanding this allows us to see why even well-intentioned efforts to inject cultural relevance into education may be met with strong, multifaceted resistance. This understanding also primes us to better strategise how to mitigate this resistance, armed with the deep insights provided by renowned scholars across various fields.

A Designer's Autoethnographic Journey through Culturally Relevant Pedagogy: Strategies and Roadmaps

In my studio, surrounded by the tools of the trade—drafting pencils, grids of screen pixels, and sheets of tracing paper—I find myself entangled in a web of connections far beyond the technical aspects of design. Each line I draw or shape I mould reflects a broader mosaic: one that includes my cultural identity, educational background, and a variety of societal structures. In this sense, the act of design is inseparable from the lived realities of identity and cultural background. When I engage with design software or sketch a new concept, I'm navigating an intricate terrain of personal and collective experiences.

You see, design for me is not merely a skill or a job but a conversation— a dialogue between my own heritage and the world around me. The layers of this dialogue are thickened by the reality that design education is so often constructed within a framework that prioritises a singular, often Eurocentric, set of aesthetics and principles. As a result, design and design education become arenas where cultural narratives either find expression or face erasure.

The drafting table, therefore, is not just a piece of furniture; it's a battleground and a meeting place, a site of tensions and harmonies. Each project I embark on becomes a microcosm of the larger debates about cultural relevance and representation in education. Can the principles of modernism coexist with Indigenous African aesthetics? How does the Bauhaus movement dialogue with the intricate patterns found in Islamic art? These are not just theoretical inquiries. They are lived questions that surface every time I, or any other designer influenced by diverse cultural histories, sit down to create. For many years, I felt like an outlier in design classes where the curricula seemed detached from the multifaceted realities of a global society. This was not because of a lack of talent or interest among diverse students, but because of a pedagogical framework that was narrow in its scope. It's one thing to discuss design theories; it's another entirely to see how they come to life in different parts of the world, influenced by distinct cultural narratives.

I realised that this sense of alienation wasn't just a personal problem but a symptom of a system that needed reconsideration. If design is to be truly universal, design education must be inclusive and sensitive to a broad range of cultural values and aesthetics. The classroom can be a starting point for this transformation, where educators and students alike acknowledge and embrace the plurality of design—its histories, its present, and its future potentials.

As we move forward, the structural barriers come into sharper focus. I recall my initial encounters with design education, where the syllabi were replete with canonical Western designers and movements. My attempts to integrate non-Western influences were often met with puzzlement or outright dismissal. This was not a deliberate act of exclusion by my educators, but rather a consequence of a system that had been designed with a narrow scope of what "good design" means. Within this system, my work—and the work of others who drew from varied cultural wellsprings—was often marginalised, relegated to the realm of the "exotic" or "alternative," rather than as valid contributions to the design canon.

And yet, despite these barriers, opportunities for transformation shimmered through the cracks. I remember one particular project where I decided to incorporate visual motifs inspired by my own cultural heritage. Rather than isolation, the project generated interest and sparked a conversation among faculty and students alike. That simple act of aesthetic resistance became a point of entry for discussions about the limitations and potential expansiveness of our design education.

In my experience, these aren't just isolated moments but tiny revolutions that have the potential to recalibrate the coordinates of design education. They demonstrate the powerful role that educators and institutions can play if they become aware of their potential for inclusivity. I often think about the responsibility of educational policymakers to recognise and break down these systemic barriers. By widening the curriculum and integrating a more diverse set of design influences, we make room for a richer, more nuanced understanding of what design can be.

Let's also not underestimate the grassroots level movements that are gaining traction. Student-led initiatives, such as exhibitions focusing on non-Western design traditions or guest lectures from designers who bring diverse perspectives, are starting to fill the gaps left by traditional curricula. These efforts should not be seen as extracurricular but should be integrated into the educational framework itself.

So, as we delve deeper into the structural, pedagogical, and societal intricacies in the upcoming sections, keep in mind that these aren't abstract challenges but lived experiences. They're apparent in every design project that challenges traditional norms, in every classroom dialogue that acknowledges the diversity of our cultural fabric, and in every policy that aims to democratize our collective perception of design. This journey may be fraught with tension, but it's in navigating these tensions that we find avenues for meaningful change.

Decolonised Design in Action: A Practical Classroom Guide

When delving into the complexities of implementing decolonised design practices, one does not have to look far to find success stories that can serve as blueprints for actionable change. Drawing from real-world scenarios, this section offers step-by-step practical examples demonstrating how educators can embed these practices within the classroom.

Case Study 1: Embracing Indigenous Patterns

Consider a scenario in a design course classroom:

1. **Identification of Gap:** An instructor recognises the predominantly Western focus of the curriculum and sees an opportunity to incorporate Indigenous patterns.
2. **Research & Consultation:** Before introducing these patterns, the instructor spends time learning about their origins, meanings, and significance. They might even reach out to Indigenous community leaders or experts for insights and guidance.
3. **Classroom Introduction:** The instructor presents the patterns to students, contextualising them within their cultural and historical framework. This is not just about design; it is about respecting and understanding the narratives behind each pattern.
4. **Student Engagement:** Students are encouraged to discuss, critique, and explore these patterns. A class discussion could be initiated, where students share their perceptions, ask questions, and express their viewpoints.
5. **Application in Design:** Tasked with a project, a student chooses to integrate these patterns in their design. But rather than using them as mere decorative elements, they showcase the patterns" deeper cultural and aesthetic significance.
6. **Reflection & Feedback:** After project completion, students reflect on their design choices, discussing challenges faced, the thought process behind their design decisions, and feedback from peers and the instructor.

Through such a structured approach, what unfolds is not just an academic exercise but a meaningful engagement with design that is rooted in cultural appreciation and sensitivity.

Scalability & Replication

The success of such classroom experiences holds valuable lessons for broader application. By documenting these steps, other educators can replicate this model, tailoring it to their specific contexts. The key is to discern the principles at play: respect for Indigenous knowledge, active student engagement, and continuous reflection.

However, the journey to integrate decolonised design is not without its challenges. For every success story, there might be hurdles, setbacks, or even failures. But these are equally valuable. For instance, a similar approach might face resistance in a different educational setting due to pre-existing biases or lack of resources.

Behind-the-Scenes Decisions

Beyond the visible classroom activities lie numerous decisions and processes. Consider faculty meetings where curricula are debated, or budget discussions determining resource allocation. Such behind-the-scenes moments provide a fuller picture of the practical challenges and compromises faced when striving for a decolonised design curriculum.

These narratives are not just anecdotal; they provide a detailed roadmap. They highlight both the practical steps taken and the underlying ethos that should guide such endeavours. Understanding the intertwined nature of these decisions—pedagogical, administrative, and even financial—is crucial for a holistic appreciation of the decolonisation journey in design education.

Student Creativity: A Portfolio of Outcomes

Do not just take my word for it—let us turn the pages of a portfolio, revealing the creative outcomes born from culturally relevant pedagogy. These are projects I have witnessed first-hand—students engaging with design through the lens of their own cultural contexts, thereby enriching both their work and the educational setting. From digital artwork inspired by African geometric patterns to urban planning projects that respect Indigenous histories, these are more than just assignments; they are affirmations of identity and capability.

This portfolio does not merely showcase finished works but outlines the process, the layers of thought, creativity, and cultural input that go into each project. Let me walk you through an example, a project in which a student used design thinking to create a community garden plan inspired by permaculture principles of her native culture. The garden was not just designed to be sustainable; it was a reproduction of a farming system used in her ancestral land. She combined contemporary design tools with traditional ecological knowledge, resulting in a project that was technologically up to date yet deeply rooted in her cultural background.

Here is another: a student project aimed at redesigning a public transportation system. Drawing upon the student's own experiences with accessibility and crowding in public transport back in their home country, the design incorporated features that would make public transit more inclusive for people of different physical abilities, ages, and social strata. The plans even included QR codes linking to oral histories of the neighbourhood, blending the functional and the historical in a way that honoured the community's diverse experiences.

These projects do not just earn grades; they earn a sense of ownership and belonging among students. They reflect the pluralism that is not just tolerated but celebrated and leveraged for educational benefit. And because these projects often focus on solving real-world issues that resonate with the students, they are intrinsically motivated, driving a more effective and engaging learning process.

The importance of this portfolio is in its capacity to serve as both a repository and a spotlight. It archives the varied ways in which culturally relevant design education can manifest, and it highlights the kind of meaningful work that can be produced when students are permitted—and encouraged—to incorporate their complete selves into their academic endeavours. The portfolio challenges the often-monolithic view of what constitutes "good design" by showcasing a kaleidoscope of aesthetic and functional approaches that are culturally rooted and socially responsive.

This is not merely a selection of student projects; it is a gallery of possibilities, a testament to the impact of aligning pedagogical strategies with cultural relevance. Each entry serves as evidence that this approach does not just make for better designers but creates more engaged and thoughtful citizens, capable of understanding and addressing the complex challenges of our diversifying world. If you were to flip further into this portfolio, you would also find an array of collaborative projects that speak to the potential of intercultural exchange within a design education framework. For instance, one project features a cross-cultural design collaboration between students from diverse ethnic backgrounds who developed a multi-language emergency response app. This was not merely an exercise in software design but a lived example of how various cultural perspectives can coalesce to solve a universal problem. Through the collaborative process, the students navigated language barriers, reconciled differing design aesthetics, and debated the ethical implications of data usage. The resulting app became a microcosm of the world they are preparing to enter, one that is interconnected and multifaceted.

What is particularly striking about these collaborative efforts is the pedagogical value they offer. They serve as real-world simulations where students must negotiate, adapt, and merge different cultural logics and ethics, thereby fostering a level of intercultural competence rarely achieved in traditional design curricula. It is in these collaborative spaces that students learn to see their cultural identities not as limiting factors but as strengths, as viewpoints that enrich the collective outcome. While the portfolio predominantly features digital and physical projects, it also includes reflective essays and self-assessments, encouraging students to articulate their experiences and challenges in navigating culturally relevant pedagogy. These reflective pieces serve a dual purpose. First, they provide a metacognitive element, allowing students to think about their thinking, thereby deepening their learning experience. Second, they offer educators valuable feedback for refining this pedagogical approach. In essence, the portfolio becomes a dialogic space, a cyclical feedback loop that benefits both students and educators.

Another significant element worth noting is how the portfolio extends its impact beyond the academic setting. Many of these projects find their way into community presentations, local exhibitions, and even policy proposals, thereby creating ripples in broader societal ponds. Students, often marginalised in traditional academic settings, find their voice amplified, their work validated, and their cultural capital recognised and celebrated. By showcasing their projects in these external forums, we are not just validating their academic efforts but advocating for a more inclusive and diverse design industry and, by extension, society.

In sum, this portfolio is not just a collection of student work. It is a narrative, a layered story that provides compelling evidence for the power and necessity of culturally relevant pedagogy in design education. It tells us that when we make room for diverse cultural voices, we are not diluting academic rigor or design excellence. On the contrary, we are enriching it, making it more robust, more comprehensive, and significantly more relevant in a globalised world.

A Spoken Word Finale: Mother Africa Speaks

The journey through this chapter has been both an intellectual exploration and a deeply personal narrative, aimed at unearthing the intricate layers of culturally relevant pedagogy within the context of design education. While the discussions have ranged from theoretical frameworks to practical strategies, from policy-level interventions to grassroots initiatives, the underlying urgency of this discourse has been most palpable when talking about its application in the African context. Africa is a continent rich in history, culture, and diversity, yet its educational systems often bear the imprint of colonial legacies, side-lining Indigenous knowledge and cultural context. The need to realign these systems with locally relevant pedagogy is not just a moral imperative but a practical one. This realignment has the potential to unlock a reservoir of creativity, innovation, and community engagement that is profoundly rooted in the very essence of what it means to be African.

In this chapter, the autoethnographic and storied ethnographic approach has allowed us to delve into the complexities that make this subject both challenging and essential. The successful case studies, illustrated as graphic narratives, serve as beacons, lighting the path forward with proven strategies. They are a testament to what is possible when education is envisioned as a pluralistic endeavour. Likewise, the showcased student portfolios are more than a collection of academic assignments; they represent a newfound sense of identity and capability, showing the transformative power of culturally relevant design education. The inclusion of historical and contemporary African artworks is not a mere aesthetic choice; it is an acknowledgment of the intellectual and cultural contributions that Africa offers to the world. It is also a call to action to dismantle the often-Eurocentric paradigms that have long dominated design and educational narratives.

So, what is the call to action? For educators, it is to adopt and advocate for a pedagogical approach that recognises and celebrates the diversity of your student body, especially if you are operating within the African context. You can shape curricula, to choose which artists and designers are studied, and to create an environment where every student feels seen and valued. For policymakers, the charge is to institute and support policies that allow for a more inclusive, culturally sensitive educational system. This is not merely about revising textbooks or modifying syllabi; it is about rethinking the very framework within which education operates.

Community leaders and organisations can play a critical role too. Support educational reforms that aim to be more inclusive. Build platforms that celebrate and disseminate culturally relevant content. Be a voice that continuously advocates for an education that is a mirror and window—reflecting the students it serves while offering them a view into the wider world. In essence, we all have a role to play in shifting the axis of educational discourse toward a more equitable and culturally attuned direction. The time for this change is not in some distant future; it is now. The urgency is both moral (that is, tied to the ideals of justice and inclusivity) and practical (that is, linked to the tangible benefits that such an approach brings to educational outcomes and societal cohesion). This chapter may be a single waypoint on a longer journey, but it is also a call to collective action. The path ahead may be complex, but as has been demonstrated through lived experiences, practical case studies, and theoretical grounding, it is navigable. Let us move forward, equipped with the knowledge and urgency that this work requires.

Notes

1 In an endnote that employs simulated ficto-ethnography, various authors engage in a dialogical conversation. They agree that these case studies serve as rich, empirical nodes in the interconnected web of cultural, educational, and social reform. They argue that these examples should be seriously considered in scholarly discourse, offering both the texture of lived experiences and quantifiable metrics that can inform educational policy.

Endnote Conversations

2 **Ngũgĩ wa Thiong'o:** This reflects my argument that language plays a crucial role in shaping consciousness and that embracing our own languages can free us from the linguistic colonisation our educational systems have long perpetuated.
Noam Chomsky: While I agree that language is fundamental to thought, we must also consider that bilingualism can be a resource, not a hindrance. The point is to empower students to navigate multiple linguistic landscapes.
3 **Chinua Achebe:** This is a welcome change. As I have always argued, until the lions have their own historians, the history of the hunt will always glorify the hunter.
Paulo Freire: The pedagogy of the oppressed comes full circle here. Education becomes an act of liberation and not just a depositing of facts.
4 **Albert Einstein:** "Pure mathematics is, in its way, the poetry of logical ideas." It is fascinating to see cultural diversity extending to this "poetry."

Gloria Ladson-Billings: Here, culturally relevant pedagogy moves beyond the social sciences and enters a realm often considered culturally neutral—math. A potent counternarrative to the Eurocentric standard.

Endnote Conversations

5 **Paulo Freire:** Resource constraints undoubtedly compromise the pedagogical efficacy of design education. It is in well-resourced settings that my theory of education as a "practice of freedom" can fully manifest. The lack of such resources renders the practice transactional, thus blunting its transformative potential.
John Dewey: Paulo, your thoughts resonate with my own emphasis on experiential learning. In design education, the lack of resources not only limits freedom but also stifles the kind of engaged, hands-on learning that I consider vital for personal and intellectual development.
Paulo Freire: I agree, John. Your point about experiential learning is well taken. When resources are constrained, design education risks becoming a rote exercise, devoid of the critical engagement necessary for true learning and liberation.
Nel Noddings: This conversation brings to mind my focus on care ethics in education. If the ultimate aim of education is to nurture capable, caring individuals, then the scarcity of resources in design education is not just an operational issue but a moral one. The inability to provide the right educational environment effectively withholds care, preventing students from reaching their full potential.
John Dewey: Nel, your observation adds another layer to this issue. The lack of resources directly conflicts with the very ethics of education. By limiting the ability for experiential learning, we are essentially impeding the moral development of students.
Henry Giroux: Let us not forget that these constraints are often not neutral but are informed by broader sociopolitical decisions about who gets what resources. This links back to Freire's notion of education as a practice of freedom—or in constrained settings, a practice of oppression.
Paulo Freire: Precisely, Henry. The resource limitations in design education can be seen as a form of systemic injustice, reflecting broader socioeconomic inequities.
Martha Nussbaum: I would like to bring in the idea of capabilities. Education should aim to expand individuals' freedoms to achieve the lives they have reason to value. The absence of resources, particularly in something as applied and tactile as design education, severely limits these capabilities, undermining the broader objectives of education.
Henry Giroux: Martha, that's an invaluable point. The resource constraints thus become an ethical dilemma, affecting the kind of citizens we are shaping through education.
Paulo Freire: The philosophical implications of resource constraints are indeed vast. They intersect with the theories of education, freedom, and social justice, revealing the multifaceted challenges of implementing culturally relevant pedagogy in design education.

Endnote Conversations

6 **Paulo Freire:** The "banking model of education" captures how education systems perpetuate oppressive power dynamics by treating students as passive receptacles. The resistance to culturally relevant pedagogy can be seen as a refusal to challenge these power dynamics.

Michel Foucault: Yes, Paulo, I would add that this resistance is not merely a matter of inertia but serves a calculated purpose. Institutions like schools exist to normalise specific behaviors and ideologies. Any resistance to changing pedagogical methods is intimately tied to preserving these norms and the power structures they uphold.

Judith Butler: Foucault, your idea about the normative functions of schools resonates with my notion of "performativity." Schools perform their own identities through the methods and curricula they employ. Shifting toward culturally relevant pedagogy would require a change in this performance, a change that could be tantamount to an identity crisis for the institution.

Ivor Goodson: That identity crisis you mention, Judith, is not just cultural but also economic and political. My research on the politics of curriculum shows that choices are often dictated by considerations other than pure educational value. Economic factors can heavily influence which subjects and approaches are given prominence, often sidelining the importance of cultural relevance.

Paulo Freire: Goodson, your point about economic factors is crucial. We often ignore the economics of education when discussing pedagogical change. The system is geared towards what it perceives as productive, which unfortunately might not align with the broader aims of human liberation and cultural relevancy.

Michel Foucault: This is where my argument circles back. The choices about what is productive and what isn't are again tied to the types of individuals the system aims to produce and the power structures it aims to uphold.

Judith Butler: Absolutely, and changing these deeply entrenched norms and structures would necessitate a thorough re-evaluation not just of pedagogical approaches but also of the foundational purposes of educational institutions.

Ivor Goodson: In the end, it becomes clear that resistance to culturally relevant pedagogy isn't an isolated issue. It is a node in a complex web of social, cultural, political, and economic factors that define the broader educational landscape.

References

Butler, J. (2009). Performativity, precarity and sexual politics. *AIBR. Revista de Antropología Iberoamericana, 4*(3): i–xiii.

Dewey, J. (1916). Nationalizing education. *Journal of Education, 84*(16): 425–428. https://doi.org/10.1177/002205741608401602

Foucault, M. (2016). *The punitive society: Lectures at the Collège de France, 1972–1973.* Springer.

Goodson, I. F. (2005). *Learning, curriculum and life politics: The selected works of Ivor F. Goodson.* Routledge.

Ladson-Billings, G. (2022). *The dreamkeepers: Successful teachers of African American children.* John Wiley & Sons. https://doi.org/10.2307/2077209

Wa Thiong'o, N. (1992). *Decolonising the mind: The politics of language in African literature.* East African Publishers. https://doi.org/10.2307/524049

3
SPIRITUALITY, RELIGION, AND ARTISTIC PRACTICES IN AFRICAN DESIGN EDUCATION

In the heart of Accra, Ghana, there lived a young aspiring designer named Kwame. His journey in design began in the bustling markets of Makola, surrounded by vibrant colours, intricate patterns, and the symphony of a thriving community. Kwame's grandmother, Esi, a revered textile artist, was his first mentor. She taught him that every thread woven into her fabrics was a story, a prayer, a piece of ancestral wisdom passed down through generations.

As Kwame grew, his talent and passion for design led him to a prestigious design school. The curriculum was rigorous, focusing on modern techniques and Western design principles. Yet, Kwame felt a disconnect. The designs he created lacked the soul and depth of Esi's textiles. He yearned for something more, something that resonated with his spirit and heritage.

This longing led Kwame to embark on a journey back to his roots, to the wisdom of his grandmother and the spiritual traditions of his people. He learned about the symbols in Esi's textiles—the Adinkra symbols, each carrying profound philosophical and spiritual meanings. He discovered how these symbols were not just decorative but were a language of wisdom, an expression of the collective consciousness of his people.

Inspired, Kwame began to integrate these spiritual elements into his designs. He designed a series of chairs, each inspired by a different Adinkra symbol, embodying concepts like unity, perseverance, and harmony with nature. These weren't just pieces of furniture; they were storytelling mediums, imbued with the wisdom of ancestors.

However, integrating spirituality into his work was not without challenges. Kwame faced criticism from some of his professors, who saw his approach as

DOI: 10.4324/9781032692647-3

unconventional. Yet, he persisted, believing in the value of bridging the gap between the traditional and the modern, the spiritual and the material.

Kwame's designs began to gain attention. People were drawn to the depth and authenticity of his work. He realised that his designs did more than just fill spaces; they connected people to their heritage, their spirituality, and to each other.

Years later, as an accomplished designer, Kwame opened a school of design in Accra. He built a curriculum that honoured both the technical aspects of design and the rich spiritual and cultural heritage of Africa. He taught his students to see design as a holistic practice, one that involves not just creating functional and aesthetically pleasing objects but also understanding and honouring the cultural and spiritual narratives that shape our world.

Kwame's journey came full circle when he invited Esi to his school to share her wisdom. As she spoke to the young designers, weaving her stories with threads of wisdom, Kwame realised the true essence of his journey. It was about rekindling a connection to the past to illuminate the path forward, about weaving the spiritual and cultural sensitivities into the fabric of modern design.

In Kwame's school, students from diverse backgrounds came together, learning to create designs that were not just physically appealing but also spiritually resonant and culturally meaningful. They were taught to design with empathy, respect, and a deep understanding of the interconnectedness of all things.

Through Kwame's story, the essence of spirituality, religion, and artistic practice in African design education comes alive. It's a story of returning to the roots, of embracing ancestral wisdom, and of transforming the practice of design into a spiritually and culturally rich endeavour. Kwame's journey exemplifies the transformative power of integrating spiritual and cultural dimensions into design, creating a more holistic, inclusive, and resonant form of education and practice.

The intersection between religion, spirituality, and design in the African context presents a rich, intricate relationships that defy simplistic categorisation. Unlike the often-secularised settings of Western design education, where functionality and aesthetic value tend to dominate discourse, African design sensibilities inherently enmesh with spiritual and religious considerations. This profound connection links not just to the final design outcomes, but influences every stage of the design process, from conceptualisation to execution and public reception. It is an engagement that is both vertically historical (drawing from ancestral traditions) and horizontally present (connected to contemporary contexts and future implications).

This complexity is further magnified when one considers the sheer diversity of Africa—geographically immense and culturally multifaceted, with each region having its unique spirituality and design ethos. From the ancestral wisdom carried forth in the beadwork of the Maasai in Kenya to the intricate Islamic geometric patterns in Moroccan architecture, design cannot be detached from the spiritual and the sacred. These manifestations serve as both a mirror and a canvas, reflecting the society that creates them while also shaping its spiritual narratives. Such interdependency extends the roles and responsibilities of the designer beyond mere creation to become a keeper of tradition, an interpreter of faith, and even a spiritual guide in some senses. Given this intricate relationship, decolonised design education cannot help but become a more nuanced affair. It involves not only imparting technical skills but also navigating a matrix of spiritual, ethical, and cultural considerations. To genuinely appreciate this, imagine a design classroom where students are grappling with questions about how their work fits within their spiritual worldview, or how it advances or interferes with communal values. It becomes a pedagogical challenge and opportunity, not just to produce skilled designers but also spiritually aware, culturally competent individuals. It is a form of education that does not just stop at how to design but advances to asking the questions: Why design? For whom? and Within what spiritual framework?

The question then arises: How can this interplay be managed or facilitated within the educational landscape, especially when the curriculum often follows a Western-centric model less accustomed to integrating spirituality? This challenge becomes an avenue to explore the boundaries and potentials of design education. It raises an array of complex questions: Should spiritual principles guide the aesthetics and functionalities of design? If so, how can such principles be embedded in pedagogy without imposing a particular religious view or exoticising the spiritual aspects of African culture? The ensuing chapters will delve into these complexities. They will journey through historical footprints, theoretical frameworks, and current practices, interrogating the layered relationships between religion, spirituality, and design. Along the way, they will also consider the implications of these relationships for those charged with the crucial role of educating the next generation of African designers. It is a fascinating and challenging landscape, one that holds the promise of deepening our understanding of the intersections between the spiritual, the aesthetic, and the functional in design education in Africa.

Overview of the Intersection between Religion, Spirituality, and Design in Africa.

In exploring the historical context of the interplay between spirituality and design in Africa, one finds a deeply rooted relationship that spans across eras, transcending mere form and function to imbue designs with spiritual symbolism and ritual significance. Notable scholars such as Abiodun (2014) in "Yoruba art and language: Seeking the African in African art" have illustrated how Yoruba artworks, for instance, are not simply aesthetic endeavours but encapsulations of broader cosmic views. Similarly, scholars like Pogoson (1990) and Picton (2021) have devoted considerable attention to the study of the spiritual aspects in African art and design, particularly focusing on how these creations were intended as media through which spiritual powers could be accessed or invoked. The myriad of ancient African artifacts, ranging from Nok sculptures in Nigeria to the Rock Churches in Ethiopia, are often more than mere representations of artistic skill; they are an assemblage of spiritual significance, collective memory, and communal ethos. For example, the Akan gold weights from Ghana are not just functional objects used for weighing gold dust; they are also miniature storytellers depicting proverbs, spiritual truths, and social norms. Their shapes often incorporate Adinkra symbols, which have specific meanings and are used to convey complex spiritual and philosophical ideas. A notable example is the intricate beadwork of Sulu, showcasing their rich cultural heritage. As Harney (2004) outlines in "In Senghor's shadow: Art, politics, and the avant-garde," the beadwork is not just ornamental but communicates intricate messages about the wearer's social status, age, and even intentions. Beadwork colours have particular meanings that could relate to emotions, political conditions, or ancestral spirits. Therefore, wearing such beadwork can act as a form of both personal expression and spiritual connection, blending the aesthetic and the numinous in a complex weave of meaning. The concept of "Kule", explored by Strother (1999) "Inventing masks: Agency and history in the art of the central Pende," points out that in Pende cosmology, masks were not simply carved wooden structures. They were "invented" in dreams and then brought to life through design, thus serving as a bridge between the physical and the spiritual world. The artistic process was itself considered a spiritual endeavour, a form of worship or veneration. A common underpinning in these diverse examples is the spiritual ethos that deeply influences traditional African design. Whether it is in the intricate beadwork, the carving of masks, or the sculpting of gold weights, there exists a common spiritual resonance—a sense of unity between the material and the metaphysical, between the craftsman and the cosmos. It is not merely about creating something beautiful or functional but also spiritually meaningful.

This notion of design as a spiritually integrative practice does not stand in isolation but rather exists within a broader framework of religious and philosophical systems that guide and govern life in traditional African societies. Here, the concepts of unity, balance, and harmony, often encapsulated in philosophies like Ubuntu in Africa, underscore the importance of interconnectedness, not just among humans but also between humans and the spiritual world. As we delve further into notions of spirituality and design, it becomes essential to appreciate the continuity of these traditions into contemporary practice, but also to recognise the influence of external, often Western, perspectives on African design paradigms. Walker (2020) seminal work, "Design and spirituality: A philosophy of material cultures," provides a useful lens to view this. While Walker's focus is not exclusively African, his ideas can be readily mapped onto the African context (Walker, 2020). He emphasizes that materials are not just passive substances shaped by human hands but are active participants in creating meaning. In traditional African design, this resonates with the spiritual life breathed into artifacts, masks, or beadworks. Walker (2020)'s ideas harmonise with what scholars like Enwezor and Okeke-Agulu (2009) discuss in "Contemporary African Art Since 1980," as they explore how modern African artists and designers engage in a dialogue with their materials in ways that extend beyond the tactile into the spiritual realm. These dialogues can often involve invocations, offerings, or rituals that are aimed not just at creating an object but at manifesting a spiritual entity or force. For example, the sculpting of a Chiwara antelope headdress among the Bamana people of Mali is more than a creative endeavour; it is a ritualistic practice. This relates back to Walker (2023 p. 54)'s notion that design is a "philosophy of material cultures," where spirituality, materiality, and craftsmanship are intertwined (Walker, 2023).

It is also worth mentioning the often-heated debates surrounding the individualism versus collectivism in design approaches, especially when these traditions intersect with modern education systems. While traditional African designs heavily lean towards collectivism, reflecting the collective spiritual ethos of the community, the often Western-centric methodologies introduced in contemporary design education promote individual creativity. These dichotomies are not merely academic; they raise substantive questions about the ethics of design practice. If a design is created with spiritual intention within a community, can an outsider, who uses it merely for aesthetic or functional purposes, ever engage with it ethically? This connects with broader dialogues about cultural appropriation and ethical considerations that many scholars, like Basu (2017) in "The inbetweenness of things: materialising mediation and movement between worlds," have been investigating. It is evident that the ancestral wisdom permeating traditional African designs is not a relic of the past but continues to be a dynamic part of the present, negotiating its space in a globalised world. As new generations of African designers receive their education in increasingly international and multicultural settings, the questions become: How do they reconcile their ancestral spiritual heritage with the secular and often individualistic philosophies they encounter? and How do educators help facilitate this synthesis to create a design philosophy that is both contemporary and deeply rooted in the richness of African spirituality? In extending the discussion, one might consider the role of digital technologies in the modern landscape of African design, particularly how they intersect with traditional spiritual practices. If the artifact in a traditional sense served as a conduit for spiritual meaning, can a digital design—say, an app or website—achieve something similar? Can digital pixels convey the same weight of spiritual depth as a meticulously crafted ancestral mask? The nature of the digital realm offers both challenges and opportunities for integrating spirituality into design. It is largely secular and utilitarian but can be adapted to mirror or even enhance spiritual traditions.

The democratisation of design tools also opens new avenues for the global dissemination of African spiritual philosophies. Before, a spiritually significant artifact might reside in a single village, appreciated by a small community. Now, a digital version of that artifact can be seen, shared, and even interacted with by people across the globe. This has implications not just for the spread of African spirituality, but for the way that spirituality is incorporated into designs that may not be rooted in African traditions. In this context, a new symbiosis can emerge where spiritual designs are not just maintained but evolved in dialog with a broader range of cultural and technological influences. Furthermore, the field of experiential design, focusing on creating immersive environments, offers a fresh platform for bringing spiritual principles to the forefront. Imagine a virtual reality experience designed to emulate an African ritual, complete with intricate designs modelled after traditional artifacts. While it can never replace the actual ritual, this digital approximation could serve as an educational tool, helping to both preserve traditional practices and explain them to those outside the community. Here, design serves as a bridge between worlds, tangible and intangible, past and present, local and global.

Additionally, From the Yoruba spiritual tradition, we can incorporate the concept of interconnected realms of existence—Orun (the sky) and Aiye (the earth). This duality suggests a design approach that respects both the celestial and the terrestrial, encouraging a balance between the spiritual and the material in product creation. Additionally, the veneration of ancestors and the role of diviners (Babalawo) who consult the Ifa corpus, covering diverse fields like medicine, science, metaphysics, and cosmology, could inspire designs that are both spiritually meaningful and grounded in practical wisdom. The Sulu spiritual tradition offers the belief in a supreme being (*Unkulunkulu*), and a nuanced understanding of the human condition, recognising the body (*Umsimba*), spirit (*Idlosi*), heart/emotion (*Inhlisiyo*), mind (*Ingqondo*), and personality (*Isithunsi*). This holistic view of human existence can be reflected in designs that cater to the multifaceted nature of human needs and experiences. Moreover, Sulu practices of ancestor veneration and the use of sacrifices and magic in maintaining a bridge with the spiritual world could inspire designs that foster a sense of continuity with the past and a deep connection with natural and supernatural realms.

The Igbo spirituality, characterised by the veneration of the earth goddess Ala and a pantheon including Chukwu (a creator god), Anyanvu (sun god), and Igwe (sky god), presents a worldview where nature is revered and closely linked with the divine. The Igbo belief in the continuum of the living, the dead, and the unborn, and the role of diviners and priests holding the Ofo (a symbol of authority, justice, and truth) could guide design practices towards creating products that honour natural elements, reflect a deep respect for history and tradition, and embody principles of justice and truth. In summary, tapping into the rich spiritual traditions of African cultures such as the Yoruba, Sulu, and Igbo can offer new pathways in design. By integrating these diverse spiritual beliefs and practices, designers can create products that not only serve practical purposes but also resonate with the spiritual and cultural dimensions of life. These traditions emphasize a holistic understanding of existence, the significance of ancestry and nature, and a harmonious balance between various aspects of life, all of which can profoundly influence modern design to be more inclusive, meaningful, and culturally rich.

In conclusion, as the boundaries between the traditional and the modern, the material and the digital, and the local and the global continue to blur, the historical spiritual ethos of African design offers not just a rich context but also a dynamic framework for innovation. It allows us to think about design as an inherently holistic endeavour, one that melds form and function with meaning and spirituality, inviting us to not just look at design differently but to feel and experience it in entirely new ways. To bridge the conceptual exploration of African design's spiritual ethos to the tangible evidence of this philosophy, a thoughtful transition emphasizes the continuity of tradition and innovation. This segue highlights the enduring relevance of spiritual and cultural symbols through the ages, setting the stage for a deeper investigation into their manifestations and significance in contemporary design practices. By drawing attention to the intricate relationship between ancient artifacts and modern interpretations, I underscore the holistic approach that integrates form, function, meaning, and spirituality in African design, inviting a comprehensive understanding and appreciation of its rich heritage and its potential for future innovation.

Examination of Ancient African Artifacts and Spiritual Symbolism

The inquiry into the intersection of spirituality and design in Africa inherently takes us back to ancestral wisdom manifested through various forms of art and artifacts. To understand this relationship fully, it is vital to examine these historical elements in detail. Ancient African artifacts, whether they be masks used in spiritual rituals, sculptures representing deities, or even textiles with particular geometric patterns, often serve as tangible expressions of a community's spiritual ethos. These are not merely decorative items, but powerful cultural icons infused with symbolic meanings and spiritual energies. One can consider the meticulous craftsmanship behind the Akan gold weights, traditionally used by the Akan people in West Africa. These were small, sculpted objects made of brass or gold, used as a measuring system. Though their primary function was utilitarian, the shapes they took were often symbolic, representing proverbs, ethical ideas, or elements from nature. They served as a medium for teaching societal values, embodying the philosophy that even everyday objects could serve spiritual and ethical ends.

Similarly, consider the Yoruba's beadwork in Nigeria, often created to adorn royalty and divinities during ritualistic ceremonies. The meticulous designs, comprised of vividly colourful beads, are not merely aesthetic choices; they contain specific spiritual messages and historical recounts. The use of colour, form, and texture in these pieces is not arbitrary but grounded in spiritual beliefs about power, divinity, and existence. The vibrant wall paintings of the Ndebele people in South Africa present a similarly fascinating example. Often created by women, these intricate designs are a ritualistic practice intended not merely for beautification but as a spiritual exercise that connects the individual with their ancestors and community. The colours and patterns, handed down from generation to generation, have specific meanings and are believed to protect the household and attract positive energies. The underlying spiritual ethos in these traditional designs can be summed up as a deeply rooted belief in interconnectedness—that objects and beings exist not just in a physical realm but are nodes in a network of spiritual relationships. In this context, design takes on a highly participative and performative role, serving as a bridge between the human and the divine, the physical and the metaphysical. Continuing our exploration, the theoretical underpinning of these spiritual elements in design can be linked to the broader philosophy of material cultures. This perspective encourages us to view materials not just as passive substances waiting to be shaped, but as active participants that bring with them intrinsic meanings, histories, and even spiritual dimensions. In this context, African design serves as a powerful conduit for both intentional and unintentional spiritual expression. The object, once crafted, is no longer merely an object; it becomes a manifestation of a spiritual ethos deeply ingrained in the culture and traditions of its origin.

For example, let us consider the Dogon doors from Mali. These are not merely functional wooden doors but contain intricate carvings that tell stories, often of cosmological significance, and are believed to protect the home from spiritual harm. These carvings on the wood, their patterns, and the stories they encapsulate, become an act of transference: transferring spiritual and cultural knowledge from the material world to the spiritual realm, and vice versa. Here, the door becomes not just a physical barrier but a spiritual one, guarding against malevolent forces while embracing the good. If we juxtapose this with contemporary design thinking, which often emphasizes the function and aesthetics of an object, it is clear that the African spiritual ethos offers a more holistic approach. It considers not just the how and what but also the why, the very purpose behind each stroke, colour, or shape. This is an acknowledgment of design as an inherently spiritual act, linking creator, creation, and the community in a network of meaningful relationships. This idea directly feeds into broader debates in the philosophy of material cultures, particularly concerning the materiality of spirituality. In African design, materiality does not just stop at the utilitarian or aesthetic level but is inherently recognised for its ability to convey spiritual truths and principles. The artifact, in essence, becomes a living embodiment of the divine, the community, and the natural world. This comprehensive approach demands a shift in how we conceive design education. Design is not just about mastering technical skills but involves cultivating a nuanced understanding of the deeper, often spiritual, implications of our work. This spiritual depth does not restrict but enriches the design process, offering multifaceted layers of meaning and function that can only be achieved when one recognises the inherent spirituality in every creative act. As we delve into the pedagogical implications of acknowledging the spiritual ethos and material philosophies that underlie African design traditions. This necessitates a shift from conventional design education models, which are often overly focused on technique and formal principles, towards a more holistic approach. Such an approach would recognise the intrinsic meanings and spiritual dimensions woven into the fabric of design practice, treating them not as supplementary but integral to the design process itself.

Think of a pedagogical approach that allows students to explore not just different materials and techniques but also the cultural and spiritual significance of these choices. The teaching approach could draw from indigenous methodologies like the mentor-apprentice systems common in African traditional settings, alongside modern, often Western-centric design education paradigms. In these hybrid classrooms, assignments would not just demand technical prowess but also a thoughtful engagement with the spiritual and cultural dimensions of design. Students could be tasked with projects that require them to work with local artisans, thereby providing them with firsthand exposure to ancient techniques and spiritual beliefs that have shaped these practices for generations. This multilayered approach to design education is in line with the concept of Ubuntu, an African philosophy emphasising communal values, shared destiny, and mutual respect. Imagine a design process that reflects this ethos of interconnectedness, where students are taught to see themselves not as isolated entities but as part of a broader spiritual and cultural tapestry. Such an education could help cultivate designers who are not just technically proficient but also spiritually aware, capable of producing works that resonate on multiple levels—functional, aesthetic, and spiritual.

However, introducing spiritual elements into design education is not without challenges. Ethical dilemmas may arise, such as cultural appropriation or the imposition of particular religious or spiritual views. But these challenges are not insurmountable; they are an invitation to engage more deeply, critically, and respectfully with the diverse spiritual traditions that students bring into the classroom. To conclude, the integration of spiritual elements, rooted in the philosophies of material cultures and the ancestral wisdom of African design, offers a richer, more nuanced approach to design education. It calls for an interdisciplinary method, one that brings in ethical considerations, spiritual awareness, and cultural sensitivity alongside technical expertise. Such an approach does not merely add another layer to design education; it fundamentally transforms it, making room for a holistic understanding that is both deeply rooted and far reaching. It is not just an incorporation of spirituality into design but a reimagination of what design education can and should be. Navigating the complexities of integrating spirituality into design education, we find ourselves at a crossroads of tradition and innovation. This pivotal moment, rich with potential ethical dilemmas, subtly transitions us towards a new chapter in design pedagogy. Here, the essence of Ubuntu emerges as a guiding light, embodying the spirit of community, interconnectedness, and mutual respect. This seamless shift from theoretical considerations to the practical application of Ubuntu principles in design education illustrates a profound journey, transforming challenges into opportunities for growth, understanding, and holistic innovation in the classroom and beyond.

Embracing Ubuntu in the Spiritual Framework of Design Education

Incorporating Ubuntu into design education transcends traditional teaching methodologies, imbuing the curriculum with a spirit of community, interconnectedness, and mutual respect. This spiritual interpretation of Ubuntu in design education is not merely an academic exercise but a profound journey into understanding how design impacts and is impacted by the communities it serves. By grounding design projects in the principles of Ubuntu, educators and students embark on a path that views design as a communal act—a process that nurtures and is nurtured by the intricate web of human relationships and natural ecosystems. This approach encourages a reflective practice where every design decision is evaluated not just on its aesthetic or functional merits but on its capacity to foster unity, support mutual growth, and respect the dignity of all involved. Through community-driven projects, such as the Land, Letšema, and Leola initiative, the application of Ubuntu in design education reveals its potential to create solutions that are deeply resonant with the values and needs of the community, embodying a holistic vision for a sustainable and equitable future (Magoro & Bidwell, 2022).

The project Land, Letšema, and Leola, exemplifies how digital transformation can be achieved on a rural community's terms, embodying the principles of Ubuntu in every phase of the design process. The journey from understanding Ubuntu and Botho in abstract terms to witnessing their profound impact in tangible design initiatives is both enlightening and transformative. Land, Letšema, and Leola exemplifies how digital transformation initiatives, when approached through the lens of Ubuntu, can flourish on terms set by the community itself (Magoro & Bidwell, 2022). This project does not merely incorporate technology into a rural setting; it weaves digital tools into the social fabric, respecting and enhancing local traditions, knowledge systems, and environmental stewardship.

In this light, the design process becomes a deeply spiritual act, a conduit for reinforcing the sacred triad of creator, creation, and community. It is here, in the harmonious interplay of innovation and tradition, that the project shines, offering invaluable insights into how design education can be both a reflective and forward-thinking endeavour. Through this lens, students learn not just to create but to connect, embedding their work within the broader narrative of societal growth and communal wellbeing. Expanding on the notion that the design process can be a deeply spiritual act, we delve deeper into the essence of creating with consciousness, where every design decision reflects the harmonious balance between innovation and tradition. This perspective envisions design not merely as a task of creation but as a profound journey of connecting deeply with the roots of community, culture, and the natural world. The sacred triad of creator, creation, and community encapsulates a holistic view of design, where the designer steps into a role much akin to a caretaker or steward, nurturing the relationships between their work, the people, and the environment. In this framework, design becomes a medium through which these relationships are celebrated, strengthened, and evolved. The emphasis on this interconnectedness invites a deeper level of thoughtfulness and intentionality into the design process, encouraging creators to consider the wider implications of their work on societal growth and communal wellbeing.

In educational settings, this approach transforms the learning experience, guiding students to not only acquire technical skills but also to cultivate a profound sense of empathy, responsibility, and community engagement. By embedding their work within the broader narrative of societal development, students learn to view their creations through the lens of impact, asking not just, Can we? but Should we? and For whom? This shift towards a more reflective and forward-thinking practice prepares students for the challenges of designing in a complex, interconnected world, equipping them with the skills to create solutions that are not only innovative but also sustainable, equitable, and culturally resonant.

Integrating the spiritual essence of Ubuntu and Botho into design education necessitates a curriculum that not only imparts technical skills but also immerses students in the spiritual and cultural ethos of their communities. This approach fosters a holistic understanding of design as an act deeply rooted in communal values, mutual respect, and interconnectedness. By drawing upon the decolonization efforts in Botswana's and Nigeria's design curricula, Moalosi et al. (2017) discuss the infusion of local knowledge into design curricula, focusing on a cocreation process guided by Ubuntu, which emphasizes collaboration and communal values. In Okofu and Fakere (2022) explore the transformation of architectural education, introducing negotiated pedagogy as a means to incorporate local cultures and contexts into the learning process. Both projects are significant steps towards an education system that respects and uplifts

African epistemologies and cultural practices within the framework of design. The innovative dissemination of indigenous knowledge as seen in the "Audio Pacemaker" project, we can illustrate the transformative power of integrating spirituality into design education (Bidwell & Winschiers-Theophilus, 2012). This curriculum embraces the complexity of cultural heritage, ensuring that students emerge as designers who not only create with innovation and efficiency but also with a profound respect for the spiritual and communal dimensions of their work. This project, by leveraging oral traditions and indigenous knowledge through digital means, exemplifies how design can serve as a bridge between the old and the new, honouring the past while innovating for the future (Bidwell & Winschiers-Theophilus, 2012). It showcases the spiritual act of preserving and sharing wisdom, emphasizing design's role in sustaining the cultural and communal fabric. This narrative strengthens the chapter on spirituality, underscoring that design, when imbued with the values of Ubuntu and Botho, transcends mere creation. It becomes a spiritual journey of connection, respect, and care for the community and its heritage, illustrating the profound impact spirituality can have on shaping design practices that are not only technologically advanced but also deeply human and respectful of the interconnectedness of all beings.

Ultimately, embracing this spiritual aspect of design fosters a new generation of designers who are not only skilled creators but also compassionate community members and thoughtful stewards of the planet. This approach heralds a future where design transcends its traditional boundaries, becoming a force for positive change, deeply embedded in the fabric of societal advancement and the pursuit of a more harmonious world. This initiative showcases the power of community-driven design projects in promoting a holistic approach to education, where learning is not just about acquiring technical skills but also about fostering a deep connection with the community, environment, and cultural heritage. By prioritizing local needs, values, and knowledge systems, the project highlights the importance of creating meaningful relationships between the creator, creation, and community. Incorporating a case study of this project into our curriculum can inspire students to approach design as an inherently spiritual act, where the focus is on achieving harmony and balance within the community. It serves as a tangible example of how Ubuntu/Botho can guide the development of pedagogies that are not only relevant to African communities but also resonant with the global discourse on sustainable and inclusive design.

Concepts of Materiality and Their Spiritual and Cultural Meanings

In the realm of design, materiality is not just a matter of physical attributes; it often carries with it a range of intrinsic meanings that are deeply influenced by culture, spirituality, and religion. Walker (2020), in his seminal work *Design and*

Spirituality: A Philosophy of Material Cultures, challenges us to consider materiality as a complex interplay of form, function, and deeper spiritual significance. In the African context, this idea gains additional layers of meaning, given the continent's rich spiritual traditions and diverse cultural landscapes. This leads us to a point of contested grounds: the tension between secular and spiritual design in the context of modern design education. In traditional African settings, design and spirituality were almost inseparable. Artifacts, whether utilitarian or purely aesthetic, often bore spiritual symbolism and were crafted with a specific cultural or religious context in mind. However, as design education has globalised, often taking cues from Western-centric models, a certain sterilisation of spiritual elements has occurred. The focus has leaned heavily towards the technical, functional, and commercial aspects, leaving little room for spiritual expression.

This presents a complex challenge: how do we reconcile the secular ideals of modern design education with the deeply spiritual nature of traditional African design practices? The secular viewpoint argues for a neutral ground where design is divorced from any religious or spiritual affiliations, allowing for universal application and avoiding potential sectarian conflicts. This perspective holds that design education should be a space for the development of technical skills and critical thinking, where spiritual beliefs have no formal role. On the other hand, the spiritual perspective posits that separating design from spirituality results in a loss of depth and context, leading to designs that may be technically sound but lack soul or cultural relevance. It challenges the notion of neutrality in design, arguing that all design is rooted in some form of worldview, whether acknowledged or not. From this vantage point, excluding spirituality is itself a form of bias, one that disregards the rich of spiritual traditions that have informed design practices for centuries, particularly in Africa.

Navigating this tension requires a nuanced approach. One possible avenue is to develop an integrated curriculum that allows room for both secular and spiritual approaches, recognising the value in each. Assignments and projects can be designed to offer different tracks, allowing students to engage with design problems through various lenses—technical, spiritual, or a synthesis of both. Moreover, educators can provide contextual courses that delve into the spiritual and cultural significances of different materials and design elements, informed by indigenous wisdom as well as modern design theories. The dichotomy between secular and spiritual perspectives on design raises a series of ethical and pedagogical questions. If spirituality is integrated into design education, how should it be done in a way that respects diverse belief systems and avoids potential issues of cultural appropriation or imposition? On the flip side, if spirituality is left out, do we risk perpetuating a form of epistemic injustice, where specific forms of knowledge—rooted in spiritual traditions—are marginalised? One possible path forward is to consider an integrative approach, one that acknowledges the multifaceted nature of design as both a technical and spiritual endeavour.

This could manifest as modules or courses that explore design through various cultural and spiritual lenses, inviting students to interrogate their own biases and expand their perspectives. It might also involve more community-based projects where students engage directly with different spiritual and cultural communities, allowing for a more nuanced understanding of how design serves various human and spiritual needs.

However, an integrative approach also carries risks. For example, there may be challenges in adequately representing diverse spiritual traditions without simplifying or commodifying them. Also, the very act of inclusion might seem to some as a form of endorsement or prioritisation of certain spiritual perspectives over others, creating a new set of ethical quandaries. The debate over secular versus spiritual design in education is not one that will be easily resolved. However, as the field of design continues to evolve and globalise, the need for a more nuanced, inclusive approach becomes increasingly urgent. This is particularly relevant for the African context, where the fusion of design and spirituality has a long, intricate history that offers valuable insights into how material culture can serve as a conduit for spiritual expression. In essence, the tension between secular and spiritual design perspectives presents an opportunity for growth and enrichment in design education. It calls upon educators, students, and practitioners to engage in ongoing dialogue, questioning the paradigms we have inherited and forging new paths that honour both the technical and the spiritual dimensions of design.

Debate on Incorporating Spirituality into Modern Design Curricula

The debate on incorporating spirituality into modern design curricula is complex and multifaceted, with scholars and practitioners offering a range of opinions. On one end, proponents argue that spirituality enriches design by adding layers of meaning, context, and depth. Walker (2020) lays the groundwork for understanding how materiality can embody spiritual principles. In line with this, Gloria Kondrup of Art Centre College of Design suggests that integrating spirituality can push design beyond commercialism and towards humanistic values. On the other end, critics, such as Kenneth FitsGerald, whose work often examines the professional and academic practices in graphic design, caution against such incorporation. The argument is that it could potentially muddle the educational focus and introduce elements that are inherently nonuniversal, subjective, and potentially divisive (Fitzgerald, 2010). The pros of incorporating spirituality revolve around the idea that it can enrich the design process. As Walker outlines, considering spiritual aspects could lead to designs that are not only functional but also emotionally and spiritually resonant (Walker, 2020). Such an approach could make room for a more holistic understanding of user needs, incorporating not just physical or utilitarian requirements but also deeper human desires for meaning and connection.

However, the cons cannot be overlooked. One major concern is the risk of essentialising or stereotyping spiritual traditions, reducing complex practices and beliefs to simplistic visual or symbolic elements. This is a particular concern when discussing religious iconography and symbolism in African design, where traditional symbols are rich in meaning and context. Misappropriation or misuse could lead to cultural degradation or commercialisation of sacred elements. A further challenge lies in the practicality of integrating spirituality into a classroom environment, traditionally focused on secular and empirical learning. How do educators navigate the plurality of spiritual beliefs among a diverse student body? Is it even possible to teach spirituality without crossing ethical boundaries of imposing beliefs? Incorporating spiritual elements, particularly from specific traditions like those in Africa, also raises the question of authenticity. Appiah (1993) has delved into issues of identity and authenticity in African art and the ethical quandaries these present. When design education attempts to integrate traditional African religious iconography and symbolism, it must be wary of falling into traps of exoticism or tokenism. Designers like Mpho Vackier and Porky Hefer have often utilised motifs and symbols deeply ingrained in African spiritual traditions. For Vackier, her furniture designs are not just functional elements but a medium for storytelling that draws heavily from African folklore and spiritual practices. In a similar vein, Hefer's design objects often blur the lines between functional design and symbolic representation. The use of religious symbols in African design, however, opens an ethical debate, which can be framed using the arguments of scholars such as Edward Said and Leora Auslander. Said's concept of "orientalism" warns against the exotification and misinterpretation of non-Western cultures, including their religious symbols (Said, 1978). While Said (1978) focused primarily on the Middle East, the concept is highly applicable to the African context. Auslander and Zahra (2018), on the other hand, discusses the "authenticity" of material culture, which can be compromised when religious symbols are used outside of their intended context or without a deep understanding of their meaning.

The incorporation of these religious symbols in design curricula could, therefore, be seen as both an opportunity and a risk. On one hand, it offers the potential for a more enriched educational experience that goes beyond technical skills to encompass cultural and spiritual literacy. On the other hand, there is the risk of superficial engagement with these symbols, which could lead to cultural appropriation or trivialisation of deeply held beliefs.

Yet, this is precisely why some scholars like Bhabha (2012) argue for a "third space" in design education, a pedagogical area where differing viewpoints can be reconciled or at least coexist. In this space, students would not only be trained in the technicalities of design but also engaged in the ethical and spiritual dimensions of their work. Bhabha's ideas could serve as a theoretical foundation for a more holistic approach to design education, that neither dilutes the cultural richness of designs nor promotes a one-size-fits-all model.

Thus, the debate over incorporating religious iconography and symbolism in African design into modern curricula becomes not just a pedagogical question but also an ethical one. It raises issues that go beyond the design classroom to touch on broader societal values and norms. On one end of the spectrum is the argument for cultural preservation and spiritual depth. By integrating these elements into modern design curricula, educators have the potential to offer a more holistic education. Here, design is not seen merely as an instrument of utility but as a complex interplay of form, function, and philosophy. This multidimensional view is often closer to traditional African perspectives on design, which do not draw sharp boundaries between the secular and the sacred. However, this integration is not without its challenges. The most evident is the risk of superficiality or even cultural appropriation. How can educators ensure that such deeply symbolic elements are handled with the gravity they deserve? Without thorough contextual understanding, there is a danger that these symbols become mere aesthetic choices, stripped of their depth and meaning. This could be perceived as a form of cultural dilution or even disrespect.

Then, there is the question of universality versus specificity. A design curriculum that leans too heavily into a particular spiritual tradition could risk alienating students from different backgrounds or beliefs. It is a delicate balance to maintain, and one that raises the question: Can a design curriculum be both globally relevant and culturally specific? The idea of a third space in education, where differing cultural, secular, and spiritual viewpoints coexist, becomes increasingly appealing in this context. This pedagogical approach allows for the exploration of spirituality and culture without forcing a singular perspective upon students. It provides room for critical engagement and personal growth, offering a rounded education that respects both the complexities of design as a discipline and the multifaceted nature of human experience. By engaging these considerations, we aim to pave the way for a pedagogical model that neither negates the importance of religious and spiritual symbolism in African design nor risks the pitfalls of cultural appropriation or dilution. The debate remains complex and fraught with challenges, but it is precisely this complexity that makes it a rich area for academic exploration and practical innovation in design education.

Role of Religious Symbols in African Design

Religious symbols in African design serve as an intriguing intersection of faith, culture, and artistry. They are not merely aesthetic choices; these symbols carry the weight of spiritual doctrines, tribal histories, and communal ethics. Whether it is the Ankh symbol from ancient Egypt, representing life and immortality, or the Adinkra symbols in West Africa, each conveying unique wisdom or moral teaching, the significance runs deep. These symbols permeate various forms of design: from textiles and fashion to architectural structures and furniture. However, it is not just about the visual appeal or even the spiritual meaning in isolation; the incorporation of these symbols into design involves a broader, more intricate sociocultural dialogue. These designs serve as both an educational and mnemonic tool, promoting communal values and connecting present generations with ancestral wisdom. In a traditional setting, where oral traditions often take precedence over written records, symbols embedded in design elements serve as a form of language unto themselves, communicating complex layers of meaning that go beyond mere ornamentation.

This communicative power of religious symbols in African design suggests that the line between the sacred and the secular can often blur. Consider how these symbols could serve in both religious ceremonies and everyday utilitarian objects. A textile might adorn a sacred space but also serve as a functional item in a household. A pot or utensil might carry spiritual motifs, used in everyday cooking but also in religious rites. This dual function presents a unique challenge in decoding the symbol's purpose: is it merely functional, purely spiritual, or a nuanced blend of both? The question becomes more complex when we consider the growing trend of commercialising these religious symbols. In today's globalised market, African designs are increasingly finding their way into mainstream fashion, home decor, and even digital media. While this offers an opportunity for African artistry to gain global recognition, it also raises ethical questions. Is the symbol being used respectfully and contextually, or is it being appropriated, stripped of its original meaning and value?

For example, the Maasai tribe's intricate beadwork has been duplicated in high-fashion contexts without acknowledgment or compensation to the Maasai people. Such ethical quandaries underline the need for a responsible approach to incorporating religious symbols in design. It is not just a matter of artistic license; it is a dialogue that involves the custodians of these symbols, the designers who adapt them, and the consumers who engage with them.

The ethical dimension of using religious symbols extends into pedagogical practices as well. If design education incorporates these elements without a nuanced understanding or without giving due credit to their origins, it risks perpetuating a cycle of cultural misappropriation. It is crucial for educational curricula to include ethical guidelines, not just for the sake of political correctness, but as a profound engagement with the complex layers of spirituality, ethics, and cultural respect that these symbols carry. In essence, the role of religious symbols in African design is multifaceted. It serves to connect, educate, and inspire, but it also challenges designers and educators to think critically about the ethical implications of their choices. Ethical considerations begin with the intent behind incorporating a religious symbol. When used within the community that understands and respects its meaning, the symbol serves as a unifying cultural or spiritual element. However, problems may arise when these symbols are taken out of context or used in ways that disrespect their original significance. For instance, using a religious symbol purely for its aesthetic appeal, without acknowledging its deeper meaning, can be viewed as a form of cultural appropriation. This is not just a theoretical concern; real-world instances have led to controversies that question the ethical boundaries of artistic freedom.

A nuanced ethical approach would involve understanding the origins and significance of these symbols and engaging with them in a manner that respects their cultural context. This is easier said than done, especially in a globalised world where designs easily cross cultural and religious boundaries in the blink of an eye. This brings us to the domain of intellectual property rights and the complexities of attributing cultural ownership to design elements. For example, should a non-African designer pay royalties or seek permission to use an African religious symbol? Or is it sufficient to acknowledge the symbol's origins and treat it respectfully? The issue also extends to the classroom, where educators bear the responsibility of teaching not just the technical aspects of design but also the ethical nuances. It is a pedagogical challenge to impart the skills necessary to navigate the fine line between cultural appreciation and appropriation. Should curriculum developers include case studies that expose students to the controversies and ethical dilemmas that have arisen in the past? Or should they incorporate exercises that require students to research the cultural and spiritual significance of elements they wish to include in their designs? It is worth considering the concept of informed consent, particularly from the communities that are the custodians of these symbols. Just as ethical norms in research require informed consent from participants, could a similar principle apply in the design context? Could consultations with community leaders or spiritual authorities be a part of the design process when religious symbols are involved, particularly if the design is intended for commercial use or broader dissemination? Furthermore, there is an ethical consideration related to the consumer. When a consumer buys a product adorned with a religious symbol, they engage in a form of dialogue with the designer and the culture from which it originates. It is an indirect, material-based dialogue, but a form of communication, nonetheless. Do designers have a responsibility to educate their audience about the significance of these symbols? Should products come with tags explaining their cultural and religious significance?

As we have established, navigating the cultural and spiritual dimensions of these symbols is far from straightforward. So, how can design education rise to the challenge? One approach could be experiential learning, a pedagogical strategy that emphasizes active engagement over passive reception of information. This could involve field trips to cultural heritage sites, museums, or even religious institutions where students can firsthand observe the role of religious symbols in traditional and contemporary African designs. Immersing students in the environment where these designs originate offers them a more nuanced understanding than classroom instruction alone could provide. Community involvement stands out as a pivotal strategy in educational literature, recognized for its significant role in boosting learning achievements. In the context of design education, this could involve students partnering with local communities on design projects that serve those communities' needs. Such engagements would not only allow students to apply their skills in real-world settings but also give them the opportunity to learn directly from the custodians of the religious symbols they may be incorporating into their designs. It teaches respect for cultural context and, ideally, fosters a sense of responsibility toward ethical considerations.

Reflective practice serves as a crucial teaching technique, prompting students to critically evaluate their design decisions. By regularly documenting and reflecting on their design process, students can become more aware of their assumptions, including those concerning the use of religious symbols. Assignments could include reflective essays or journals that prompt students to consider the ethical implications of their design decisions. The use of case studies can also be effective. These could range from examining controversies arising from misuse of religious symbols to success stories where designers have successfully and respectfully incorporated these elements. Analysing these cases would provide students with real-world examples to dissect, discuss, and learn from, honing their critical thinking skills in the process. Role-playing exercises could also serve as an effective pedagogical tool. Students could be given scenarios that place them in the role of designers who must navigate ethical dilemmas involving the use of religious symbols. This can help students understand the complexities involved and think through the ethical considerations they would need to account for in real-world practice.

In summary, the teaching methodologies to address the complex ethical terrain around the use of religious symbols in African design need to be as multi-faceted as the issue itself. Experiential learning, community engagement, reflective practice, case studies, and role-playing exercises each offer valuable perspectives that can help students navigate the complexities involved. These methods should not be viewed as mutually exclusive but as complementary strategies that, when skilfully integrated, offer a holistic educational experience. This multipronged approach not only equips students with the technical skills they need but also cultivates an ethical awareness and cultural sensitivity that are just as crucial in the world of design.

Traditional African Mentor-Apprentice Systems

In traditional African educational settings, the mentor-apprentice system has been a cornerstone. Unlike the more formal, institution-based educational systems prevalent in many Western societies, the mentor-apprentice relationship in Africa is often deeply personal and multifaceted. The mentor is not just a transmitter of technical skills but often serves as a moral and spiritual guide. The relationship is inherently practical, rooted in real-world activities, but it is also steeped in the cultural and spiritual ethos of the community.

Contrast this with mainstream Western-centric approaches to design education, where the focus is often on individual achievement, detached from spiritual and community contexts. The educational setting is formalised, with structured curricula and evaluation metrics. While this system has its advantages, such as scalability and standardised assessment, it often lacks the deep, experiential, context-based learning that characterises the mentor-apprentice system. How then can we integrate these seemingly disparate approaches into a cohesive teaching methodology, particularly in the context of design education? One fresh idea could be to adopt a hybrid model that combines the structured, theoretical training of Western education with the experiential, spiritual, and community-centred ethos of the African mentor-apprentice system. Imagine a curriculum that incorporates community service projects, where students are paired with local mentors who guide them in both the technical and ethical aspects of design. This not only gives students real-world experience but also embeds them within a specific cultural and spiritual context, enriching their understanding of design as a multidimensional activity. The Yoruba spiritual tradition, which encompasses the interconnected realms of Orun and Aiye and a holistic understanding of human existence, could serve as a philosophical foundation for this integrated approach. This tradition emphasizes a balance between the spiritual and the material, values that can bring a more harmonious and inclusive focus into design education. This can manifest in collaborative projects that solve real community issues, guided by principles of sustainability and ethical awareness. It not only trains students in technical skills but also helps cultivate a sense of social responsibility and spiritual connectedness, attributes that are integral to African design traditions.

The essence of Ujamaa lies not only in fostering strong interpersonal relationships but also in nurturing a harmonious bond with the environment, objects, and artifacts. In the field of design, this translates to a deep consideration of the ethical and communal implications of one's work. Design under the Ujamaa philosophy is not solely focused on problem solving or aesthetic creation; it is an endeavour to enhance the welfare of the community, thereby contributing to the moral and ethical vigour of the individual designer. The challenge here is to cultivate a pedagogical approach that balances individual creativity with communal welfare, achieving both technical excellence and spiritual fulfilment. The aim is to develop designers who are not just adept craftsmen, but also moral beings profoundly connected to their communities and their cultural traditions. Integrating Ujamaa principles and elements of traditional cooperative workmanship, we can envision a more comprehensive approach to design education. This approach would encompass not just practical skills but also ethical discourse, community involvement, and spiritual contemplation, offering a well-rounded, contextually rich education for aspiring designers. This is more than a fusion of Western and African methodologies; it is an advancement that respects the intricacies of contemporary life while embracing timeless wisdom and cultural traditions.

Furthering the integration of Ujamaa and traditional cooperative systems in modern design education, it is crucial to explore how this model interacts with existing educational frameworks. In many Western institutions, accreditation and formal evaluations are standard. A key challenge is to formulate assessment criteria that respect the depth and subtlety of an education inspired by Ujamaa. This presents a chance for creative innovation. Traditional evaluation models, typically centred on individual accomplishment, could be broadened to include communal impact. For example, a student's design project could be assessed not just on aesthetics and functionality but also on its beneficial influence on the community and its ethical considerations. This aligns with the Ujamaa philosophy, underscoring that one's work reflects communal contribution, not just personal ability.

It also tackles a major discussion point in contemporary education: the balance between standardisation and customisation. Western education often leans towards standardisation for the sake of scalability and equality of assessment. But a truly integrated, Ubuntu-inspired system would require a more personalised approach, acknowledging the unique strengths, interests, and cultural backgrounds of each student. While this is more resource-intensive, advances in educational technology might provide tools to manage this complexity. Platforms that track not just grades but also interpersonal skills, ethical considerations, and community engagement could offer a more rounded view of a student's abilities and contributions. Moreover, the value of experiential learning, a cornerstone of the mentor-apprentice system, could be formally recognised through such a platform. Beyond traditional classroom settings, this opens doors for fieldwork, internships, and community projects to become essential components of design education. What if students, as part of their coursework, are required to spend time in local communities, working on real-world design problems under the guidance of experienced mentors? Such experiences could be incredibly enriching, providing hands-on experience while also deeply embedding students in a cultural and ethical context. In this way, an integrated educational approach does not just produce technically competent designers; it nurtures socially responsible and ethically aware citizens. It recognises that design is not an isolated activity but a deeply interconnected one. A chair is not just a chair; it is a statement of values, a product of its cultural context, and a contributor to the wellbeing (or detriment) of its users. A building is not just a structure; it is a space that shapes social interactions and impacts the environment.

The integrated approach calls for a revolution in how we think about design and education. It challenges the boundaries we have erected between academic and practical, between technical and ethical, between individual and community. In the end, it proposes a design education that is as complex, rich, and interconnected as the African tapestry that inspired it, driven by the timeless principles of Ubuntu and traditional wisdom. In the journey toward an integrated approach to design education, Ubuntu offers just one philosophical lens among many rich African traditions that can contribute to a more holistic model. Alongside Ubuntu, we have traditions such as Negritude, which originated as a literary and ideological movement among French-speaking black intellectuals but has philosophical implications for valuing black culture and heritage. Similarly, the concept of *Maat* from ancient Egyptian philosophy, emphasising harmony, balance, and order, could serve as another foundation. Negritude emphasizes the importance of connecting to one's cultural roots and encourages resistance to cultural assimilation. In the design context, this could inspire curricula that prioritise indigenous design languages and techniques over Western or global trends. This is not to perpetuate a division between "Western" and "African," but rather to foster a space where students can explore their identity and heritage as informing factors in their design choices. Maat, on the other hand, emphasizes ethical and social harmony. The philosophical implications for design are immense, especially in an era of increased awareness of sustainable and ethical design. It could inspire a pedagogical approach where ethical considerations are not just an add-on to the design process but are integrated from the very beginning. Imagine a design class where the first lessons are not about line, shape, or colour, but about ethics, sustainability, and social harmony, considered not as restrictions but as creative challenges.

An additional perspective worth exploring is the African principle of Sankofa from the Akan people of Ghana, which means "go back and retrieve it." Sankofa represents the idea that progress requires an acknowledgment and understanding of the past. In design education, Sankofa could encourage a curriculum where historical and cultural explorations are not peripheral but central to the learning experience. This could manifest in research projects that involve studying ancient African design artifacts or traditional crafting techniques as a foundational part of any new design endeavour. There is also the Yoruba concept of *Ase*, which signifies the power to create change and produce effects. This notion can lend itself to an empowerment model in design education, where students are not passive recipients of knowledge but active creators and changers of their environment. By engaging with Ase, students are imbued with the sense that their work carries both creative and transformative power. Drawing from these diverse African philosophies, design education becomes not merely a mechanical impartation of skills, but an invitation into a complex web of cultural, ethical, and spiritual considerations. It becomes a crucible for nurturing not just technical proficiency, but wisdom—an essential quality often overlooked in conventional educational settings. This holistic model would be revolutionary in its scope and impact, producing designers who are not only skilled but deeply rooted in ethical and cultural contexts. By integrating these rich philosophical underpinnings into modern design education, we pave the way for a more meaningful, impactful, and grounded approach to design—a truly revolutionary shift that honours the complexity and richness of African intellectual heritage.

Introduction to Spiritual Principles

In the discourse around design, spiritual principles often appear as a peripheral concern. However, when it comes to African design traditions and practices, the spiritual cannot be easily divorced from the aesthetic or the functional. This symbiosis reflects broader African cosmologies where the spiritual world is not a detached realm but interwoven with everyday life. Therefore, the design process is not merely an act of creating functional or aesthetically pleasing objects but is a deeper practice that can reflect, convey, and even engender spiritual values and communal ties. This spiritual ethos brings us to a compelling debate on the principles of individualism versus collectivism in design, a topic that transcends geographical and cultural boundaries but finds unique expression in Africa. Individualism in design often celebrates personal creativity, innovation, and the distinctiveness of the designer's voice. It is a model widely recognised in Western-centric design paradigms, which often champion the designer as an autonomous creator, distinct and separate from the community. This concept has been critically examined by scholars like Esio Mansini, who discusses the role of the designer in society and argues for more collaborative and community-oriented approaches (Manzini, 2015).

On the other side, collectivism in design has strong roots in many African traditions, where the act of creating is often communal and bound up with spiritual and ethical principles that prioritise the wellbeing of the community over the individual. For instance, traditional crafts like beadwork or weaving are not just acts of individual expression but are often community activities imbued with spiritual meanings. The design then becomes not an assertion of individual ego but a contribution to the ongoing, collective act of making culture, history, and even spirituality tangible. This divergence is not simply a binary choice between Western individualism and African collectivism; rather, it is a spectrum where design can be a harmonious blend of both. The challenge lies in how modern African design education can integrate these seemingly contrasting viewpoints into a holistic pedagogical approach. Can a space be created where individual creativity flourishes while still being tethered to community needs and spiritual sensitivities?

Diving into case studies illuminates the intricate interplay between individualism and collectivism within spiritually informed design practices in Africa. For instance, consider an artist collective in Senegal that integrates ancestral wisdom and indigenous spiritual motifs into contemporary furniture design. Here, each designer contributes their unique vision but does so within a framework that honours shared cultural and spiritual values. The output is neither a sole expression of individual artistry nor an undifferentiated product of communal effort. Instead, it embodies a delicate balance between individual creativity and collective ethos, enriched by the spiritual threads that run through it. A remarkable instance includes Daffonchio Architects in South Africa, an architectural firm that specializes in eco-friendly building techniques inspired by traditional African cosmologies. While Western green design principles often focus primarily on environmental impact, this firm incorporates rituals and spatial arrangements that facilitate a sense of spiritual wellbeing for the community. This is collectivism in action, yet each building is also a testament to the innovative spirit of its individual architects.

In examining these case studies, the role of education becomes a focal point. How can design curricula accommodate this richness of spiritual, individual, and collective considerations? Traditional educational approaches often risk compartmentalising these complex relations, especially under the influence of Western-centric pedagogical models that lean towards specialisation and individual assessment. It might be valuable to consider more integrative, interdisciplinary approaches. Courses could be designed to allow for collaborative projects that encourage individual expression while requiring students to engage with community needs or spiritual principles. Fieldwork could be integrated, connecting students directly with local communities and spiritual leaders to explore how design functions in different cultural and spiritual contexts. Here, a comparative analysis becomes instrumental. Comparing mainstream, often Western-centric, methodologies with traditional African approaches, such as mentor-apprentice systems, reveals the advantages and disadvantages of each, setting the stage for a synthesis of methodologies. The question is not whether modern design education should be spiritual, individualistic, or collectivist. Instead, the question is how it can be authentically all three, honouring the complexities and nuances that these dimensions offer. By carefully crafting educational experiences that reflect this multifaceted reality, we can prepare future designers for a world that is not only increasingly interconnected but also spiritually and culturally diverse.

Examples Showcasing the Work of Designers Who Integrate Spiritual Elements

The integration of spiritual elements into design practices has manifested in strikingly diverse yet deeply resonant ways across Africa. The works of specific designers offer tangible evidence of the layered impact of spirituality in design. For example, consider a Nigerian designer who specialises in textile designs based on Yoruba cosmology. Such textiles serve multiple functions: they are visually appealing, yes, but they also act as storytelling mediums that encapsulate Yoruba spiritual beliefs and narratives. Imagine these textiles imprinted with intricate designs that map out the Yoruba cosmological view of the universe, depicting not just traditional symbols but also encapsulating oral traditions, myths, and legends. When used in religious ceremonies, for instance, the textiles are not mere accessories; they are key elements that facilitate spiritual connection and meaning making. They have the power to transform ordinary experiences into spiritual journeys, providing a multisensory engagement that includes visual splendour, tactile interaction, and cultural relevance.

In Kenya, an innovative architect is redefining community spaces through the Kikuyu principle of *harambee*, signifying "all pull together." Community centres, libraries, and even open squares are designed in ways that promote social cohesion, encourage communal rituals, and allow for personal solitude simultaneously. In essence, these spaces function not merely as physical entities but as spiritual and social ecosystems, enhancing collective wellbeing. Now, what is the utility of such spiritually informed designs? At the most basic level, these designs serve functional needs efficiently. The textiles can be used as garments, decorations, or ceremonial accessories. The community spaces facilitate a variety of activities from community gatherings to individual solitude. But these designs offer a more profound impact that extends beyond their functional utilities. They resonate emotionally and spiritually with the people who interact with them. The Yoruba-themed textiles evoke a sense of cultural pride and spiritual connection among those who understand their symbolism. The Kenyan community spaces, designed under the harambee ethos, promote values like unity, collaboration, and mutual respect. It is a complex layering of functionality, emotional resonance, and spiritual depth, creating ecosystems rather than just objects or spaces. In educational contexts, such examples can provide compelling case studies for students, offering real-world applications of how spiritual considerations can be incorporated into design without sacrificing functionality or aesthetic value. By analysing these cases, students can gain insights into how to negotiate the complexities that come with incorporating spiritual elements into their work. They learn how to balance form and function with deeper spiritual or cultural meanings, a skill that has become increasingly important as design reaches into ever more diverse settings and audiences. The value of integrating these real-world applications into a curriculum cannot be overstated. Students gain more than just theoretical knowledge; they develop an understanding rooted in practical realities. They learn that design is not an isolated practice but a complex interplay of various factors, including cultural, spiritual, and social elements.

It is a multifaceted utility, one that operates at multiple levels—from the individual user to the broader community and even to the level of spiritual and cultural frameworks that underlie societal norms and values. For example, the Nigerian designer's textiles could also have economic benefits, empowering local artisans and contributing to cultural preservation efforts. Similarly, the Kenyan architect's designs could foster social capital, strengthening community bonds and contributing to collective wellbeing. Moving beyond the case studies and their utility, we delve into the pedagogical implications of incorporating spiritually informed designs in design education. The cases we have looked at—whether it is the Yoruba-inspired textiles or community spaces based on the concept of harambee—do more than offer examples of good design. They raise crucial questions about what it means to educate designers for a world that is not only diverse but also deeply spiritual.

The traditional Western-centric curriculum, which emphasizes a universalist and largely secular approach to design, often falls short in addressing these questions. Not that universal principles are not important; they are. However, the absence of cultural and spiritual considerations creates a gap in the education of a well-rounded designer, one who can engage with communities at a deeper, more nuanced level. In practical terms, what might the inclusion of spirituality in design education look like? First, the curriculum could incorporate modules that examine the role of spirituality in traditional and contemporary design practices across different cultures. The goal here is not to turn design students into theologians but to enrich their understanding of how spiritual values can influence design choices. Such modules could include hands-on activities that challenge students to design products or spaces that reflect specific spiritual or cultural values. They might, for example, be tasked with designing a product that aligns with the principle of Ubuntu, the concept emphasising communal values over individualism. Additionally, ethical considerations would be at the forefront of such a curriculum. Designers wielding the power to integrate spiritual elements into their work must do so respectfully and ethically. The commodification or appropriation of spiritual symbols for commercial gain, for instance, would be a topic of study and debate. Students must grapple with the complexities of how to ethically include spiritual elements, navigating the fine line between appropriation and appreciation, and between universal design principles and specific cultural needs. Assessment methodologies would also need to evolve to evaluate student designs not just on technical proficiency but also on their ability to integrate cultural and spiritual elements in a meaningful, respectful manner. For instance, peer and community reviews could be included as part of the evaluation process, providing feedback on how well the design resonates with the targeted cultural or spiritual community. Integrating spirituality into design education also has broader, systemic implications. The industry as a whole could benefit from a workforce trained to think beyond the material and functional aspects of design. This form of education can contribute to creating more sustainable, culturally relevant designs and can even push the industry towards a more ethical orientation. For example, a designer educated in this manner may prioritise community-led projects that align with local spiritual beliefs over commercially lucrative but culturally insensitive opportunities.

The potential challenges in incorporating spirituality into a modern design curriculum are not to be underestimated. Questions of representation, potential bias, and the complexity of interpreting spiritual symbols are real issues that educators must navigate. However, the alternative—ignoring the richness of spiritual traditions that influence design—seems a far more problematic approach, one that risks perpetuating a narrow, Eurocentric perspective on what design is and can be. Ultimately, it is about equipping future designers with the tools to create not just aesthetically pleasing or functionally effective designs, but ones that resonate on a deeply spiritual level with the communities they serve. It is about recognising that design is, at its core, a human-centred discipline, one that benefits from an understanding that extends beyond the physical and into the realm of the spiritual.

Approaches for Integrating Spirituality into Design Education

The quest to create a more comprehensive design education that integrates spirituality into the curriculum has led scholars and educators through a fascinating journey of exploration and experimentation. David Orr's contributions to ecological literacy also offer a critical narrative, emphasising that ethical and spiritual perspectives can serve as foundational elements in sustainable design (Orr, 1991). One of the key approaches to infuse spirituality into design education is the focus on experiential learning. The fundamental idea here is that learning is not just an intellectual exercise but a lived experience. Taking cues from educational theorist Paulo Freire's emphasis on praxis, experiential learning enables students to engage with the spiritual dimensions of design through direct, hands-on activities (Freire, 2021). Freire's pedagogical philosophy argues for an interactive learning environment where students are active participants rather than passive recipients of knowledge. This environment not only engages students in practical tasks but also encourages them to critically reflect on their experiences, subsequently informing their future actions.

Community engagement further enriches this experiential learning process. In this model, students do not just work on theoretical projects but participate in real-world design problems that require them to consider the spiritual and cultural elements inherent in the communities for which they are designing. The term "engaged pedagogy," coined by bell hooks, resonates here (hooks, 1996). It refers to an educational approach where teaching and learning occur in a way that not only benefits the student but also has a broader social impact. In this pedagogical setting, students are not the only beneficiaries; the community also gains from the students' work, fostering a symbiotic relationship. This notion is supported by participatory design principles, which encourage collaborative efforts in design processes. Scholars like Pelle Ehn have advocated for a participatory design methodology that functions as a democratised space, creating an environment where both learners and community members act as cocreators of both knowledge and tangible design solutions (Ehn et al., 2014).

The intertwining of experiential learning and community engagement in spiritually informed design education offers an enriched learning landscape. However, it also poses several pedagogical challenges and ethical considerations that need to be addressed thoughtfully. The aim is not merely to add a spiritual 'layer' to the existing curriculum but to fundamentally rethink how we approach design education. This shift will require ongoing scholarly discussion, carefully designed pedagogical strategies, and a willingness to iteratively refine educational practices. The goal is a transformative design education that is as deeply engaged with spirituality and ethics as it is with aesthetics and functionality. The incorporation of reflective practice into design education holds particular promise for an in-depth integration of spirituality. Borrowing from Donald Schön's compelling work, *The Reflective Practitioner*, which calls for an ongoing, introspective examination of one's own design processes and outcomes (Schön, 1984). This exercise is not just an academic one; it is a deeply personal and ethical exploration. Students, through reflective practice, engage with their designs not just as functional or aesthetic objects but as manifestations of spiritual, ethical, and cultural intentions and impacts. The objective is a deeper self-awareness that allows them to recognise their biases, including cultural and spiritual ones, and to navigate the ethical dimensions of design more responsibly. However, as we thread spirituality into design education, there are formidable challenges that accompany the promise. One of the most pressing is the ethical quagmire of cultural appropriation and misrepresentation. Here, the critiques outlined by Edward Said in his ground-breaking work, *Orientalism*, serve as a cautionary framework (Said, 1978). He points out the risk of othering or stereotyping cultures, especially when interpreting them through a Western lens. This ethical consideration is pivotal for design educators who want their students to respect the spiritual traditions they are incorporating into their work.

A further educational obstacle is the evaluation of designs influenced by spirituality. Traditional assessment criteria typically focus on technical skill, aesthetic quality, and functional utility. These benchmarks are likely to be insufficient when dealing with designs aimed at fulfilling deeper spiritual or cultural objectives. A more comprehensive assessment model is required, one that encapsulates a myriad of criteria ranging from ethics to cultural resonance. In this context, Nigel Cross's ideas in *Designerly Ways of Knowing* could offer a fresh avenue for exploration (Cross, 2001). Cross suggests a more fluid and open-ended approach to design evaluation, one that accommodates multiple forms of knowledge and various metrics of success (Cross, 2001). Combining all these dimensions—experiential learning, community engagement, reflective practice, and a nuanced approach to assessment and ethical considerations—yields a complex but richly textured mosaic for spiritually-informed design education. This is not a minor modification of existing curricula but rather a transformative shift that demands an equally transformative pedagogical approach. It calls for a holistic and deeply integrative pedagogical strategy, one that treats the design process not just as a technical endeavour, but as a complex interplay of aesthetics, functionality, ethics, and spirituality. Yet, this complexity is not without its frayed edges; ethical pitfalls and practical challenges will necessitate ongoing vigilance, scholarly discourse, and iterative refinement in both pedagogical and practical realms. This multi-layered, spiritually informed design education constitutes a pedagogical frontier that holds as much promise as it does complexity.

Ethical Dilemmas like Cultural Appropriation and Religious Imposition

Embarking on the integration of spirituality into design education unearths ethical complexities that cannot be ignored. The pitfalls of cultural appropriation and religious imposition, for instance, become areas of keen concern. When students are exposed to designs rooted in different spiritual traditions, there is a temptation to incorporate these into their own works. However, without adequate understanding or cultural context, this runs the risk of trivialising or misrepresenting sacred symbols, rituals, or philosophies. Similarly, the academic environment, often a melting pot of varied cultural and spiritual beliefs, raises the issue of religious imposition. How can educators impart knowledge about the spiritual aspects of design without appearing to impose a specific belief system? The academic setting aims to respect the diversity of belief systems among students; integrating spirituality in such a setting, therefore, can be akin to walking on a tightrope. So how can these complexities be navigated? One strategy involves deep cultural immersion as part of the design education curriculum. Rather than just reading about a spiritual tradition, students could be exposed to it through field trips, interviews with community leaders, or even temporary apprenticeships. This would serve a dual purpose: it enriches the students' understanding of the spiritual tradition they are studying and mitigates the risk of unintentional cultural appropriation by providing a richer, more nuanced understanding. An additional strategy is found within the concept of dialogical learning. Creating a classroom environment where open dialogue about these ethical concerns is encouraged can go a long way in fostering ethical sensitivity among budding designers. Students can be urged to share their own spiritual and cultural backgrounds and perspectives, and how these influence their understanding of design. This sharing of diverse viewpoints can create a vibrant insight that not only enriches everyone's perspective but also naturally weeds out any tendencies toward cultural appropriation or religious imposition by making students more aware of the weight their design choices carry.

As we delve deeper into the issue, it becomes evident that the ethical and spiritual considerations in design are not merely add-ons but core components that can significantly influence the outcome and impact of design projects. This observation leads us to the discussion of pedagogical models that can successfully marry the spiritual with the technical in design education. One possibility is a project-based learning model where students take on design challenges rooted in real-world spiritual or cultural contexts. This educational setup would encourage students to think holistically from the get-go, considering the social, ethical, and spiritual dimensions as they work through the design process. For example, a student tasked with designing a community centre might consider not just the utilitarian aspects like spatial efficiency but also the spiritual aspects like communal rituals, symbolic elements, and cultural practices that the space must accommodate. At the same time, fostering a culture of self-reflection can further enrich this learning experience. Here, students would regularly engage in reflective exercises that prompt them to consider the ethical implications of their design choices. In addition to written reflections, this could be facilitated through group discussions, one-on-one mentoring sessions, or even the use of digital portfolios that document not just the product but the entire thought process behind a design. The challenges of integrating spirituality into the curriculum also present an opportunity for interdisciplinary learning. Given the complex nature of the ethical issues at hand, collaborations with departments focused on ethics, philosophy, or religious studies could provide design students with a well-rounded understanding that goes beyond surface-level aesthetic considerations. For instance, a course module on ethics could be co-taught by faculty from the philosophy department, bringing in fresh perspectives on moral philosophy and ethical decision making.

Thus, a multidisciplinary, project-based, and reflective pedagogical model presents itself as a viable route for integrating spirituality into design education. Such an approach would not only arm students with the technical skills they need but also equip them with the ethical and spiritual sensibilities that are essential in today's interconnected, culturally diverse world. As design challenges become increasingly complex and laden with ethical considerations, the need for designers who can navigate these intricacies becomes even more crucial. Moving forward, there is a palpable need to consider how technology can serve this integrated approach to design education. Digital platforms could facilitate a more nuanced and expansive dialogue around the spiritual and ethical dimensions of design. Imagine a virtual space where students can showcase their designs alongside narratives that articulate the spiritual ethos driving their choices. Such a platform could also host virtual symposiums where students, educators, and experts from various disciplines can engage in conversations that probe the spiritual underpinnings of design in different cultural contexts.

In terms of assessment, breaking away from traditional grading systems might offer more room to evaluate the multifaceted nature of spiritually informed designs. Portfolio assessments, where students are evaluated based on a body of work rather than a single project, can provide a more comprehensive view of a student's ability to integrate spiritual and ethical considerations into their designs. This can be coupled with peer reviews that involve not only fellow students but also community members and experts in related fields like anthropology, religious studies, and ethics. Such a diversified approach to assessment recognises the inherently subjective and community-based nature of spiritual considerations. There is also an opportunity to explore partnerships with community organisations and spiritual leaders. These collaborations could offer students unique platforms to apply their learning in real-world scenarios, thus serving both educational and community-building objectives. For instance, a collaboration with a local church or temple could involve students in the redesign of a community space, where they would have the direct experience of dealing with spiritual and cultural intricacies. Importantly, this integrated pedagogical approach would require educators to engage in continuous professional development. Keeping up to date with ever-evolving ethical guidelines and cultural sensitivities is essential for guiding students through the minefield of ethical and spiritual considerations in design.

To sum up, the incorporation of spirituality into design education is not a one-off effort but an ongoing process that calls for innovative pedagogical strategies, cross-disciplinary collaborations, and a commitment to continuous learning and adaptation. While fraught with complexities and challenges, this integrative approach offers a path towards a more holistic, ethically grounded, and culturally sensitive design education. In conclusion, the challenge of integrating spirituality into design education goes beyond merely adding a new layer to the curriculum. It demands a fundamental rethinking of pedagogical strategies, assessment models, and the very ethos that guides design education. This is not merely an academic exercise but an essential undertaking that has the potential to enrich the field of design in immeasurable ways, making it more inclusive, ethically responsible, and culturally sensitive. By embracing an integrated approach that combines experiential learning, community engagement, and reflective practice, we stand a better chance of training designers who are not only technically competent but also spiritually and ethically grounded. These are the designers who can truly serve the diverse and complex needs of a global society. This quest is fraught with complexities, but its promise makes the journey worthwhile. It is an ongoing endeavour, one that will require the collective wisdom and effort of educators, scholars, students, and communities alike.

Integrated Approach Combining Spirituality, Culture, and Design

In the nexus of design, culture, and spirituality, there is an urgent call to re-imagine what design education can be and should be. The current paradigm, often rooted in Western-centric ideals, leans heavily on technical prowess and commercial viability. While these elements are undeniably important, they do not encapsulate the full scope of human experience and the diverse cultural landscapes we inhabit. By incorporating spirituality and cultural awareness into the design curriculum, we not only enrich the educational experience but also equip future designers to create work that resonates on a deeper, more universal level.

Curriculum changes could be multi-fold. First, courses that explore the historical and spiritual context of design in various cultures can be introduced, thereby providing a broader foundation. Second, experiential learning should be integrated, where students are placed in different cultural and spiritual settings to engage in design practice. This can range from local community projects to international collaborations. Third, the assessment criteria should be revised to include considerations for spiritual and cultural relevance in addition to functionality and aesthetics. Assignments that encourage students to reflect on their designs from these angles can help them become more conscientious creators. Moreover, students should be encouraged to critically analyse their work through a spiritual lens as part of their reflective practice. This could be facilitated through journaling, peer reviews, or guided discussions. Community-based projects could also serve as a platform for students to practice culturally and spiritually sensitive design, while simultaneously contributing to social good.

Yet, the most significant curriculum change could be the pedagogical shift toward an integrated approach. By blending spirituality, cultural studies, and design, we cultivate a learning environment that nurtures holistic designers who can navigate the intricacies of a pluralistic world. The implication here is far reaching: from fostering greater empathy and ethical mindfulness to driving innovations that are not merely technologically advanced but also culturally and spiritually resonant. In conclusion, the need for a new paradigm in design education is clear. One that not only teaches students how to make but also inspires them to think about why they make and for whom they make. An education that prepares them to engage with the world, in all its spiritual and cultural diversity, in a meaningful and respectful way. This is not just a pedagogical challenge but a moral imperative. It requires a collective effort among educators, scholars, practitioners, and communities to reshape the contours of design education, to be more inclusive, holistic, and ultimately, transformative. It is a bold vision, but one that is increasingly essential as we move further into a world defined by its interconnectedness and complex social fabric. This is our call to reimagine design education for the betterment of all.

Summary and Call to Action for a More Nuanced, Spiritually Aware Design Education

In summary, the current landscape of design education, heavily influenced by a Western-centric approach, often fails to consider the intricate layers of spirituality and culture. As we navigate an increasingly interconnected world marked by cultural and spiritual diversity, there is a pressing need to cultivate designers who are not just skilled artisans but also thoughtful curators of experiences that respect and celebrate this diversity. Curriculum changes that incorporate spirituality, cultural awareness, and ethical considerations are not just additive; they are transformative. They can enrich the design process, add depth to the educational experience, and create designs that resonate more profoundly with a broader audience. As we look toward the future, the question is not whether we can afford to integrate these elements into design education but whether we can afford not to.

Therefore, the call to action is clear: educators, scholars, and design practitioners must collectively strive to reimagine and reform design education. By integrating spirituality and cultural understanding as core components of the curriculum, we can foster a new generation of designers equipped to create meaningful, impactful, and inclusive designs. It is not merely about a curriculum overhaul but a fundamental shift in how we conceive design's role in society. Let us embark on this essential journey, meeting the moral imperative to produce not just functional but also spiritually and culturally resonant designs. This is a call to action for a more nuanced, spiritually aware design education.

References

Abdelnour-Nocera, J., Ondieki Makori, E., Robles-Flores, J. A., & Bitso C., *Innovation practices for digital transformation in the Global South: IFIP WG 13.8, 9.4, Invited Selection*. 59–78. Springer.

Abiodun, R. (2014). *Yoruba art and language: Seeking the African in African art*. Cambridge University Press.

Appiah, K. A. (1993). *In my father's house: Africa in the philosophy of culture*. Oxford University Press. https://doi.org/10.2307/1581314

Auslander, L., & Zahra, T. (2018). *Objects of war: The material culture of conflict and displacement*. Cornell University Press.

Basu, P. (2017). *The inbetweenness of things: materializing mediation and movement between worlds*. Bloomsbury Publishing.

Bhabha, H. K. (2012). *The location of culture*. Routledge. https://doi.org/10.4324/9780203820551

Bidwell, N. J., & Winschiers-Theophilus, H. (2012). Audio pacemaker: walking, talking indigenous knowledge. Proceedings of the South African Institute for Computer Scientists and Information Technologists Conference: 149–158. Pretoria, 1–3 October.

Cross, N. (2001). Designerly ways of knowing: Design discipline versus design science. *Design Issues, 17*(3): 49–55.

Ehn, P., Nilsson, E. M., & Topgaard, R. (2014). *Making futures: Marginal notes on innovation, design, and democracy*. The MIT Press.

Enwezor, O., & Okeke-Agulu, C. (2009). *Contemporary African art since 1980*. Damiani Bologna.

Fitzgerald, K. (2010). *Volume: Writings on graphic design, music, art, and culture*. Chronicle Books.

Freire, P. (2021). *Pedagogy of hope: Reliving pedagogy of the oppressed*. Bloomsbury Publishing.

Harney, E. (2004). *In Senghor's shadow: Art, politics, and the avant-garde in Senegal, 1960–1995*. Duke University Press.

hooks, b. (1996). Teaching to transgress: Education as the practice of freedom. *Journal of Leisure Research, 28*(4): 316. https://doi.org/10.4324/9780203700280

Magoro, K. D., & Bidwell, N. J. (2022). Land, Letšema and Leola: Digital Transformation on a Rural Community's Own Terms. In J. Abdelnour-Nocera, E. O. Makori, J. A. Robles-Flores, C. Bitso (Eds.), *Innovation Practices for Digital Transformation in the Global South*. IFIP Advances in Information and Communication Technology, vol 645. 59–78. Springer. https://doi.org/10.1007/978-3-031-12825-7_4

Manzini, E. (2015). *Design, when everybody designs: An introduction to design for social innovation*. MIT press.

Moalosi, R., Marope, O., & Setlhatlhanyo, K. N. (2017). Decolonising Botswana's design education curricula by infusing indigenous knowledge: Ubuntu co-creation process. In M. T. Gumbo, & V. Msila (Eds.), *African voices on indigenisation of the curriculum: Insights from practice*. 66–96. Reach Publisher.

Okofu, N. P., & Fakere, A. A. (2022). Decolonising the Curriculum of Architectural Education in Nigeria: A Case of Negotiated Pedagogy. *Journal of Asian and African Studies, 59*(3). https://doi.org/10.1177/00219096221124939.

Orr, D. W. (1991). *Ecological literacy: Education and the transition to a postmodern world*. State University of New York Press.

Picton, J. (2021). *African textiles*. Routledge.

Pogoson, O. I. (1990). The question of outside origins for the Esie stone carvings. *African Notes: Bulletin of the Institute of African Studies, University of Ibadan*, 14(1–2): 42–51.

Said, E. (1978). *Orientalism*. Routledge.

Schön, D. A. (1984). The architectural studio as an exemplar of education for reflection-in-action. *Journal of Architectural Education, 38*(1): 2–9.

Strother, Z. S. (1999). *Inventing masks: agency and history in the art of the Central Pende*. University of Chicago Press.

Walker, S. (2020). *Design and spirituality: a philosophy of material cultures*. Routledge.

Walker, S. (2023). *Design for resilience: Making the future we leave behind*. MIT Press.

4
POLITICS AND THE POSTCOLONIAL IDEALS

Use of Design to Fight Injustice, Racism, and Apartheid

Chapter 3 took a focused look at how the internal worlds of spirituality and culture deeply influence the practice and perception of design. It illuminated the pedagogical underpinnings that are shaped by experiential learning, community engagement, and reflective practice. In that context, design was perceived as an extension of one's internal belief systems and community norms, intricately tied to spiritual and cultural identities. Now, as we venture into chapter 4, the scope expands to include the external political and social forces that shape and are shaped by design. These forces, often deeply rooted in historical contexts and carrying substantial sociopolitical implications, influence design decisions and their broader impact on society. It is critical to appreciate that the shift from spirituality and culture to politics is not a departure but an expansion. Spirituality and politics are not isolated domains but rather operate on a continuum where individual beliefs and cultural norms intersect with broader social and political structures. In this chapter, the aim is to navigate the complex terrain where design meets politics, specifically focusing on postcolonial contexts that bear their own unique sets of challenges and opportunities. Here, we will explore how design can either perpetuate systemic inequalities or serve as a catalyst for change and empowerment. By doing so, this chapter aims to weave the more abstract, spiritual, and cultural aspects discussed in chapter 3 into the concrete, tangible, and often contentious realm of politics and social justice.

Importance of Understanding Design's Role in Political and Social Contexts

The realm of design is a complex interplay of functionality, aesthetics, and messaging that extends far beyond mere appearance or utility. At its core, every design decision is a pronouncement of values, a delineation of priorities, and a distribution of resources. Whether it is the materials chosen for a building, the user accessibility of a digital interface, or the spatial arrangement of a public square, these choices are inherently fraught with political meaning. For instance, the design of a public square can either facilitate democratic ideals by encouraging free assembly and speech, or it can stymie them through the strategic placement of physical barriers and surveillance infrastructure. Essentially, design can either uphold existing power dynamics or serve as a conduit for social change and emancipation.

Understanding this intrinsic political dimension is crucial but becomes even more critical in postcolonial contexts. In such settings, the political implications of design decisions are compounded by the enduring legacies of colonialism. Whether It is the remnants of architectural styles that privilege Eurocentric aesthetics or urban planning strategies that marginalise indigenous communities, the residues of colonial imposition are palpably present. In these scenarios, the act of designing is never merely a neutral professional practice; it is a deeply political act that can either reinforce historical injustices or contribute to their dismantling. In societies still struggling with the long-lasting impacts of colonial rule, understanding the politics of design becomes more than an academic endeavour—it evolves into a moral imperative and social responsibility. Designers, educators, and policymakers in such contexts are endowed with the complex task of navigating this nuanced landscape, making conscious choices that can either perpetuate systemic inequalities or challenge and eventually break down these entrenched hierarchies.

Overview of the Postcolonial Ideals as They Pertain to Design

Postcolonial ideals in design are intrinsically about decentring. This involves questioning the canon, problematising the assumed universality of Western design principles, and paying homage to the richness of indigenous design vocabularies. In practical terms, this could mean several things: sourcing local materials for construction projects to benefit local economies, acknowledging and integrating traditional aesthetic principles into modern designs, or involving community members in the design process to ensure that their needs and cultural sensitivities are met. The framework of postcolonialism offers a lens to dissect how design serves as a form of expression that can either perpetuate or challenge colonial legacies. When integrated thoughtfully, these ideals can lead to a more equitable design practice that respects cultural diversity and champions social justice. Thus, this chapter aims to explore how design can be reoriented to meet the ethical and political challenges of our time, particularly in contexts that have suffered the brunt of colonial exploitation. It will do so by examining historical instances, contemporary case studies, and proposing future-forward strategies.

In summary, the objective is to move beyond mere aesthetics or functionality, towards a more politically conscious, ethically responsible, and socially equitable design paradigm. This transition is not just an expansion but a necessary evolution, forging a link between the spiritual-cultural considerations discussed in chapter 3 and the broader sociopolitical landscape that forms the focus of this chapter.

Historical Context: Design in the Age of Colonisation

In chapter 2, we laid the foundational understanding of how design is deeply interwoven with political and societal fabrics. As we move deeper into the topic, this section aims to excavate the specific layers of history that have significantly impacted design paradigms. We delve into the colonial period, a crucial era that has left an indelible imprint on the realm of design.

Colonial Exploitation and Its Impact on Indigenous Design Practices

In broadening the scope of our inquiry, we uncover the intricate ways in which the colonial period distorted indigenous design philosophies. Beyond the overtly visible impositions of colonial rule, the subtle shifts in design approaches had lasting effects that are often overlooked. While resource extraction and direct economic gain were undoubtedly pivotal motivations for colonial enterprises, the lesser-known tale is the subversion of indigenous design practices (Smith, 2021). Upon arrival in new territories, colonial powers usually encountered cultures that had refined their design sensibilities over centuries. These indigenous design frameworks, as highlighted by King (2019), were holistic and purposeful, deeply embedded in communal identities and serving functional roles while also sustaining ethical and spiritual aspects of life.

However, colonial rulers saw these practices not as complex systems worth studying and understanding but as rudimentary techniques needing improvement (Andreotti, 2011). The imposition of Eurocentric design principles, often justified under the guise of so-called civilising missions, a term now recognised as synonymous with cultural eradication, was environmentally unsustainable in many cases. For instance, the British colonial rule in India led to the deforestation of vast tracts of land, disregarding local, sustainable woodcraft practices (Kumar, 2018). By devaluing and often dismantling indigenous design systems, colonial powers effectively severed the links between communities and their ancestral wisdom, leading to the decay of native crafts and the disempowerment of local artisans (Papachristodoulou, 2023). This was not a mere shift in aesthetics or utility; it led to the decline of their status within their communities. The effects of this design appropriation were not only immediate but had a snowballing impact over generations, making colonised communities economically reliant on their colonisers for even basic necessities (Begum, 2015). This cycle further entrenched the inferiority of indigenous designs in the collective psyche, making it increasingly challenging to resurrect these practices in the postcolonial era (Breidlid, 2013). Thus, examining colonial exploitation through the lens of its impact on indigenous design gives us a fuller understanding of its long-lasting effects. While the economic and political dimensions have been thoroughly discussed, this facet opens up new avenues for appreciating the depth of cultural dislocation and loss that took place, affecting the design landscape in ways still manifest today (Brock-Utne, 2005).

The Erasure and Marginalisation of Traditional Design Methods and Aesthetics

In discussing the erasure and marginalisation of traditional design methods and aesthetics, It is pivotal to weave in contemporary perspectives, particularly those of African scholars who offer critical insights into this complex landscape. Integrating the scholarly contributions of African academics such as Achille Mbembe (Mbembe, 2017), Felwine Sarr (Sarr, 2023), and Nkiru Nsegwu (Nzegwu, 1994) brings a multidimensional understanding to this topic. Achille Mbembe, known for his seminal work on postcolonialism, presents a theoretical framework that helps us understand how colonial power dynamics facilitated the erasure of indigenous design traditions. Mbembe (2017) articulates that design was not merely functional; it was symbolic, reflecting local cosmologies, social orders, and philosophies. Yet, colonial powers disregarded these layers of meaning, enforcing a decontextualization that led to the degradation of traditional designs. Sarr (2023), meanwhile, delves into how economic models during the colonial era contributed to the devaluation of indigenous craftsmanship (Sarr, 2023). In many African societies, design was a collective enterprise, interwoven with communal values. Sarr argues that the shift to market-based economic systems, as imposed by colonial rulers, fragmented this social fabric, leading to the commodification and subsequent marginalisation of indigenous designs. In many African societies, design—be it in textiles, pottery, or architecture—was a gender-inclusive practice. Nzegwu (1994) highlights how colonial regimes imposed patriarchal structures that excluded women and marginalised their contributions to traditional design, thereby altering the aesthetics and techniques that were handed down through generations. Combining these insights with our existing framework, we recognise that the marginalisation of indigenous designs was not an accidental by product of colonial rule but a targeted effort. From the transformation of economic systems that devalued traditional crafts to the imposition of patriarchal norms, colonial powers employed multiple avenues to dismantle indigenous design paradigms. These changes were not superficial; they struck at the core of social, economic, and spiritual systems that had sustained these traditions for centuries.

Even today, the effects of this marginalisation are palpable. Indigenous craftspeople struggle to maintain traditions in a global market that often privileges Western aesthetics. Museums, often situated in the West, house invaluable artifacts of these marginalised designs, further detaching them from their native contexts and reducing them to mere objects of curiosity rather than lived cultural heritage. Extending the discussion, one of the crucial dimensions often overlooked in the discourse surrounding the erasure of indigenous designs is the role of education. The educational systems in many postcolonial countries still operate under curricula that were initially designed during colonial times, often marginalising or entirely omitting the rich history and complexities of indigenous designs, aesthetics, and crafts (Dennis, 2018). Consequently, newer generations grow up with limited exposure to their own cultural heritage, further amplifying the erasure that started centuries ago. Another essential point is the influence of globalised media, which often perpetuates Western design standards as the ideal (Enwezor & Okeke-Agulu, 2009). Whether in fashion, architecture, or digital design, these international norms subtly reinforce the notion that indigenous aesthetics are "less than" or "outdated," which has a real-world impact on local artisans and designers trying to keep traditional practices alive. The ubiquity of such messages creates a perceptual barrier for indigenous design to be seen as equally valid, contemporary, or desirable. Additionally, the role of intellectual property rights in the marginalisation of indigenous designs cannot be underestimated (Moreton-Robinson, 2015). Traditional knowledge and designs often fall into the realm of common goods in indigenous communities. However, the Western legal framework around intellectual property commodifies this knowledge, making it possible for entities to own and sell designs that have been communal heritage for centuries. This not only leads to cultural appropriation but also strips away any economic incentives that local communities might gain from their indigenous designs, driving yet another wedge between traditional artisans and their craft.

In conclusion, the marginalisation of traditional designs is a multifaceted issue with economic, cultural, and social dimensions. It is not only the echo of a colonial past, but a present and persistent reality shaped by contemporary educational systems, global media, and legal structures. Understanding this complex web is vital for any serious attempt to reclaim, revive, and honour these invaluable aspects of indigenous culture in the postcolonial era (Woolman, 2001). Therefore, the conversation must move beyond merely identifying the issue to actively seeking interdisciplinary, culturally informed solutions that address the root causes and offer sustainable paths for revival. In summary, by infusing our analysis with the contemporary perspectives of African scholars, we gain a richer, more nuanced understanding of how traditional design methods were marginalised. Their voices add critical depth, helping us see that this marginalisation is not merely historical but ongoing, impacting the cultural, economic, and social spheres of postcolonial societies. Thus, to genuinely understand the erasure of traditional designs, we must listen to those most affected by it, so as to find pathways for restoration and reclamation in the postcolonial era (Arnold, 2021; Mbembe, 2001; Nzegwu, 1994).

Case Studies: Colonial Impact on African, Asian, and Indigenous American Designs

To fully appreciate the colonial impact on design across different cultures, examining specific case studies from African, Asian, and Indigenous American contexts can provide a comprehensive understanding. These examples not only elucidate the variances in how colonialism affected different regions but also highlight some common themes, including the suppression of indigenous designs and the imposition of foreign aesthetics and methods.

African Design: Kente Cloth and Modern Fashion

Take, for instance, the production of Kente cloth in Ghana, a traditional form of weaving with vibrant patterns and colours, each with its unique meaning. Kente was traditionally a royal fabric, worn only by kings and dignitaries. However, the colonial period saw the commercialisation and mass production of Kente-inspired products, which were often produced outside Ghana using synthetic materials. This not only devalued the cultural significance of Kente but also led to a decline in traditional weaving techniques. However, postcolonial designers are now reclaiming Kente by incorporating it into modern fashion, thereby striving to balance cultural preservation with innovation.

Historical and Cultural Significance of Kente Cloth

Kente cloth, originating from the Ashanti Kingdom of Ghana, is more than just fabric; it is a visual representation of history, philosophy, ethics, oral literature, religious beliefs, social values, and political thought. Traditionally, Kente was woven from silk and cotton, with each colour and pattern symbolising specific cultural concepts. For instance, gold represents status and serenity, green signifies renewal and growth, and blue denotes peacefulness, harmony, and love. The intricate patterns are not random but are carefully designed to convey messages and stories, each a distinct expression of the weaver's artistic vision and the community's heritage.

Kente in the Royal Context

In its origins, Kente cloth was a symbol of prestige and exclusivity, reserved primarily for royalty and the elite. It was worn during significant events and ceremonies, such as coronations, festivals, and important gatherings. The exclusivity of Kente reflected its intricate production process and the time required to weave these elaborate patterns. This exclusivity and significance made Kente a treasured item, reflecting the wearer's high social status and connection to their cultural roots.

Introduction of Mass-Produced Textiles

During the colonial era, European powers introduced mass-produced textiles to the African market. These textiles were often cheaper and more readily available than traditional handwoven fabrics like Kente. The influx of these foreign textiles significantly disrupted the local textile industry. The traditional process of Kente weaving is labour intensive and time consuming, making it difficult for these artisans to compete with the cheaper, mass-produced alternatives. As a result, many local weavers faced economic hardships, and the market for authentic Kente began to shrink.

Impact on Artisanal Skills and Knowledge

The decline in demand for traditional Kente had a direct impact on the transmission of weaving skills and knowledge. Kente weaving is not merely a craft; it is an art form steeped in cultural history and symbolism. It is traditionally learned through apprenticeships, with skills and knowledge passed down from one generation to the next. As the market for Kente declined, fewer young people took up weaving, leading to a gradual erosion of these traditional skills. This not only affected the economic wellbeing of the weavers but also threatened the preservation of an important cultural practice.

Dilution of Cultural Authenticity

The production of Kente-inspired designs using synthetic materials further diluted the cultural authenticity of Kente cloth. These imitations, often produced outside of Ghana, lacked the intricate symbolism and quality of authentic Kente. Each pattern and colour in traditional Kente has specific meanings and is tied to the history and values of the Ghanaian people. The mass-produced versions, lacking these cultural nuances, contributed to a misunderstanding and misrepresentation of Kente's cultural significance in the global market.

Devaluation in the Global Market

As Kente-inspired textiles flooded the market, the perception and value of authentic Kente cloth were adversely affected. The inability of the global market to distinguish between authentic Kente and mass-produced imitations led to a devaluation of the craft. This not only had economic implications for the weavers but also cultural implications, as the unique identity and significance of Kente were undermined.

Loss of Economic Independence

Prior to colonialism, Kente weavers in Ghana enjoyed a certain level of economic independence and prestige. The craft was not only a source of livelihood but also a source of pride and cultural identity. The shift towards mass-produced textiles undermined this independence, making weavers and their communities economically vulnerable and dependent on the colonial economy.

Resistance and Adaptation

In response to these challenges, some Kente weavers began to adapt their techniques and designs to suit the changing market. This included the incorporation of new materials and the creation of designs that were less labour intensive. While this allowed some weavers to sustain their craft, it further contributed to the departure from traditional Kente weaving practices.

Contemporary Repercussions

The legacy of colonialism in the realm of Kente weaving is still felt today. The struggle to preserve traditional weaving techniques and the challenge of competing with mass-produced textiles continue to impact weavers in Ghana. There is, however, a growing awareness and appreciation of the cultural and historical significance of authentic Kente, both within Ghana and internationally. This has led to efforts to revive traditional weaving practices and educate consumers about the value of authentic Kente cloth.

Postcolonial Reclamation and Modern Fashion

In the postcolonial era, there has been a renaissance in African fashion, with designers keen to explore and celebrate their heritage. Contemporary African designers are now integrating Kente into modern fashion in innovative ways. They are not just using the fabric; they are weaving new stories and meanings into it, making it relevant to contemporary lifestyles and fashion trends. This integration serves a dual purpose: it preserves the cultural significance of Kente while making it accessible and appealing to a global audience.

Innovative Use of Kente in Modern Design

Today's designers are blending Kente with other fabrics and incorporating it into various clothing styles, from casual wear to high-end fashion. They are experimenting with Kente patterns in non-traditional colours, adapting them for a broader range of garments such as jackets, dresses, and accessories. This innovative use of Kente not only pays homage to the traditional craft but also showcases its versatility in contemporary fashion.

Economic and Social Implications

The resurgence of interest in Kente has significant economic and social implications. It provides a boost to local economies, supporting weavers and artisans who preserve these traditional techniques. It also fosters a sense of pride and identity among African communities, reinforcing the importance of cultural heritage in an increasingly globalised world. Furthermore, the global recognition of Kente as a luxury and culturally rich fabric helps to rectify the historical devaluation experienced during the colonial period.

Challenges and Future Directions

Despite these positive trends, challenges remain. The global market is flooded with imitation Kente fabrics, which undermines the value of authentic handwoven Kente. Addressing issues of intellectual property, ensuring fair trade, and raising awareness about the authenticity and cultural significance of true Kente are essential steps in preserving this heritage. Additionally, encouraging and supporting the next generation of weavers is crucial for the craft's survival and evolution.

Role of Education and Community Engagement

Educational initiatives that teach the history and techniques of Kente weaving can play a vital role in preserving this tradition. Community engagement, through workshops and exhibitions, can also help in spreading awareness about the cultural and historical importance of Kente. Such initiatives ensure that the knowledge and skills are passed down to younger generations, keeping the tradition alive and evolving.

Global Recognition and Cultural Exchange

The global fashion industry's recognition of Kente cloth as a symbol of African heritage is a positive step toward cultural exchange and appreciation. International designers collaborating with African artisans and incorporating Kente in their collections can foster a respectful exchange of ideas and promote cultural diversity in the fashion industry.

Conclusion

In conclusion, the journey of Kente from a royal, culturally significant fabric to a symbol of African heritage in modern fashion is a testament to the resilience and adaptability of cultural traditions. By reclaiming and innovatively integrating Kente into contemporary fashion, designers are not only preserving a rich cultural heritage but also opening new avenues for creative expression. This harmonious blend of tradition and modern

The Essence of Traditional Indian Architecture

Traditional Indian architecture is a diverse and complex field, reflecting the country's vast geographical, cultural, and historical diversity. Indian architects historically emphasized functionality, aesthetics, and spirituality. Structures were designed with a deep understanding of local climates, materials, and socio-cultural needs. For instance, in the arid regions of Rajasthan, traditional homes featured 'Jharokhas'—overhanging enclosed balconies that provided shade, facilitated air circulation, and offered a vantage point for inhabitants. Similarly, in the wetter regions like Kerala, houses were built with steeply pitched roofs and large overhangs to protect against heavy rain.

Sustainability and Community in Design

A key aspect of traditional Indian architecture was its sustainability. Local materials like mud, wood, bamboo, and stone were predominantly used, ensuring that the buildings were ecologically harmonious and resource efficient. Community involvement in building processes was also typical, reflecting a collective approach to habitat creation. This community-centric approach fostered a sense of belonging and identity, as seen in the layout of traditional Indian villages where homes were clustered around central communal spaces like temples or courtyards.

British Colonial Influence on Indian Architecture

The British colonial period marked a significant shift in Indian architecture. The introduction of Victorian and European architectural styles was more than a mere aesthetic change; it represented a cultural imposition and a statement of power. These styles, characterised by heavy masonry, gothic arches, and extensive use of glass, were ill-suited to the Indian climate. Colonial buildings often required extensive resources for maintenance, particularly in regulating temperatures, which was a stark departure from the climatically adapted traditional structures.

Postcolonial Struggle with Architectural Identity

Postindependence, Indian architecture faced the challenge of forging a new identity. There was a tension between embracing modern, international architectural trends and reviving traditional practices. This period saw a blend of styles, with some architects attempting to integrate traditional elements into modern designs. However, the rapid urbanisation and desire for modernity often led to the sidelining of traditional architectural wisdom.

Contemporary Efforts in Reviving Traditional Practices

In recent years, there has been a growing awareness of the value of traditional Indian architectural principles, especially in the context of sustainability and climate adaptation. Modern Indian architects are increasingly seeking to blend traditional techniques with contemporary designs. The use of Jharokhas, courtyards, verandas, and locally sourced materials is re-emerging as a response to the challenges posed by climate change and resource constraints.

Challenges in Modern Adaptation

One of the primary challenges in this modern adaptation is balancing the aesthetics and functionality of traditional designs with the demands of modern building standards and urban lifestyles. There is also a need for education and awareness among both architects and the public about the benefits of traditional architectural practices, especially in terms of sustainability and cultural preservation.

Role of Government and Educational Institutions

The Indian government and educational institutions play a crucial role in this revival. Policies that encourage the use of traditional designs and techniques in new constructions can be instrumental. Architectural education that integrates traditional Indian concepts with modern architectural theories can prepare a new generation of architects who are well-versed in both worlds.

Technology's Role in Reviving Traditional Architecture

Advancements in technology can also aid the revival of traditional Indian architecture. Digital tools and new materials can be used to reinterpret traditional designs, making them more adaptable to contemporary needs. For example, using advanced software to model traditional cooling techniques like Jharokhas can help integrate them effectively into modern high-rise buildings.

Cultural and Heritage Preservation

Preserving traditional Indian architecture is not just about maintaining a building style; It is about preserving a cultural heritage. These architectural styles tell the stories of India's past, its social structures, its climate adaptations, and its artistic sensibilities. Efforts in preservation also include restoring and maintaining old structures, which are a part of India's rich historical legacy.

Conclusion

In summary, traditional Indian architecture offers invaluable lessons in sustainability, community-centric design, and climate adaptation. The colonial period's imposition of European styles disrupted this tradition, leading to a period of architectural identity crisis. However, contemporary Indian architecture is increasingly seeking to rediscover and integrate these traditional elements. This endeavour is not only about aesthetic preferences but also about responding to environmental challenges and preserving a rich cultural heritage. The synthesis of traditional wisdom with modern techniques and materials presents a promising path for Indian architecture, one that respects its past while looking towards a sustainable future.

Common Threads

The exploration of colonial impact on indigenous designs across various cultures unveils a complex web of cultural dislocation, economic upheaval, and challenges brought by modernization and globalization. These shared experiences reveal a pattern where indigenous designs, once deeply rooted in communal heritage, transformed into commodities for a global market. A critical consequence of this shift was the weakening of cultural identity. Traditional designs, with rich histories and meanings, were often simplified or modified to appeal to foreign tastes, leading to misrepresentation of their cultural significance and a loss of identity, as the original contexts and meanings of these designs were either overlooked or forgotten. This alteration was not just aesthetic; it signified a deeper erosion of cultural narratives and practices that had been nurtured over generations. Economically, the shift towards mass-produced goods significantly impacted local artisans and craftspeople. These individuals, who were the custodians of traditional techniques and knowledge, found themselves competing against cheaper, industrially produced alternatives. The resulting economic disparities often forced artisans to abandon their crafts or significantly alter them to survive in the new market. This decline in traditional craftsmanship contributed to a loss of economic independence within these communities, undermining their cultural sustainability. In the postcolonial era, efforts to reclaim and modernise traditional designs have been fraught with challenges. The loss of ancient techniques, a significant issue, arose as many traditional skills were not passed down through generations due to decreased demand or the allure of more profitable, modern professions. Additionally, the globalised design standards, often dominated by Western aesthetics, continue to overshadow traditional designs, making it difficult for them to be seen as contemporary or relevant in a global market.

The influence of colonial design paradigms persists in contemporary design practices. This is evident in the ongoing preference for Western aesthetics in global fashion, architecture, and other design fields. This preference often marginalises indigenous designs, relegating them to the status of exotic or ethnic artifacts rather than recognising them as equally valid and contemporary forms of expression. In an increasingly globalised world, the line between cultural exchange and cultural appropriation has become blurred. While globalisation has facilitated the spread of diverse design practices, it has also led to instances where indigenous designs are co-opted without proper acknowledgment or understanding of their cultural significance. This appropriation often strips designs of their meaning and further contributes to the erosion of cultural heritage.

These case studies serve as both a cautionary tale and a call to action for a more conscious and inclusive approach to design in a global context. This involves recognising and respecting the cultural significance of indigenous designs, ensuring fair compensation and acknowledgment for artisans, and fostering an environment where traditional and modern design practices can coexist and enrich each other. It also involves educating designers and consumers about the history and meaning behind indigenous designs to promote a deeper appreciation and understanding. Understanding these dynamics is crucial for addressing the lingering effects of colonialism and fostering a design landscape that is diverse, equitable, and respectful of all cultural expressions. As such, these historical insights not only serve as a cautionary tale but also as a guide for shaping a more inclusive and culturally sensitive future in design.

Deconstructing the Colonial Mindset in Design

Deconstructing the colonial mindset in design demands a profound, insightful exploration into the depths of human consciousness and the psychological mechanisms underpinning colonialism. This endeavour extends beyond surface-level changes, requiring a fundamental shift in how we perceive, value, and engage with different design philosophies.

Ingrained Bias in Design Education

The colonial mindset in design education is deeply rooted, often unconsciously so. Educational systems that predominantly favour European and Western methods reinforce a cognitive framework where these approaches are seen as the benchmark of quality and innovation. This bias is not merely about the inclusion or exclusion of certain styles or histories; It is about the underlying value systems that are being communicated. Students, absorbing these values, often develop a cognitive schema that places Western designs at the top of a hierarchical ladder of design excellence. This leads to a form of cultural myopia, where the appreciation and understanding of non-Western designs are diminished or even completely overlooked. In the exploration of ingrained biases within design education, it is essential to understand the multifaceted nature of this issue, encompassing cognitive, linguistic, global, and technological dimensions. This section aims to uncover these varied aspects, examining their impacts and proposing solutions through alternative pedagogical models and industry-academia collaborations. The cognitive and psychological impacts of a biased design education on students are profound and often underestimated. As McPartlan et al. (2021) assert, students subjected to a Eurocentric curriculum may develop a constrained creative process, biased problem-solving approaches, and a skewed perception of global design challenges. This internalization of biases not only shapes their design outlook but also imprints on their professional identity and practice. The overemphasis on Western design principles, as highlighted by Albarrán González (2020), can lead to a lack of confidence in exploring and valuing indigenous or local design traditions. This aspect necessitates a deeper understanding of the psychological dimensions in developing educational strategies that foster a more balanced and inclusive design mindset. Language and semiotics play a pivotal role in shaping design education narratives, as argued by Dorner et al. (2023). The terminologies, symbols, and imagery used in design materials can subtly reinforce Eurocentric biases. The glorification of certain design styles or eras, predominantly from Western contexts, in textbooks and lectures can create a perception that these are the only 'valid' forms of design. As suggested by Utuk (2018), analysing and revising the language and symbols used in design education can help in unearthing and addressing these underlying biases. Globalization has a significant impact on design education, often overshadowing local and indigenous design practices. As observed by Dahmani et al. (2022), the global market demands and international design trends can create a homogenized view of what is considered 'good' or 'relevant' design. This global influence calls for a re-evaluation of how design curricula can balance global trends with local relevance and diversity. It is about fostering a design education that acknowledges and integrates the richness of global cultural diversity.

Rethinking pedagogical models is essential to combat the ingrained biases in design education. Models that emphasize experiential learning, community co-creation, and interdisciplinary approaches can be transformative. Incorporating methods from anthropology or environmental studies, as recommended by Dache-Gerbino et al. (2019), can provide students with a broader, more holistic understanding of design. These approaches not only encourage a more inclusive view of design but also prepare students to tackle complex, real-world problems that require multifaceted solutions. The role of technology and digital tools in design education is a double-edged sword. While they have the potential to perpetuate biases—through default settings, templates, and interfaces—they also hold the power to challenge and overcome these biases. As discussed by Kotok and Kryst (2017), the critical examination and adaptation of these tools can facilitate a more inclusive design process. Digital platforms, for instance, can be utilized to expose students to a diverse range of design traditions and practices from around the world. Collaborations between academic institutions and the design industry can play a crucial role in reforming design education. These collaborations can provide students with practical, real-world perspectives and help in integrating a more balanced curriculum. Industry input in curriculum development, joint research initiatives, and practical internship models, as proposed by Bakker et al. (2019), can bridge the gap between theory and practice, ensuring that students are exposed to a variety of design approaches and challenges. Including case studies of institutions or programs that have successfully integrated a more inclusive approach to design education can offer valuable insights. These case studies, as exemplified in the work of King and South (2017), provide tangible evidence of the benefits and challenges of implementing such reforms and can inspire and guide similar efforts elsewhere. In conclusion, addressing the ingrained biases in design education is a complex but essential task. By exploring its cognitive, linguistic, global, technological, and pedagogical dimensions, and proposing collaborative efforts between academia and industry, we can move towards a more inclusive, diverse, and realistic understanding of design. This shift, crucial for fostering a richer and more equitable design landscape, is imperative for preparing designers to effectively address the multifaceted challenges of our increasingly globalized world.

Consumer Psychology and Market Dynamics

Market forces significantly contribute to reinforcing the colonial mindset in design. When designs that align with Western aesthetics are more prominently showcased and financially supported, it not only creates economic disparities but also reinforces a psychological narrative of Western superiority in design. This phenomenon can be understood through social psychology concepts like the halo effect,[1] where the perceived prestige of Western designs influences consumer preferences and choices. The market, thus, becomes an echo chamber, amplifying Western aesthetics and marginalising non-Western designs, further entrenching the colonial mindset. In exploring the intricate relationship between consumer psychology and market dynamics in the context of design, it is essential to delve into various psychological theories, global branding strategies, the impact of social media, economic factors, and the concept of cultural capital. These elements collectively contribute to reinforcing the colonial mindset in design, shaping consumer preferences and choices in ways that often go unnoticed.

The concept of 'confirmation bias,' a psychological phenomenon where individuals favour information or products that affirm their existing beliefs and values, plays a significant role in consumer preferences for design. This bias, as elucidated by Nickerson (1998), can perpetuate the preference for Western designs if consumers are conditioned to view them as superior. This conditioning is not just a matter of personal taste but is deeply rooted in the cultural narratives that consumers are exposed to throughout their lives. Global branding and marketing strategies significantly impact consumer perceptions. Major brands that showcase Western aesthetics in their global campaigns reinforce the idea that such aesthetics are universally desirable, overshadowing non-Western designs. This global marketing approach, as highlighted by Haugtvedt et al. (2018), contributes to the colonial mindset by marginalizing designs that do not conform to Western standards. Social media platforms are influential in shaping consumer perceptions of design. The prominence of Western designs on these platforms can contribute to a feedback loop that reinforces the colonial mindset. However, as noted by Nwagwu and Akintoye (2023), social media also offers opportunities to showcase and popularize non-Western designs, providing a platform for challenging existing biases and democratizing design representation. Economic factors, such as production costs and market access, also play a crucial role in perpetuating biases in design. Western designs, which often receive more financial support and market access, create economic barriers for non-Western designs. This disparity not only affects the market viability of non-Western designs but also reinforces the notion of Western superiority in design, as discussed by Porter (2011). The concept of 'cultural capital,' as proposed by Bourdieu (1986), is particularly relevant in the context of design. Western designs are often perceived as having more cultural capital, which consumers associate with higher social status or sophistication. This perception influences consumer choices, further entrenching Western dominance in the field of design.

Educational initiatives have the potential to play a role in shifting consumer perceptions. Integrating discussions about the value and uniqueness of non-Western designs into educational curricula can help future generations develop a more balanced and inclusive view of design excellence. This approach, as suggested by Giroux (1983), can be instrumental in breaking the cycle of bias and fostering a more diverse understanding of design quality. The interplay between consumer demand and design education is a bidirectional relationship. While consumer preferences influence what is taught in design schools, the education that designers receive also shapes consumer preferences through the products they create. This interplay, as explored by Nelson and Stolterman (2014), is crucial in understanding how to break the cycle of bias in design. In conclusion, the relationship between consumer psychology and market dynamics in the context of design is complex and multilayered. By examining psychological theories like confirmation bias, global marketing strategies, the role of social media, economic factors, cultural capital, educational initiatives, and the interplay between consumer demand and design education, we gain a deeper understanding of how the colonial mindset in design is perpetuated and reinforced. Addressing these issues requires a concerted effort across multiple fronts, from rethinking marketing strategies to reforming design education, in order to foster a more inclusive and diverse design landscape.

Technology's Double-Edged Sword

Technology, particularly in the context of algorithms and digital platforms, plays a dual role. It has the potential to democratise design by providing platforms for underrepresented voices. However, it can also entrench colonial biases, particularly through algorithmic bias. Algorithms, often designed with a Western-centric perspective, can perpetuate the dominance of Western design aesthetics, inadvertently marginalising non-Western designs. This creates a digital environment where colonial legacies are perpetuated under the guise of 'user preferences' or 'quality content.' In the exploration of technology's impact on design, it becomes evident that while it has the potential to democratize and diversify the field, it also holds the risk of entrenching colonial biases. This dichotomy, often overlooked, is crucial in understanding the role of technology in shaping modern design landscapes. Emerging technologies such as virtual reality (VR), augmented reality (AR), and artificial intelligence (AI) offer new avenues for challenging traditional biases in design. These technologies can create immersive and interactive experiences that bring non-Western design aesthetics and philosophies to the forefront. For example, VR and AR can be used to showcase the historical and cultural contexts of non-Western designs in an engaging and educative manner, providing a counter-narrative to the dominant Western-centric design paradigm. As Dourish and Bell (2011) note, these technologies can help bridge cultural divides and enhance understanding and appreciation of diverse design traditions. The issue of algorithmic transparency and ethical design is another critical aspect of technology's role in design. As Friedman and Nissenbaum (1996) argue, algorithms must be designed not just for efficiency, but also for fairness, and their decision-making processes should be transparent. This transparency is essential for identifying and rectifying biases, ensuring that designs are inclusive and representative of diverse perspectives. Ethical design principles advocate for systems that consider the cultural and social implications of design, moving beyond mere functionality. User-centred design (UCD) principles, when applied in a global context, ensure that design solutions are tailored to the needs of diverse user groups, including those from non-Western backgrounds. Gulliksen et al.

(2003) emphasize the importance of involving users in the design process, suggesting that this can lead to more inclusive and representative design outcomes. Involving users from diverse cultural backgrounds is essential in overcoming inherent biases and ensuring that the designs are relevant and sensitive to different cultural contexts. The digital divide, the disparity in access to digital technology, significantly influences who participates in the design process and whose voices are heard. Addressing this divide is key to democratizing design. Efforts to provide equitable access to design tools and technologies, as Tacchi (2020) discusses, are essential in empowering a broader range of voices in the design field and challenging the Western-centric narrative.

Data diversity in algorithmic design is crucial in overcoming biases. The data used to train algorithms greatly influences their outputs, and as such, ensuring diversity in these data sets is paramount. This involves not only a quantitative increase in data from non-Western sources but also a qualitative improvement in how this data represents diverse cultural contexts and design philosophies. Collaboration between designers from diverse cultural backgrounds can lead to more balanced and inclusive design outcomes. Cross-cultural teams bring a variety of perspectives and experiences to the design process, helping to identify and challenge biases that a homogenous team might overlook. As Taras et al. (2023) suggests, such collaboration is essential in fostering a multicultural approach to design, one that is more reflective of a globalized world.

In conclusion, technology in the realm of design is indeed a double-edged sword. While it has the potential to perpetuate colonial biases, it also offers significant opportunities to challenge and transform these biases. By exploring emerging technologies, advocating for algorithmic transparency and ethical design, applying user-centred design principles in a global context, addressing the digital divide, ensuring data diversity, and promoting collaborative design with cross-cultural teams, technology can be leveraged to create a more inclusive and diverse design landscape. These efforts are not only crucial for overcoming colonial legacies in design but are also imperative for fostering innovation and creativity in a world that is increasingly interconnected and culturally diverse.

Narrative Psychology in Reclaiming Design Histories

The field of narrative psychology, which explores how stories shape human understanding and perception, is crucial in deconstructing the colonial mindset in design. The history of design, predominantly narrated from a Eurocentric perspective, has skewed our understanding and appreciation of global design heritage. Reclaiming and centring indigenous and non-Western narratives is not just about adding diverse stories; It is about reconfiguring the very framework through which we understand design. This reclamation challenges the existing narrative structures and offers a more pluralistic and inclusive view of design history. The field of narrative psychology offers a profound lens through which the history and evolution of design can be re-examined and recontextualized. This approach is instrumental in deconstructing the colonial mindset that has long permeated design education and practice, allowing for a more inclusive and pluralistic understanding of design history.

Narrative reconstruction and historical contextualization play a pivotal role in this process. By critically examining and reinterpreting historical design events and figures, the contributions and influences of non-Western cultures can be more accurately acknowledged and integrated into the broader narrative. Herman (2004) emphasizes the power of narrative in shaping our understanding of the world, suggesting that reconfiguring design narratives can lead to a more balanced and comprehensive view of design history. In the context of education and pedagogy, narrative techniques can be transformative. Incorporating storytelling into design education engages students more profoundly, allowing them to grasp the complex interplay of cultural, historical, and social factors in design. McAdams (1993) highlights the role of stories in constructing identity and understanding, suggesting that a similar approach in design education can foster empathy and cultural sensitivity.

The advent of digital media opens new avenues for narrative psychology in design. Digital storytelling and multimedia narratives can effectively showcase non-Western design philosophies and histories, reaching a global audience and challenging entrenched biases. Robin (2008) points out the efficacy of digital storytelling in conveying complex ideas and emotions, making it a powerful tool for presenting diverse design narratives. Narrative empathy, as Keen (2006) explores, is vital in building cross-cultural understanding in design. By engaging with stories and narratives from different cultures, designers and consumers can develop a deeper emotional connection and appreciation for non-Western designs. This empathetic engagement is key to fostering a more inclusive design environment. Museums and design exhibitions also play a crucial role in shaping public perceptions of design history. By curating exhibitions that focus on non-Western design narratives and contextualizing them within the broader history of design, museums can challenge the Eurocentric narrative and promote a more inclusive understanding of design history. This approach not only rectifies historical inaccuracies but also enhances public appreciation for the richness and diversity of global design traditions. Community engagement in the co-creation of design narratives ensures that the voices and perspectives of diverse cultures are authentically represented. Hartley and McWilliam (2009) advocate for participatory approaches in narrative creation, emphasizing that such collaboration can lead to narratives that more accurately represent the diverse spectrum of human experience and design philosophy.

Furthermore, promoting counter-narratives in design criticism and media is essential to challenge the dominant Eurocentric perspective. Encouraging critical discourse that questions established narratives and highlights the contributions of non-Western cultures to the field of design can significantly shift public perception and appreciation of global design heritage. In conclusion, narrative psychology offers a rich and multifaceted approach to reclaiming and reconfiguring design histories. Through narrative reconstruction, educational storytelling, digital storytelling, narrative empathy, museum exhibitions, community engagement, and counter-narratives in criticism and media, we can foster a more inclusive and holistic understanding of design history. These efforts are crucial not only for rectifying historical inaccuracies but also for shaping a more diverse and equitable future in the field of design.

Towards a Holistic Reformation

Deconstructing the colonial mindset in design necessitates systemic and holistic changes. This includes reforming educational curricula to value diverse design philosophies, fostering market environments that celebrate and support diverse designs, using technology to promote a more equitable representation of design traditions, and rewriting the narratives of design history to include a more diverse range of perspectives. This endeavour is as much about internal reflection and re-evaluation as it is about external structural changes. It requires a deep introspection of ingrained biases and perceptions. By acknowledging and actively challenging these colonial legacies, the goal is to cultivate a design ecology that is equitable, inclusive, and diverse. Such an ecology would not only recognise but also celebrate the unique contributions of multiple design philosophies, enriching the global discussion of design and fostering a more harmonious and inclusive world. The journey towards a holistic reformation in design extends beyond the restructuring of educational curricula and market dynamics; it encompasses a broader spectrum of cultural, psychological, and ethical dimensions. This reformation is not merely a series of external adjustments but also an introspective process that requires individuals and institutions in the design field to confront and re-evaluate deep-seated biases and assumptions.

One crucial aspect of this holistic approach is the integration of cultural empathy and sensitivity into design practices. As highlighted by researchers like Sun (2012), understanding and appreciating the cultural contexts in which designs are created and used is key to developing products and services that are truly inclusive and respectful of diversity. This cultural empathy extends beyond mere awareness; it involves actively engaging with and learning from diverse cultures, incorporating their values and aesthetics into design practices. Ethical considerations in design have become increasingly important, especially as designs impact not just consumers but also broader societal and environmental aspects. As Manzini (2015) posits, designers must adopt a more responsible approach, considering the ethical implications of their work. This includes sustainability, respect for cultural heritage, and the avoidance of cultural appropriation. Designers have a responsibility to ensure that their creations do not perpetuate stereotypes or misrepresent cultures. The role of collaborative and participatory design is another key element of holistic reformation. Sanders and Stappers (2008) advocate for co-design practices, where designers work alongside users and stakeholders from diverse backgrounds to create solutions. This collaborative approach ensures that designs are not only functional but also culturally relevant and meaningful to those who use them. Furthermore, the global interconnectedness of the design industry necessitates a re-evaluation of how design influences and is influenced by international trends and markets. As Friedman and Nissenbaum (1996) notes, the globalization of design requires a balance between maintaining local cultural identities and embracing global aesthetic trends. Designers must navigate this complex landscape, ensuring that their work reflects a harmonious blend of local traditions and global influences.

In conclusion, the holistic reformation in design is a multifaceted endeavour that transcends traditional boundaries and approaches. It requires a concerted effort across cultural, ethical, collaborative, and global dimensions, necessitating a shift not only in external practices but also in internal mindsets. By embracing cultural empathy, ethical responsibility, participatory design, and global awareness, the design community can move towards a more inclusive, respectful, and responsible future. This reformation is not just about creating designs that are aesthetically pleasing or functionally superior; It is about fostering a design ecology that truly respects and celebrates the diversity of human experience and creativity.

Emphasis on Indigenous Knowledge, Practices, and Aesthetics

Indigenous African aesthetics present a rich and intricate array of design, deeply rooted in the continent's diverse cultures and histories. This aesthetic is not merely about visual appeal but is intrinsically tied to deeper meanings, cultural narratives, and philosophical underpinnings. The vibrant and dynamic use of colour, pattern, and symbolism in African art and design is reflective of a profound connection to nature, spirituality, and communal values. The work of scholars like Ramkelewan (2020) delves into how African art and design encapsulate this deep-seated connection. For instance, the use of colour in African art is not arbitrary; each hue often has a specific meaning, associated with elements of nature, spiritual beliefs, or societal structures. This symbolic use of colour creates a visual language that communicates beyond the aesthetic, speaking to the viewer on a cultural and emotional level.

Patterns in African design are equally significant. They are often geometric and repetitive, representing the rhythm and continuity of life. These patterns can be seen in various forms of African art, from textiles to pottery to body art, each carrying its own cultural significance and story. The Adinkra symbols of the Akan people of Ghana, as highlighted by Ofosu-Asare (2023), exemplify this aspect. Each Adinkra symbol encapsulates a complex philosophical concept, reflecting values, proverbs, or historical narratives important to the Akan people. These symbols are used in textiles, pottery, and architecture, serving as a means of preserving and communicating cultural wisdom. Furthermore, African design often extends beyond the visual to encompass functional and communal aspects. Objects and structures are designed with a deep understanding of their intended use and their role within the community. This practical aspect of African aesthetics reflects the overarching philosophy that design is an integral part of daily life and communal existence.

This integration of art, functionality, and community is particularly evident in African architecture. Traditional African structures, from the mud houses of the Ndebele people to the thatched roofs of the Maasai, are designed not just for shelter but as expressions of cultural identity and social organisation. The designs are adapted to the local environment and resources, showcasing an intrinsic understanding of sustainability long before it became a global concern. African aesthetics, therefore, represent a holistic approach to design, where form, function, and meaning are deeply interconnected. This approach challenges the often compartmentalised and aesthetics-focused perspective of Western design paradigms. By integrating these indigenous African principles and practices into broader design discourses, there is an opportunity to enrich the field with perspectives that emphasize sustainability, community, and cultural depth. The philosophical foundations of indigenous African design, deeply embedded in communal values and social wellbeing, present a stark contrast to the individualistic focus that is often seen in Western design philosophies. While the concept of Ubuntu, which emphasizes interconnectedness, community, and humaneness, is a well-discussed topic in this context, there are other dimensions and new ideas that can be explored to refresh the discussion around the philosophical underpinnings of African design.

In African cultures, design is not seen as a mere aesthetic or functional undertaking; it is a holistic process that embodies the cultural, social, and ethical values of the community. This approach to design is deeply rooted in the philosophy of life that prioritises collective wellbeing over individual gain. It extends beyond the tangible aspects of design and delves into the intangible aspects of human relationships, community bonds, and harmony with the natural world. One aspect that could be explored further is the relationship between African design and storytelling. In many African cultures, storytelling is a vital tool for preserving history, imparting wisdom, and fostering a sense of community. This narrative aspect is often integrated into design, where objects, structures, and patterns serve as mediums for telling stories and conveying cultural values. For instance, the intricate patterns on traditional African textiles are not just decorative; they are symbolic representations of historical events, proverbs, and social values.

Another area of exploration could be the African concept of time and its influence on design. Unlike the linear and future-oriented perception of time prevalent in the West, many African cultures have a more cyclical and present-focused understanding of time. This perspective influences design in various ways, from the creation of spaces that encourage living in the moment to objects that are designed to be durable and timeless, reflecting a sustainable approach to resource use. Furthermore, the relationship between African design and the natural environment presents an interesting area for discussion. African design often exhibits a profound respect for and harmony with nature. This is evident in the use of local, sustainable materials and the design of spaces that are in tune with the local climate and landscape. There is a recognition that human beings are a part of the natural ecosystem, not separate from it, and this understanding is reflected in the design practices that seek to minimise environmental impact and promote sustainability.

The concept of communal craftsmanship and collaborative creation in African design also offers a fresh perspective. Unlike the Western emphasis on individual creativity and authorship, many African design practices involve communal participation, where the creation process is as important as the final product. This approach fosters a sense of community and collective ownership, and serves as a means of knowledge and skill transmission within the community. Finally, the ethical dimensions of African design, particularly in terms of equity, justice, and social responsibility, can be a rich area for discussion. African design often incorporates principles of fairness and equity, ensuring that the benefits of design are accessible to all members of the community, and that design practices do not exacerbate social inequalities.

In essence, the philosophical underpinnings of indigenous African design unfold a wealth of concepts that transcend the widely discussed principle of Ubuntu By exploring these various dimensions, we can gain a deeper and more nuanced understanding of African design philosophies and their potential contributions to the global discourse on design. In conclusion, the exploration of indigenous African aesthetics reveals a world where design is deeply intertwined with cultural identity, spirituality, and communal values. It offers a perspective where aesthetics is not just about visual appeal but are imbued with meaning, functionality, and a deep connection to the environment and community. Understanding and integrating these principles into contemporary design practices can lead to more holistic, sustainable, and culturally rich design solutions.

Reclaiming Cultural Narratives through Design

The conversation about the future of African design in a postcolonial setting presents a complex and vibrant array of differing perspectives, delving into discussions around cultural identity, tradition, and modernity. It raises pivotal questions: Is it too late to reclaim traditional African design as an indigenous artform? Should there be a fuller embrace of Western design concepts? and Does colonisation represent a transition from a metaphorical Dark Age for African design? These questions are not just reflective but also indicative of the evolving nature of African design in a globalised world. The complexity of reclaiming traditional African design lies in understanding the dynamic nature of culture and art. Critics who view the influence of Western aesthetics and values as permanently altering the trajectory of African design may consider the revival of traditional forms a pursuit of a bygone era. However, this stance might not fully appreciate the fluidity and resilience of cultural expressions. Reclaiming African design is less about resurrecting an unchanged past and more about integrating traditional elements into contemporary realities. It is an ongoing process of cultural rediscovery and redefinition, where traditional elements are reinterpreted to resonate with current societal contexts.

Conversely, the argument for adopting Western design concepts positions this approach as essential for Africa's participation in the global economy and addressing contemporary societal needs. Advocates of this perspective suggest a forward-looking stance, aligning with global trends and technological advancements. However, this perspective risks marginalising the intrinsic value of indigenous designs and their cultural significance. A more balanced approach could be crafting a unique African aesthetic that harmoniously blends traditional and Western influences, fostering innovation and global competitiveness. The notion of colonisation as a catalyst for modernisation in Africa is a highly contentious and oversimplified perspective. It suggests a benevolent role of colonisation in introducing modernity, overshadowing the exploitative and destructive nature of colonial rule. While colonisation did bring new technologies and administrative systems, it also significantly disrupted established social, economic, and cultural frameworks. The contemporary African design landscape must navigate this complex legacy, extracting beneficial influences while addressing and healing from the adverse impacts.

The future of African design, therefore, is not about an either/or choice between African and Western concepts but about creating a fusion that respects and integrates both. This path recognises the value of traditional African aesthetics and philosophies, such as communal craftsmanship and harmony with nature, and blends them with modern design principles. Such an approach does not merely accommodate current needs and global challenges but also honours the rich cultural heritage of Africa. The intersection of design and technology provides opportunities to digitise oral histories, traditional art forms, and even rituals, thereby making them accessible to younger generations within the community as well as to a broader audience. This act of digital preservation is crucial for communities whose histories have been marginalised or erased through colonial histories. Reclaiming cultural narratives is not just a matter of looking back, but also of imagining new futures. Indigenous futurism, for instance, is a growing field where artists and designers draw from traditional knowledge to envision future scenarios that centre indigenous perspectives. This subverts the common science fiction trope where futures are often envisioned through a predominantly Western or Eurocentric lens. Community involvement is key to this reclaiming process. Open dialogues and participatory design practices can ensure that the community itself leads the efforts to reclaim its own cultural narratives, thus avoiding external imposition or misrepresentation. In many instances, traditional councils or elders can serve as invaluable resources for authentic representation and ethical guidelines.

This reclaiming process also offers an avenue for interdisciplinary collaboration. Historians, anthropologists, and community leaders can work in tandem with designers to create outputs that are not only aesthetically appealing but also culturally and historically nuanced. Such a multidisciplinary approach can add layers of depth and authenticity to the design, enriching it beyond its visual components. There is also a place for policy in reclaiming cultural narratives. Intellectual property laws can be re-evaluated and restructured to protect indigenous designs, symbols, and knowledge from being exploited without consent or benefit to the communities to which they belong.

Finally, educational curricula can be designed to include more pluralistic perspectives, starting with the history of design, to ensure that the next generation of designers is well equipped to engage with a diverse set of traditions and viewpoints. In essence, the reclaiming of cultural narratives through design is a multifaceted, dynamic process that can serve as a cornerstone for postcolonial recovery and empowerment. As it integrates indigenous wisdom, leverages modern technology, fosters interdisciplinary collaboration, and influences public policy, design emerges as a multidimensional tool capable of initiating and sustaining significant cultural and social shifts.

Design as a Tool for Social Justice

This section presents a comprehensive overview of the significant impact design has in addressing social issues, fuelling activism, and creating equitable spaces. It begins by exploring various case studies that demonstrate how design solutions have been applied to tackle pressing social challenges like poverty, environmental issues, and health crises. These examples illustrate the power of design in instigating positive social change across different contexts. The discussion then shifts to examine the role of design in activism and grassroots movements. Here, the focus is on how various design elements, such as graphic design, architectural interventions, and interactive installations, have become crucial tools in supporting social and political movements. This section highlights design's capacity to communicate messages, engage communities, and raise awareness about vital issues.

Finally, the overview explores the potential of design in creating more inclusive and equitable spaces. It delves into the principles of inclusive design aimed at fostering accessible, welcoming environments for all individuals, regardless of their background or abilities. This part also considers how thoughtful urban planning and architectural design can contribute to bridging social divides and promoting a sense of community and belonging.

Affordable housing in developing countries is a subject that extends far beyond mere architectural design; it intersects with social, economic, and cultural contexts. Alejandro Aravena, a Pritsker Prise-winning architect from Chile, presents an intriguing case study in how design can be a vehicle for social change through his "half-houses" concept (Aravena, 2005). This model is not just an innovation in architectural form but also a transformative approach to community engagement, economic empowerment, and urban planning. In the traditional housing model, low-income families often find themselves relegated to homes in poorly planned, peripheral areas with limited access to services and opportunities. The underlying issue is not just the lack of houses but the limitations in conventional design thinking that fail to address the complexities of housing scarcity. This is where Aravena's participatory design comes into play.

Aravena's half-houses are essentially incomplete structures. The basic shell—comprising a roof, exterior walls, and necessary utilities—is provided initially. The occupants are then encouraged to complete the remainder of the construction according to their individual needs, financial capacity, and timelines. This ingenious approach serves multiple objectives. Firstly, it allows for a faster construction timeline, which is critical in regions experiencing rapid urbanisation and acute housing shortages. Secondly, by allowing residents to finish their homes themselves, the model lowers the overall cost of the housing project, making it financially accessible. But the benefits go even deeper. The participatory nature of this design approach fosters a sense of ownership among residents, which is often lacking in conventional social housing projects. They are not just passive recipients of aid but active contributors to their living environments. This engagement creates a psychological stake in the community, often leading to better maintenance of individual properties and common areas. Furthermore, the incremental construction allows for a certain adaptability. Families can expand or adjust their living spaces as their circumstances change—be it family size, income, or other factors. This feature makes these houses not just buildings but evolving homes that can adapt to the changing dynamics of family life. Lastly, the idea of half-houses has positive ramifications for local economies. Because residents undertake part of the construction themselves, there is a natural influx of jobs and opportunities for local craftsmen, builders, and other service providers. This not only aids in community development but also forms a symbiotic relationship between the design and the economic fabric of the area.

The role of design in disseminating public health information became glaringly evident during the **COVID-19 pandemic**. Design moved beyond its aesthetic and functional considerations to become a crucial conduit for life-saving information. The complex, often rapidly evolving, data surrounding the virus, its transmission, and preventive measures required an approach that could effectively convey intricate details in an accessible manner. Graphic designers and information designers were at the forefront of this effort, acting as intermediaries between scientific communities, public health agencies, and the public. One of the challenges of the pandemic was the sheer volume and complexity of data. Information was coming in rapidly from various sources—scientific papers, government updates, and global health organisations. For the general population, this data was often too technical or too fragmented to be immediately understandable. Here, designers stepped in to synthesize this data into easily digestible formats, such as infographics, dashboards, and interactive websites. For example, designers collaborated with epidemiologists to create flattening the curve graphs, which helped the public grasp the importance of social distancing measures in reducing the strain on healthcare systems.

Another key role played by designers was in the development of universally comprehensible icons and symbols. The virus was a global challenge, affecting people from diverse linguistic and cultural backgrounds. Designers created icons that transcended language barriers, effectively communicating actions like handwashing, mask wearing, and social distancing without needing text. This universality ensured that critical health information was accessible to as many people as possible, including those who may not have been proficient in the language of the original data. Designers also engaged in user-experience (UX) design to streamline the navigation of health websites and apps. During the pandemic, public health agencies needed to convey a range of information—from testing centre locations to vaccination schedules. UX designers worked to ensure that these platforms were intuitive, reducing friction and frustration for users seeking vital information. Efficient design made it easier for individuals to take responsible actions, whether that meant booking a vaccine appointment or understanding current restrictions in their area.

Moreover, the role of design extended into the realm of behaviour change. Designers employed principles from psychology to craft messages that would encourage public compliance with health guidelines. For example, using contrasting colours to highlight essential data or employing layouts that guide the reader's eye to crucial points. The COVID-19 pandemic underscored how design could be a powerful tool in public health strategy. From simplifying complex information and crafting universally understood symbols to enhancing user experience and motivating behaviour change, designers were instrumental in shaping the public's understanding and response to the crisis. Their work exemplified how design can transcend its traditional boundaries to become a vital element in public health and safety.

Gender-Neutral Public Spaces

In an effort to promote inclusivity, public facilities are being redesigned to be gender-neutral. This goes beyond bathrooms to include spaces like playgrounds and community centres, signalling a break from traditionally binary norms.

In recent years, the design of public spaces has been increasingly scrutinised through the lens of social justice, particularly concerning gender inclusivity. The move towards gender-neutral public spaces represents a significant shift in design thinking, one that considers the diverse identities and experiences of the community. This progression extends well beyond the often-discussed realm of restrooms to involve more communal spaces like playgrounds, community centres, and public transit systems. The traditional design of many public spaces often reinforces gender binaries, either explicitly through signage and segregated spaces or implicitly through colours, shapes, and materials that are traditionally gender coded. For example, traditional playgrounds often segregate play areas or activities based on perceived gender interests—think of boys' jungle gyms and girls' sandboxes. This not only restricts individual expression but can also perpetuate harmful stereotypes about gender roles and capabilities. Designers are now revisiting these spaces with a more nuanced understanding of gender, creating areas that do not assign or imply a gender role. New playground designs are focusing on offering a range of activities that cater to varied interests, allowing children to gravitate toward their preferences without the burden of societal gender expectations.

Community centres are another domain undergoing redesign to accommodate gender neutrality. Previously, spaces within community centres might have been implicitly gendered, with areas for activities stereotypically associated with a specific gender. Contemporary redesigns are moving away from this by providing multiuse spaces that can adapt to different activities and groups. The language used in signage and promotional materials is also changing to be more inclusive, removing any gender-specific terms. Moreover, designers are increasingly conscious of how even small design choices can impact a user's experience in relation to their gender identity. The materials, lighting, and artwork used in a space can subtly signal who is welcome there and who is not. Newer approaches favour neutral colour schemes and inclusive art that reflects the diversity of the community.

In public transportation, gender-neutral design can increase safety and comfort for all passengers. Seats that are wider or more equitably spaced, better-lit areas, and security features that consider the varying needs of a diverse population are all part of this design shift. Public announcements and information displays are also being revised to use gender-neutral language, reflecting a broader societal change. To summarise, the push toward gender-neutral public spaces is a multidimensional effort that extends across various types of communal areas. It involves revising the physical layout, material choices, and even the linguistic elements that make up a public space. These changes not only aim to create a more inclusive environment but also serve as a powerful social statement, challenging traditionally binary norms and setting a precedent for future generations. The redesign of public spaces to be gender-neutral serves as an example of how design can be harnessed as a tool for social justice, embodying values of equality, inclusivity, and respect for all.

Community Gardens in Urban Environments

Landscape architects have worked with communities to develop public gardens in underutilised urban spaces. These projects not only beautify neighbourhoods but also offer a place for community interaction and local food production, addressing social cohesion and food security. Community gardens in urban settings offer a compelling case study in how design can serve as a vehicle for social justice. Historically, cities have often developed in ways that prioritise industrialisation and commercial land use, sometimes at the expense of community wellbeing. The rise of community gardens, facilitated by the work of landscape architects in collaboration with residents, is a conscious effort to rebalance this equation.

Design considerations in these gardens go far beyond aesthetics. A well-designed community garden aims to be functional, sustainable, and inclusive. By converting neglected or underutilised areas, often burdened with issues like littering or illegal activity, into productive green spaces, the design process directly contributes to community revitalisation. Landscape architects often have to engage in creative problem-solving, dealing with constraints like limited space, poor soil quality, and varying levels of sunlight. This often leads to innovative solutions, such as tiered garden beds, vertical gardening, or the incorporation of permaculture principles. But the gardens are not just about plants; they are also social infrastructures. Here, design plays a vital role in facilitating community interaction. The arrangement of plots, communal areas, and walkways are designed to encourage communication and mutual support among gardeners. Some community gardens also include design features like amphitheatres or open spaces that can host community meetings, educational programs, or social events, further embedding them into the social fabric of the neighbourhood.

132 Politics and the Postcolonial Ideals

Moreover, these spaces are increasingly being designed with food security in mind. In urban environments, where access to fresh produce can be limited, especially in low-income areas, community gardens offer an opportunity for local food production. They become a valuable asset for the community, providing both educational opportunities about sustainable agriculture and a source of fresh, locally grown food. This directly challenges systemic issues related to food deserts and the monopolistic hold of large supermarkets, offering a grassroots solution to a widespread social issue. Accessibility is another key design consideration. Ensuring that the gardens are accessible to people of all ages and abilities is essential for their role in promoting social justice. This could mean the incorporation of raised beds for those who cannot bend down, wide paths for wheelchairs, or sensory gardens for the visually impaired.

In summary, the design of community gardens in urban spaces reflects a multifaceted approach to social justice. Landscape architects, in collaboration with local communities, are actively transforming neglected spaces into thriving ecosystems that meet multiple social needs—from fostering community engagement and cohesion to directly addressing issues of food security and sustainability. Through thoughtful design choices, these gardens become much more than just patches of green in the urban landscape; they become hubs of community action, education, and support.

Redesigning Prison Environments

Norway's Halden Prison incorporates design principles aimed at rehabilitating rather than punishing inmates. Natural lighting, educational facilities, and more humane living conditions signify a shift in how incarceration is conceptualised. The design of prison environments has traditionally been centred around concepts of punishment and isolation. However, recent approaches, such as the one exemplified by Norway's Halden Prison, challenge these norms by employing design as a tool for rehabilitation and social justice. Halden Prison stands as a pioneering case study in how design can fundamentally alter the function and impact of a carceral institution.

One of the most immediately noticeable design elements in Halden Prison is the use of natural lighting. Traditional prison designs often use limited windows or frosted glass to prevent both escape and any interaction with the outside world. In contrast, Halden uses ample windows and even glass walls in some sections. The effect is not just aesthetic; exposure to natural light has been shown to improve mental health and wellbeing, which is particularly crucial in an environment that can be psychologically taxing. Education plays a significant role in the prison's design, offering another pathway to rehabilitation. There are well-equipped classrooms, libraries, and even vocational training centres within the prison. These facilities are designed to mimic those in the outside world, to prepare inmates for reintegration into society. This educational emphasis shifts the focus from punitive isolation to constructive engagement, with the design serving as an integral part of this new orientation.

The living conditions in Halden also diverge dramatically from those in traditional prisons. Cells are more akin to dormitory rooms, equipped with amenities such as private bathrooms, minifridges, and flat-screen TVs. Recreational spaces include a gym, music recording facilities, and even a rock-climbing wall. While critics might view such amenities as overly indulgent for a prison setting, proponents argue that these design choices are aligned with the broader goal of humanising inmates, treating them with dignity, and thereby promoting better behaviour within and beyond prison walls. Beyond the facilities for the inmates, design considerations extend to the staff's work environment as well. Offices and common areas for prison employees are designed to be pleasant and stress-reducing, acknowledging that a more positive work environment for staff contributes to a more humane and effective institution overall.

In summary, the design philosophy behind Halden Prison reimagines incarceration through the lens of social justice and rehabilitation. It uses design to break away from the punitive models that have long dominated prison systems worldwide. Instead, it adopts a humancentric approach that seeks to rehabilitate and reintegrate, reflecting a paradigm shift in how society can think about justice and incarceration. The design elements—natural lighting, education, humane living conditions—are not merely aesthetic considerations but core components of a model that aims to redefine the purpose and promise of the prison system.

The Role of Design in Activism and Grassroots Movements

Design has evolved from merely an aesthetic endeavour to a potent form of activism and a critical tool in grassroots movements. This shift has been particularly accelerated by digital technologies, which have democratised design tools and provided platforms for widespread dissemination. Here are some ways design functions as an integral part of activism and grassroots efforts. First, visual storytelling is a powerful method for conveying complex issues. Graphic designers and illustrators often collaborate with activists to create impactful visuals that simplify and clarify complicated subjects. These visuals can include infographics, animations, or digital art that break down intricate policy matters or scientific data, making them more accessible to a broader audience. For instance, during climate marches or social justice protests, well-designed signs and banners can encapsulate intricate issues in a way that is both instantly understandable and emotionally compelling.

Second, design is crucial in shaping the digital and physical environments where activism occurs. Website design, for example, can dictate how easily users can access and share resources or information. User experience (UX) principles are applied to streamline the process of signing petitions, donating, or learning about a cause. Additionally, activists are employing spatial design to create safe and inclusive places for protests or community gatherings. The use of public squares, park layouts, and street designs can significantly affect the success of a protest or public awareness campaign. Third, design intersects with activism in the development of products or services aimed at social betterment. Social design projects may involve creating low-cost medical devices, eco-friendly materials, or platforms that connect marginalised communities. For example, open-source 3D-printing blueprints for prosthetic limbs have democratised access to healthcare equipment that was previously unaffordable for many.

Lastly, branding and identity design have emerged as vital components in the longevity and impact of activist movements. A strong visual identity can help to unify participants, attract supporters, and ensure a movement's message is consistently communicated across multiple platforms and media. Branding is not just about logos or slogans; it is about crafting a cohesive and resonant visual language that aligns with the movement's goals and values. In conclusion, the role of design in activism and grassroots movements is multidimensional, ranging from visual storytelling and environment shaping to social design projects and branding. As activists increasingly leverage design in their strategies, its importance as a tool for social change continues to grow, enriching and amplifying the impact of grassroots efforts.

Iconography in Protest Movements

Symbols and logos can become potent tools for mobilisation. The clenched fist, for example, has a history of being used in various movements, from civil rights to feminism, as a universal symbol of resistance. Iconography holds immense power in shaping the narrative and influence of protest movements, serving as a visual shorthand that encapsulates complex ideologies, histories, and emotions. The potency of symbols like the clenched fist lies in their ability to transcend linguistic and cultural barriers, offering a unifying visual language that can be instantly recognised and internalised. This recognition fosters a sense of collective identity and shared purpose among movement participants. Take, for example, the clenched fist itself. Its simplicity and boldness make it a compelling visual element. The history of its use stretches back decades, if not centuries, and across various causes —from the Civil Rights Movement in the United States to anti-apartheid protests in South Africa. Its ubiquitous presence in feminist, LGBTQ+ rights, and labour movements underscores its versatility and broad appeal. It serves to amplify the voice of the marginalised, acting as a rallying cry for justice and equality.

Moreover, the adaptability of such symbols allows them to be incorporated into various forms of media —from placards and t-shirts to digital platforms like social media profiles and hashtags. This broad applicability ensures that the symbol gains traction across different demographic groups and penetrates multiple social spheres. For instance, the #BlackLivesMatter hashtag became an icon in itself, transitioning from a digital slogan to appearing on physical banners, buildings, and even official government platforms. However, the use of iconography in protest movements is not without its challenges. Symbols can be co-opted, diluted, or misrepresented. As these icons enter mainstream culture, there is a risk of them losing their original meaning or being used for commercial or political ends that deviate from the movement's goals. This raises important questions about the ownership and preservation of these symbols. Therefore, movement organisers often put significant thought into the creation, dissemination, and protection of their visual elements.

Iconography also interacts with technology, particularly with how images and symbols are disseminated in the digital age. The virality factor—how quickly an icon can be shared and recognised globally thanks to social media—can either bolster a movement or lead to its aforementioned dilution. Nonetheless, the capability for an icon to go viral endows it with unprecedented power to mobilise people on a global scale. In summary, the role of iconography in protest movements extends beyond mere visual representation. These symbols serve as a nexus of shared identities, ideologies, and aspirations, capable of galvanising collective action while navigating the challenges of co-optation and representation in the digital age. As such, they are an indispensable tool in the design arsenal of modern activism.

Design in Social Media Campaigns

The Black Lives Matter movement has leveraged design to create impactful social media campaigns. Graphic elements like banners, hashtags, and infographics amplify the message and contribute to its viral spread. Design's role in social media campaigns like those of the Black Lives Matter movement demonstrates the potential for skilfully crafted visual elements to escalate the reach and impact of social causes. Graphic elements such as banners, hashtags, and infographics serve as both informational tools and visual stimulants, helping to organise and propagate the movement's core messages. For instance, banners often use distinct colour schemes, typography, and imagery that not only garner attention but also become synonymous with the movement itself. In the case of Black Lives Matter, the black and yellow colour palette has become instantly recognisable, fostering an immediate emotional and intellectual connection with the audience. These design choices make for a stronger, more cohesive brand identity, which in turn enhances the movement's visibility and recognisability.

Hashtags offer another compelling example. They function as organisational tools that allow for the easy aggregation and discovery of related content.

When coupled with powerful graphic elements or poignant imagery, hashtags like #BlackLivesMatter or #SayHerName act as amplifiers that compound the visibility of each individual post. By serving as a unifying thread that links disparate conversations and content types, they help to build and sustain a collective digital narrative. Infographics are particularly powerful in distilling complex data or historical contexts into an easily digestible and shareable format. This is crucial for movements that seek to educate the public on systemic issues that cannot be easily summarised or understood. In the case of Black Lives Matter, infographics have been used to convey statistical data on police brutality, racial profiling, and other systemic injustices, thereby providing empirical weight to anecdotal evidence and lived experiences. This combination of qualitative and quantitative storytelling serves to legitimise the movement's claims and calls to action. Importantly, the effectiveness of design in these social media campaigns also depends on its adaptability. Given the range of platforms available—each with its own set of design constraints and audience behaviours—the ability to adapt and modify graphic elements while retaining their core identity is crucial. Additionally, these designs need to be easily replicable and shareable by the public, allowing for grassroots dissemination that extends beyond the reach of the original organisers. In summary, the convergence of design and social media in movements like Black Lives Matter offers a multifaceted approach to activism. By weaving together compelling visual elements with strategic distribution channels, design acts as a force multiplier in the modern activist toolkit, enhancing engagement, education, and mobilisation across digital landscapes.

Urban Interventions for Public Awareness

Guerilla urbanism, like tactical urbanism or activist architecture, involves making small-scale changes to the built environment to highlight issues such as public space usage or homelessness. Urban interventions for public awareness are emblematic of how design can function as a form of activism or social commentary in real-world, physical spaces. Guerilla urbanism, often seen in tactics like tactical urbanism or activist architecture, serves as a compelling example of how small-scale, temporary changes to the built environment can stimulate discussions on larger social issues such as public space usage, homelessness, and urban inequality. In the realm of tactical urbanism, interventions often include things like pop-up bike lanes, temporary parklets, and DIY public plazas. These changes are generally easy to implement and dismantle but can effectively demonstrate the utility and desirability of long-term urban design modifications. For example, a temporary bike lane made using cones or chalk may highlight the viability and benefits of such lanes, putting pressure on municipal authorities to consider more permanent installations.

Activist architecture often employs similar quick, low-cost interventions but with a sharper focus on social justice concerns. Examples include constructing makeshift shelters for the homeless using recycled materials or converting abandoned buildings into community centres. These interventions challenge conventional notions of how space is allocated, who it is designed for, and who gets to make these decisions. They also force the public and policymakers to confront uncomfortable social realities, such as the lack of affordable housing or public spaces that cater to all citizens, not just the economically advantaged.

These urban interventions often gain traction through social media or community engagement, further demonstrating the symbiotic relationship between digital and physical realms in contemporary activism. Photographs or videos of the intervention circulate online, provoking public discussions and encouraging others to undertake similar projects. In some instances, these interventions may be accompanied by QR codes or URLs that direct people to websites or digital platforms where they can access more information on the issues being highlighted, participate in petitions, or engage in community forums. Another layer to consider is the collaborative nature of many of these interventions. They often involve input and participation from the community, making them more of a collective statement rather than the vision of a singular designer or group. This communal engagement not only lends credibility and authenticity to the interventions but also empowers local communities to have a voice in their own built environments.

In sum, the phenomenon of guerrilla urbanism and related tactics exemplify the burgeoning role of design in activism and grassroots movements. By making small yet impactful changes to the built environment, these interventions serve as both a critique and a call to action, challenging society to rethink the ethics and priorities of urban design. Through their accessibility, visibility, and community-driven nature, these interventions transform design into a democratised form of social commentary and advocacy.

Design of Activist Spaces

From community centres to digital platforms, the design of spaces where activists meet and strategies can influence the efficacy and inclusivity of a movement. The design of activist spaces plays a pivotal role in shaping the dynamics, inclusivity, and ultimately, the effectiveness of social and political movements. These spaces can be physical, like community centres, or digital, such as online platforms and forums. In both instances, the layout, functionality, and aesthetics of the space can have significant impacts on how individuals interact, collaborate, and mobilise. In physical activist spaces like community centres, elements such as room configurations, signage, and accessibility features are integral. A space with open floor plans and movable furniture allows for adaptability, enabling various forms of meetings, workshops, or protests to occur in the same location.

Signage can also be vital, serving to both welcome individuals and provide critical information efficiently. Features that ensure accessibility for individuals with disabilities, such as ramps or sign language interpreters, make the space inclusive, upholding the ethos of many activist movements that often aim for broad societal inclusivity.

Digital activist spaces also have unique design considerations. The user interface, functionality, and aesthetic of a digital platform can either facilitate or hinder effective activism. For example, easy-to-navigate platforms that minimise cognitive load can enhance user engagement. Features that allow for secure, anonymous participation can be crucial for activists operating in environments where political dissent may be risky. Additionally, algorithmic design plays a role; the way information is sorted and presented can influence what issues gain traction and how resources are allocated within the activist community. The design of these spaces also intersects with psychological factors. Colour schemes, lighting (in physical spaces), and even typography can affect mood and concentration. For example, the choice of calming colours might make a space more conducive for dialogue and collaboration, while poor lighting could impede focus and contribute to fatigue.

Moreover, the role of cultural sensitivity in the design of activist spaces should not be underestimated. Symbols, language, and decor must be chosen carefully to respect and reflect the diverse identities and experiences that activists bring to the table. In some cases, the incorporation of art or cultural elements—be it murals, sculptures, or indigenous symbols—can serve to both celebrate diversity and educate those who utilise the space. In summary, the design of activist spaces is a multifaceted endeavour that goes beyond mere aesthetics or utility. The design choices made can significantly impact the inclusivity, efficacy, and even the safety of activist movements. It is a vivid illustration of how design, when thoughtfully executed, can serve as a powerful tool for social justice, reinforcing the message and goals of the activism it supports.

Exploring Design's Potential in Creating More Equitable Spaces

Prioritising accessibility ensures that spaces and products are usable by as many people as possible, regardless of age, ability, or status. This principle extends from digital platforms to public transport systems. The principle of accessibility and universal design aspires to create more equitable spaces by ensuring that products, buildings, and public services are easily usable by as many people as possible. It is a concept that goes beyond mere compliance with legal standards, like the Americans with Disabilities Act (ADA) in the United States and strives for inclusion as a cornerstone of design thinking. This shift in focus has the potential to significantly alter how we understand and implement design across various sectors.

In digital spaces, universal design can manifest in several ways. For example, website and app developers are increasingly employing colour contrast ratios that are readable for those with colour blindness or visual impairments. Likewise, text-to-speech capabilities and closed captioning can aid those with hearing or vision loss. The goal is to design user experiences that are accessible out of the box, without the need for additional adaptations or specialised technology. This approach not only expands the user base but also often improves the overall user experience, as designs that are easier to navigate benefit everyone, not just those with specific challenges. In the context of public transport, this might include buses with lower floors or ramps for wheelchairs and visual and auditory announcements for each stop to assist all riders. Moreover, stations designed with clear signage, tactile paving, and elevators can aid in making transit systems universally accessible. The potential societal benefits here are enormous, ranging from increased employment opportunities for persons with disabilities to reducing car use and its associated environmental impacts, thanks to a more accessible and therefore more extensively used public transit system.

In architectural design, universal principles often show up in features like zero-step entrances, wider doorways and hallways, and the incorporation of handrails in key areas. While these features are often thought of as accommodations for those with physical disabilities, they are beneficial for a much broader population. For example, a zero-step entrance is equally beneficial for a parent pushing a stroller, a delivery person with a cart, or an older individual with limited mobility. Educational spaces are also taking note. Universities and schools are redesigning classrooms to be more inclusive. This goes beyond physical adaptations like adjustable tables for wheelchair users; it extends into the curriculum and teaching methods themselves. For instance, providing lecture materials in various formats—audio, visual, and tactile—can accommodate different learning styles and challenges, thereby creating a more equitable educational environment.

One emerging area of interest is how universal design principles can be applied in the development of smart cities. Sensor technology, real-time data analysis, and AI algorithms have the potential to create urban environments that are more responsive to the needs of all their inhabitants. For example, traffic lights could be programmed to extend their green time if a pedestrian with mobility challenges is detected at the crossing. However, It is essential to approach these initiatives critically. Universal design is a continually evolving discipline, and its implementations can sometimes have unintended consequences, such as overreliance on digital technologies that may exclude those without access. Moreover, a truly equitable approach must consider intersectionality, taking into account how disability intersects with other social factors like race, gender, and economic status.

In summary, the potential of design to create more equitable spaces is vast and multidimensional. Universal design offers a framework for achieving this equity, and its application in digital platforms, public transport, architectural projects, educational spaces, and even future smart cities looks promising. However, the challenge remains to continually reassess and refine these designs, ensuring that they truly meet the varied and complex needs of all individuals.

Cultural Sensitivity in Design

Placemaking initiatives are increasingly considering cultural sensitivity. For instance, community consultation is critical when designing public spaces in culturally diverse neighbourhoods to ensure they meet the unique needs and preferences of all residents. Cultural sensitivity in design has gained increasing prominence as designers recognise that universal accessibility is not solely a matter of physical inclusivity, but also of social and cultural relevance. Placemaking initiatives, particularly in urban settings, are one of the arenas where the integration of cultural sensitivity can make a substantial difference. Such sensitivity often starts with active community consultation, a process that goes beyond standard public forums to include in-depth discussions, surveys, and collaborative design sessions involving the people who will be most impacted by the design.

The concept of culturally sensitive design extends the principles of universal design by emphasising the importance of local context. In culturally diverse neighbourhoods, this can manifest in several ways. For example, public spaces can be designed to accommodate various types of social interaction based on cultural norms—some cultures may value large, open spaces for gatherings, while others may prefer smaller, more intimate settings. Likewise, the choice of vegetation in public parks can reflect the native flora of the countries from which a community hails, providing not just aesthetic value but also a sense of familiarity and belonging. Cultural sensitivity is not only ethical but also practical. Designs that do not consider the cultural makeup of their audience can lead to underutilised spaces and wasted resources. For instance, a park designed without input from a predominantly Muslim community might overlook the need for shaded areas suitable for sitting, as is common in many Middle Eastern parks. Or a public building in an area with a large Hindu population might inadvertently be laid out in a manner considered inauspicious according to Vastu Shastra, the traditional Hindu system of architecture.

Institutions like museums and cultural centres also benefit from a culturally sensitive approach. Exhibits can be designed to represent multiple perspectives, rather than presenting a single, often Eurocentric, viewpoint. Texts and audio guides can be made available in several languages, and interactive displays can be designed to be intuitive across different cultural contexts. Technology provides new tools to facilitate this culturally sensitive approach. Advanced data analytics can help designers understand the nuanced preferences of different community groups. Meanwhile, augmented reality and other interactive technologies can be employed to offer personalised experiences in public spaces, adapting to the cultural background and preferences of each individual user.

It is essential to recognise that cultural sensitivity in design is not a one-size-fits-all proposition. It demands an ongoing, iterative process of community engagement and a willingness to adapt and modify designs as cultural norms evolve. It also requires designers to confront their biases and assumptions continually, engaging in a process of lifelong learning and adaptation. In conclusion, cultural sensitivity enriches the concept of universal design by incorporating the diverse needs and preferences of various communities into the design process. It makes public spaces more inclusive and equitable, ensuring that they are welcoming and functional for everyone, regardless of their cultural background. It is a critical step forward in the quest for true inclusivity in design.

Restorative Justice through Design

Restorative justice through design is an emerging area that encompasses multiple dimensions, from physical layout to psychological atmosphere, all aimed at facilitating dialogue, reconciliation, and healing. This concept stems from the broader trend of human-centred design and the understanding that design can have a substantial impact on human psychology and behaviour. When applied to spaces like peace circles or truth and reconciliation commissions, the design becomes instrumental in the process of achieving justice and community healing.

The physical layout of these spaces often deviates from the adversarial or hierarchical setups we see in traditional justice environments. For example, peace circles may be arranged so that all participants sit at eye level, facing one another in a circle, which encourages equitable conversation and emphasizes communal decision-making. These circles are often unadorned to avoid distractions and are sometimes placed in nature to help foster a sense of openness and tranquillity. The circular arrangement is not just aesthetically pleasing but rooted in various cultural traditions and psychological theories that posit how such a layout can facilitate honest, nonconfrontational dialogue. Attention is also given to the threshold or entrance of these spaces. The transition from the outside world to the restorative justice environment can be designed to prepare individuals mentally and emotionally for the experience. This may involve symbolic elements like a water feature for ritual cleansing or a specific path that one walks, helping participants to physically and psychologically leave behind the external world and prepare for open dialogue. Lighting, acoustics, and even scent can be manipulated to create an atmosphere conducive to openness and reflection. Natural lighting is often favoured for its ability to instil a sense of wellbeing, while acoustics can be engineered to ensure that voices can be heard clearly but not so sharply as to become grating or cause discomfort. In some settings, subtle natural scents like lavender or cedarwood are introduced to promote calmness, based on principles of aromatherapy.

In addition to physical space, digital and virtual platforms are increasingly being explored for restorative justice. While digital platforms lack the embodied aspect of physical spaces, they offer other advantages like anonymity and accessibility. However, they also come with design challenges such as how to facilitate meaningful interactions in a virtual environment, or how to make the platform accessible for people who may not be tech-savvy. Another critical factor is cultural relevance; the design elements must be adaptable to different cultural settings. The notion of what constitutes a healing space can differ greatly among cultures. Therefore, designers should consult with local communities and cultural experts to ensure that the space does not unintentionally alienate or marginalise participants. The process of designing restorative justice spaces often involves an interdisciplinary team consisting of architects, interior designers, psychologists, legal experts, and community leaders. This multidisciplinary approach ensures that the design meets practical requirements and is psychologically sound while being culturally sensitive and community oriented. Restorative justice design extends its impact beyond the immediate participants, influencing broader social norms and attitudes about justice and community. Well-designed spaces can serve as powerful symbols, demonstrating society's commitment to values like fairness, empathy, and collective wellbeing. They also offer educational opportunities, serving as tangible models that can be studied, critiqued, and improved upon, contributing to an evolving body of knowledge and practice in this area.

To summarise, the design of spaces for restorative justice is a complex but profoundly impactful endeavour. It incorporates a range of considerations, from physical layout and atmospheric elements to cultural sensitivity and interdisciplinary collaboration. When done right, it can create environments that not only facilitate the process of justice but also contribute to societal healing and transformation. This expands the scope and potential of design as a tool for social justice, making it an essential consideration in contemporary restorative justice practices.

Green Design for Sustainability

Ecologically responsible design not only mitigates environmental impact but also often results in more equitable access to resources. For example, sustainable urban planning can reduce pollution, thereby improving public health outcomes for marginalised communities that are often disproportionately affected. Green design for sustainability is an approach that integrates ecological responsibility into the planning, creation, and eventual use of products, systems, or spaces. The focus is not just on minimising the negative impact on the environment, but often extends to improving social equity and wellbeing. In the realm of urban planning, for example, sustainable design can create ripple effects that bring significant benefits to marginalised communities.

It is worth noting that many low-income or marginalised neighbourhoods are often located in proximity to industrial sones, highways, or waste facilities, making them more susceptible to pollution and poor air quality. Traditional design and planning approaches have often ignored these communities or have even exacerbated their challenges. Sustainable urban planning aims to correct this through various strategies such as zoning reforms, green buffer sones, and improved public transport. Zoning reforms can reallocate land use to distance industrial activities from residential areas, reducing the exposure of marginalised communities to harmful pollutants. This legislative approach can have an immediate impact on public health, reducing rates of asthma, respiratory infections, and other pollution-induced ailments.

Green buffer sones, featuring trees and vegetation, can be strategically placed to absorb pollutants and serve as a barrier between industrial and residential sones. These natural areas are not just aesthetically pleasing; they can also capture carbon dioxide and release oxygen, contributing to better air quality. Further, green spaces offer recreational opportunities, promoting physical health and community interaction. Improved public transport can offer a more equitable distribution of mobility options, breaking down barriers to employment, education, and healthcare for marginalised communities. Electric buses, cycling lanes, and well-connected metro systems also cut down on carbon emissions and reduce dependency on fossil fuels.

Another important aspect is the integration of renewable energy sources into the urban grid. Utilising solar, wind, or hydroelectric power for public utilities can significantly reduce a city's carbon footprint. Moreover, localised renewable energy projects can empower communities by offering jobs and even the possibility for residents to sell excess energy back to the grid, generating additional income. Water management systems also play a role in sustainable urban planning. Techniques like rainwater harvesting and water recycling can be crucial in areas suffering from water scarcity. This approach not only conserves natural resources but also makes water more accessible to low-income communities.

Lastly, sustainable design often incorporates community participation as a key component. Involving residents in decision-making ensures that the solutions developed are tailored to the unique needs and circumstances of the community. This participatory design process can be empowering, giving people a say in shaping their environment and future. In conclusion, green design for sustainability is a multifaceted approach that impacts both environmental conservation and social equity. From zoning reforms to renewable energy integration, each design choice can have far-reaching implications on marginalised communities. By consciously incorporating sustainable practices into design and planning, we can create more equitable and resilient urban spaces. This amplifies the importance of green design as not just an ecological necessity but a vital tool for social justice.

Data-Driven Decision Making

The use of data analytics in urban planning can identify systemic inequalities in resource distribution, from healthcare to education, and help redress these imbalances through targeted design interventions. The integration of data analytics into the design and planning process marks a significant advancement in crafting equitable and sustainable urban spaces. Data-driven decision making allows planners, policymakers, and designers to move beyond anecdotal evidence and gut feelings, offering a more objective lens through which to view systemic issues.

Traditionally, urban planning was done with a one-size-fits-all approach, often neglecting the specific needs of marginalised communities. With the advent of advanced analytics tools and the availability of big data, we can now identify disparities in resource distribution more accurately and in real time. These data sets can include variables such as income levels, accessibility to public transport, healthcare facilities, quality of schools, crime rates, and even air quality indices. Once such inequalities are identified, targeted design interventions can be implemented. For example, if data reveals that a certain neighbourhood lacks adequate healthcare facilities, plans could be made to construct a community health centre equipped with the necessary medical resources. Similarly, if high crime rates are recorded in a particular area, planners might look into designing safer public spaces, possibly through better lighting, increased surveillance, or community policing initiatives.

Data can also inform more effective resource allocation. Suppose a city is looking to upgrade its public transportation. Data on existing routes, frequency of use, and population density can help in designing a transportation system that is both efficient and equitable. Such an optimised system would make it easier for people from marginalised communities to access job opportunities, healthcare, and educational institutions, thereby improving their quality of life. Importantly, the iterative nature of data-driven decision-making allows for continuous improvement. Feedback loops can be established through the ongoing collection of data, which can then be analysed to assess the effectiveness of implemented design changes. If an intervention does not yield the expected results, adjustments can be made promptly. This adaptability is crucial in addressing systemic and often deeply ingrained inequalities.

Moreover, data analytics can make the planning process more transparent, involving community members who can access the data and understand the rationale behind design choices. This can empower communities to hold decision-makers accountable, thereby contributing to a more democratic planning process. While data analytics offers powerful tools for identifying and addressing systemic inequalities, it is essential to approach this method with ethical considerations. Data privacy and consent should be paramount, along with ensuring that the data itself does not reinforce existing biases. In summary, the integration of data analytics into urban planning and design provides an empirical foundation upon which to build more equitable spaces. By identifying systemic imbalances in resource allocation, planners and designers can target interventions that not only meet community needs but also foster greater social equity. This approach amplifies the role of design as a tool for social justice, providing a framework for continually adaptive and responsible planning.

In summary, design's multifaceted capabilities can profoundly influence social justice initiatives, from the personal level to systemic change. Whether through direct applications in case studies, its role in activism, or its potential to create more equitable spaces, design can be a powerful tool for improving lives and societies.

Design and Anti-Racism

In discussing the critique of design that perpetuates racial stereotypes and biases, it is essential to recognise that design, like any form of communication, can either reinforce societal prejudices or challenge them. Historical and contemporary design practices have often been guilty of perpetuating racial stereotypes, either through imagery, language, or context. For example, certain advertising and branding designs have reinforced harmful stereotypes by portraying people of colour in subordinate roles or using caricatured representations, thereby normalising these biases (Gammage, 2015). Design also plays a role in shaping perceptions through the environments it creates. Urban design, for instance, has often been critiqued for reinforcing segregation and racial inequality. The layout of cities, the allocation of resources, and even the aesthetics of public spaces can subtly reflect and reinforce societal biases. Scholars like Rigon and Broto (2021) have pointed out how certain urban planning decisions have historically marginalised communities of colour, leading to unequal access to services and opportunities.

In digital design, biases can manifest in algorithms and user interfaces. For instance, facial recognition technology has been criticised for racial bias, with studies showing that these systems are less accurate in identifying people of colour, leading to discriminatory outcomes (Levin, 2000). Similarly, web and app designs that fail to consider diverse user experiences can inadvertently exclude certain racial groups. Addressing these issues requires a conscious effort to create designs that are inclusive and diverse. This involves not only avoiding stereotypical representations but also actively seeking to portray people of all races in a variety of roles and contexts, reflecting the diversity of human experiences (Smith, 2021). In urban design, this might mean designing public spaces that cater to the needs of diverse communities, ensuring equitable access to resources and facilities. In the realm of digital design, inclusive design practices involve developing algorithms and interfaces that are tested for biases and ensuring that diverse user experiences are considered in the design process. This might include, for instance, ensuring that facial recognition technology is accurate across different skin tones or designing websites and apps that are accessible and user-friendly for people from a range of cultural backgrounds.

Case studies of design projects that have successfully tackled racial issues offer inspiring examples of how design can be used as a tool for promoting racial equity and justice. These projects range from advertising campaigns that challenge racial stereotypes to urban redevelopment initiatives that aim to redress historical inequalities. For example, initiatives like the Black Lives Matter street murals in cities across the United States not only made a powerful visual statement but also helped to reclaim public spaces for communities of colour (Rodrigues, 2018). In conclusion, while design has historically played a role in perpetuating racial biases and stereotypes, it also has the potential to challenge and dismantle these prejudices. By embracing inclusive design practices and consciously working to address racial issues, designers can contribute to creating a more equitable and just society.

Strategies for Creating Designs that Are Inclusive and Diverse

Decolonising African design education is an extensive process that requires integrating various strategies to ensure that the design is not only inclusive and diverse but also reflective of the rich cultural heritage of Africa. This effort involves deep engagement with the continent's diverse cultural and social contexts and a commitment to reimagining the design process from an African perspective. The process begins with expansive research and engagement, where designers and educators immerse themselves in the cultural and social contexts of their audience. This requires ethnographic research, community engagement, and collaboration with cultural consultants to ensure a deep understanding of varied African perspectives. This step is crucial in avoiding a one-size-fits-all approach and ensuring that designs are grounded in the real-life experiences and cultural nuances of African communities.

Inclusive imagery and language are also vital. Moving beyond tokenism to authentically represent people from different African backgrounds in empowering and realistic roles is essential. This entails utilizing visuals and language that genuinely capture the diversity of the continent, from vibrant urban areas to serene rural settings, and portraying the extensive range of cultures, languages, and traditions that exist throughout Africa. Accessibility is a cornerstone of this approach. Design education must cater to a wide range of cognitive abilities and sensory experiences. This involves designing for colour blindness, ensuring ease of navigation for physically challenged individuals, and simplifying language for better comprehension. Accessibility in design ensures that everyone, regardless of their physical or cognitive abilities, can access and benefit from the designed products and services.

Collaborative design processes are also crucial. Adopting a co-design approach where members of diverse African communities are active participants in the design process ensures that the final products are more inclusive and resonate with a wider audience. This collaborative process can lead to innovations that a single designer or educator might not envision and ensures that the designs are truly by Africans, for Africans. Adaptive and responsive design is another key aspect. Inclusive design is an ongoing process, requiring designers and educators to be responsive to feedback and willing to adapt their work. This might involve iterative testing with diverse focus groups across the continent and being open to evolving the design based on this feedback.

Employing an empathy-driven design thinking approach can lead to deeper insights into the needs of diverse users. This involves observing, engaging, and empathising with the target audience to create solutions that truly resonate with their needs and experiences. This approach is particularly important in a continent as diverse as Africa, where understanding the nuances of different cultures, languages, and lived experiences is essential for effective design. Cultural competence in design is also crucial. Designers and educators must strive for cultural competence, which involves understanding and respecting cultural differences and being aware of one's own cultural biases. This can be achieved through continuous learning and exposure to different cultures and perspectives across the continent.

Leveraging technology to enhance inclusivity is another important strategy. This includes using AI and machine learning to personalise experiences and using VR/AR to create more immersive and accessible design experiences. Technology can be a powerful tool in making design more accessible and engaging for a wide range of users. In conclusion, decolonising African design education is a comprehensive process that requires a commitment to understanding and incorporating the diverse cultural contexts of the continent. By integrating these strategies, designers and educators can create products, services, and experiences that are not just visually appealing but are truly inclusive, catering to the diverse needs and preferences of all users across Africa, thereby contributing to a more equitable and culturally rich design landscape. This process involves not just a change in design practices but also a fundamental shift in mindset, from viewing African design through a Western lens to appreciating and embracing the unique perspectives that African cultures bring to the table.

Facial Recognition Technologies

Facial recognition technologies have become a focal point in scholarly discussions that delve into ethical design and social justice. While the technology is promising for a variety of applications, its flaws become glaringly evident when scrutinised for racial and social equity. At the foundation of these technologies are the data sets used for training algorithms. Scholars like Joy Buolamwini point out that such systems exhibit systemic bias due to their reliance on unrepresentative data sets, often containing predominantly white and male faces. This skewness is not merely a data selection oversight but indicative of a deeper, systemic issue within the tech industry. The ramifications extend beyond technical imperfections; they constitute significant design flaws with severe implications. In particular, legal scholars express concern about how misidentifications could lead to miscarriages of justice, including wrongful arrests that disproportionately impact communities of colour. This raises ethical questions that demand attention not only during the engineering phase but also in the initial design phase. Advocacy for "ethics by design" is growing among engineers, calling for inclusivity to be a core aspect of product development. This includes diverse design teams and data sets, as well as rigorous testing protocols that evaluate racial, gender, and age biases.

Beyond the engineering and design considerations, business ethics scholars are debating corporate responsibility in deploying these biased technologies. The discussion suggests that businesses need to take a proactive stance against biases in their products, with some scholars advocating for third-party audits and full transparency in design and testing methodologies. The conversation around accountability also spills into the domain of policy and law, with scholars discussing the urgent need for regulatory frameworks. These frameworks could balance the rate of technological innovation with social responsibility and could range from complete moratoriums to strict licensing, depending on the identified risks and applications.

Furthermore, scholars from disciplines like gender studies and cultural studies are introducing intersectionality into the discourse. They argue that these design biases are not isolated issues but are part of broader structures that marginalise not just racial minorities but also women and other disadvantaged groups. These viewpoints advocate for an interdisciplinary approach to technology design, one that considers the various dimensions of social inequality. In summary, the flawed design in facial recognition technologies is attracting intense scrutiny from scholars across various disciplines. The discussions focus on systemic biases, ethical considerations in engineering, corporate accountability, and the role of regulatory frameworks. The debates collectively emphasize the need for a comprehensive, interdisciplinary approach to resolve the issues at hand, highlighting how technological design can intersect deeply with matters of social justice.

Colour Choices in Design

Colour choices in design may appear superficial, but they hold profound implications for how individuals see themselves represented or marginalised in society. This is especially pertinent when discussing products meant to be extensions or representations of the human body, such as bandages or cosmetics. The predominant availability of "flesh-coloured" items that only match lighter skin tones is a racialised design decision, whether intentional or not. This choice perpetuates a hierarchy that places lighter skin tones as the normative or default category, thereby marginalising individuals who do not fit into this prescribed definition of *flesh*. To unpack this further, one might consider the historical context of colour theory in design. Colour theory, often grounded in European fine arts traditions, has not historically been inclusive of global perspectives on colour, aesthetic, and meaning. The ramifications of this Eurocentric approach are evident today in the limited colour palettes that consider lighter skin tones as "neutral" or "standard." Aesthetic decisions, in this case, are not merely a matter of preference or tradition; they become politicised choices that have repercussions in people's everyday lives. This issue intersects with discourses in social psychology, as scholars examine how these design choices impact individual and collective identity. Studies show that representation, or the lack thereof, can significantly influence self-esteem and societal perceptions of marginalised communities. Therefore, the choice of colour in design is not merely aesthetic but psychological and sociopolitical.

Ethical design theorists are calling for a re-examination of these established norms. They argue that diversity and inclusivity should be prioritised not just in representation within design teams but also in the resulting products. Brands like Tru-Colour Bandages, which offer a variety of shades to cater to multiple skin tones, reflect a shift towards this ethical stance. However, it is crucial to note that recognising these brands as progressive uncovers the deeply ingrained racial bias that the design industry is just beginning to tackle earnestly. Critics may argue that expanding colour choices might make production more complex and costly, but economic analyses suggest that inclusivity can be profitable. The popularity of brands that have diversified their colour palettes, like Fenty Beauty, supports the case that there is a market demand for inclusive products. Furthermore, as consumer awareness about social justice issues grows, companies that insist on maintaining exclusionary practices may face backlash, impacting their reputation and bottom line.

There is a growing movement among designers and scholars advocating for conscious design practices that consider the sociopolitical implications of design decisions. This trend involves multidisciplinary approaches, including insights from ethnic studies, gender studies, and even critical theory, to inform more equitable design practices. One example of this is the rise in community-based participatory design, where end-users are involved in the design process, ensuring that products are both functional and representative of a diverse consumer base. It is important to emphasize that the discourse is broadening to involve practical initiatives aimed at dismantling systemic racial biases. One of these initiatives is education. Despite the growth in awareness, educational curricula in design schools often still reflect a Eurocentric perspective, perpetuating the cycle of exclusionary design. To truly make progress, the pedagogy must evolve to include diverse viewpoints and critical engagement with how design choices can perpetuate racial and other forms of bias.

Besides education, another pivotal factor is policy. Whether It is company policies or industry-wide guidelines, there is a need for more concrete frameworks that mandate inclusivity. These frameworks can cover various aspects such as ethical sourcing, user testing, and design evaluation metrics that prioritise diversity and social impact. Such policies can offer practical steps to ensure that design decisions are scrutinised for their social and racial implications, not just their aesthetic or functional merits. The discussion on colour choices can also benefit from technological advancements. Today, we have sophisticated tools that can provide designers with insights into how their work will be perceived across diverse user groups. Machine learning algorithms, for example, can analyse consumer sentiment more accurately and on a broader scale than ever before. While these tools are not without their challenges, including the potential to inherit biases present in training data, they represent a step toward objectivity and could be designed to flag potentially problematic design choices before they reach the market.

Then comes the role of public and consumer advocacy. Social media platforms have provided marginalised communities a louder voice in critiquing design elements that are racially insensitive. Public opinion can put pressure on organisations to revaluate their design choices, serving as a counterbalance to any internal biases that might exist within a company or design team. These public discourses often serve as catalysts for change, and their importance should not be underestimated. Finally, the metrics for evaluating design success need a revamp. Instead of solely focusing on metrics like user engagement or profitability, success metrics should also consider social impact and inclusivity. This shift would not just be ethical but also strategic, as businesses that are socially conscious are increasingly being favoured by consumers.

In sum, colour choices in design serve as a microcosm of broader systemic issues related to race, representation, and social equity. Tackling this challenge requires a multifaceted approach that goes beyond diversifying colour palettes. It involves reshaping educational curricula, implementing concrete policies, leveraging technology, and considering public and consumer advocacy. Each of these facets is integral to creating a more inclusive and equitable design landscape, thereby fulfilling the broader societal goal of racial equity.

Typography and Racial Stereotypes

Even typography, which many might consider innocuous, can become a vehicle for perpetuating racial stereotypes. Fonts that caricature cultural elements—such as Chop Suey fonts often used to denote East Asian aesthetics or exaggerated "urban" fonts associated with Black culture—can reinforce harmful clichés. These design elements trivialise and stereotype whole cultures, reducing them to dated and shallow representations. Typography, often viewed as a purely aesthetic or functional element in design, holds a more complex role that intersects with culture, politics, and social norms. The issue of typography perpetuating racial stereotypes may not be immediately evident but is deeply ingrained in the design industry's history and practices.

One way to delve into this is by considering the historical trajectory of typography. Early typefaces were often created within a specific cultural and historical context, and as such, they were reflective of the biases and beliefs of those times. Over the years, these typefaces have been imported into digital platforms and modern design tools, sometimes carrying over the stereotypes they were originally designed with. In the case of the Chop Suey fonts, these typefaces date back to a period of significant anti-Asian sentiment in the United States. They were frequently used in contexts that were derogatory or eroticising towards East Asian cultures. Even though society has progressed in many ways since these fonts were first created, their continued use signifies an unconscious perpetuation of those harmful stereotypes.

Likewise, "urban" fonts that are used to signify Black culture often resort to exaggerated, graffiti-like elements. While graffiti itself is an art form that has roots in resistance and empowerment, the way these fonts are used can stereotype Black culture as edgy, unruly, or informal. This undermines the rich tapestry of experiences and contributions that Black culture encompasses. The psychological impacts of such typographic choices are noteworthy. These stereotypes can contribute to what scholars call "stereotype threat," where individuals who are aware of stereotypes about their group may unconsciously conform to those expectations. Even if designers do not intend to marginalise or stereotype, the design choices they make can inadvertently contribute to such societal issues.

Now, how can the design community move toward more ethical typography? The first step is to become critically aware of the historical and social connotations of typefaces. Designers need to ask themselves not just how a font looks, but what it communicates on a deeper level. Critically evaluating the origins and implications of a typeface would be an effective starting point. Educational reforms in design schools could play a pivotal role in this. Curricula should cover the ethics of design choices, including typography, alongside traditional elements like form and function. Students should be exposed to case studies that outline both the negative and positive impacts of design choices, encouraging a more holistic view of their work's consequences. Moreover, there should be industry standards and guidelines that explicitly address these issues. These guidelines could serve as resources for designers and firms committed to ethical practices, providing actionable steps for choosing typefaces that are inclusive and devoid of harmful stereotypes. Technological solutions can also aid in the process. Advanced text analysis tools can detect and flag potentially problematic fonts or typographic elements during the design phase, providing an opportunity to rethink and revise.

Public accountability has proven effective in other areas of design and can work in typography as well. Open dialogues, whether in scholarly journals or social media, can foster awareness and commitment to change. Continuing from the point of public accountability, one approach that has demonstrated its efficacy in recent years is that of consumer activism. As social awareness increases, consumers are more vocal about their preferences for ethical practices in the products and services they patronise. Boycotts, social media campaigns, and even shareholder activism can pressure companies to revisit their design choices, including typography. A well-coordinated public outcry can lead to impactful changes. Professional associations for designers also have a role to play in addressing this issue. By organising workshops, seminars, and even certifications on ethical design practices, they can foster a community of practitioners who are well versed in the implications of their work. Collaborative efforts between these organisations and academic institutions can yield powerful insights and methods to approach typography in a way that respects cultural diversity and avoids perpetuating stereotypes.

It is also essential to factor in global perspectives. Design is increasingly an international endeavour, and as such, typography must also adapt to be globally sensitive. Standardising ethical guidelines in typography across borders will be a complex task given the range of languages, scripts, and cultural norms. Nevertheless, international cooperation can significantly aid in combating racially and culturally insensitive designs. Another vital aspect is the role of algorithmic systems in shaping design. Algorithms increasingly automate many aspects of graphic and typographic design, and these algorithms are trained on existing datasets. If these datasets contain biased or problematic typefaces, the algorithm could unknowingly propagate these issues at scale. Designers and engineers should be vigilant in ensuring the ethical integrity of automated systems, given their potential to magnify existing societal problems. The evolving landscape of copyright law offers another avenue for change. If typeface creators are held accountable for the societal impact of their designs, they might be more incentivised to create fonts that are respectful and inclusive. However, this raises complex legal questions about freedom of expression and artistic license, which would need to be carefully navigated.

Research into the consequences of typographic choices is an ongoing need. This could involve not only surveys and social studies but also psychological research examining the impact of typography on subconscious attitudes and behaviours. Scientifically validated findings can add weight to calls for change, moving the conversation from the realm of anecdotal evidence to empirical science. In conclusion, the task of eliminating racial stereotypes from typography is a multifaceted challenge that will require concerted efforts from various stakeholders. This includes designers who must develop critical awareness, educational institutions that need to reform curricula, industry bodies that can set ethical guidelines, technology platforms that can integrate checks, the public who can hold companies accountable, and researchers who can validate claims with empirical data. By approaching the issue from these multiple angles, the design community can contribute significantly to the larger societal goal of combating racial and cultural biases. Continuing from the point of public accountability, one approach that has demonstrated its efficacy in recent years is that of consumer activism. As social awareness increases, consumers are more vocal about their preferences for ethical practices in the products and services they patronise. Boycotts, social media campaigns, and even shareholder activism can pressure companies to revisit their design choices, including typography. A well-coordinated public outcry can lead to impactful changes. Professional associations for designers also have a role to play in addressing this issue. By organising workshops, seminars, and even certifications on ethical design practices, they can foster a community of practitioners who are well versed in the implications of their work. Collaborative efforts between these organisations and academic institutions can yield powerful insights and methods to approach typography in a way that respects cultural diversity and avoids perpetuating stereotypes.

It is also essential to factor in global perspectives. Design is increasingly an international endeavour, and as such, typography must also adapt to be globally sensitive. Standardising ethical guidelines in typography across borders will be a complex task given the range of languages, scripts, and cultural norms. Nevertheless, international cooperation can significantly aid in combating racially and culturally insensitive designs.

Another vital aspect is the role of algorithmic systems in shaping design. Algorithms increasingly automate many aspects of graphic and typographic design, and these algorithms are trained on existing datasets. If these datasets contain biased or problematic typefaces, the algorithm could unknowingly propagate these issues at scale. Designers and engineers should be vigilant in ensuring the ethical integrity of automated systems, given their potential to magnify existing societal problems. The evolving landscape of copyright law offers another avenue for change. If typeface creators are held accountable for the societal impact of their designs, they might be more incentivised to create fonts that are respectful and inclusive. However, this raises complex legal questions about freedom of expression and artistic license, which would need to be carefully navigated.

Research into the consequences of typographic choices is an ongoing need. This could involve not only surveys and social studies but also psychological research examining the impact of typography on subconscious attitudes and behaviours. Scientifically validated findings can add weight to calls for change, moving the conversation from the realm of anecdotal evidence to empirical science. In conclusion, the task of eliminating racial stereotypes from typography is a multifaceted challenge that will require concerted efforts from various stakeholders. This includes designers who must develop critical awareness, educational institutions that need to reform curricula, industry bodies that can set ethical guidelines, technology platforms that can integrate checks, the public who can hold companies accountable, and researchers who can validate claims with empirical data. By approaching the issue from these multiple angles, the design community can contribute significantly to the larger societal goal of combating racial and cultural biases.

Urban Planning and Racial Segregation

When it comes to urban planning, design choices can have long-lasting impacts on racial segregation and community access to resources. Methods that may appear race neutral, like zoning laws or housing covenants, can have discriminatory effects, echoing the historic practice of redlining. For example, in many U.S. cities, highways were designed to divide white neighbourhoods from Black neighbourhoods intentionally. Such decisions have lasting socioeconomic impacts, contributing to the racial wealth gap, unequal access to quality education, and healthcare disparities. In examining the relationship between urban planning and racial segregation, It is crucial to start with the historical factors that laid the foundation for present-day inequalities. The legacy of redlining, initiated by the federal government in the 1930s, explicitly demarcated neighbourhoods based on racial demographics, labelling predominantly Black neighbourhoods as high-risk for mortgage lenders. This not only hampered investment in these areas but set the stage for decades of institutionalised racial segregation. Zoning laws and housing covenants that followed often disguised racial biases under the guise of economic factors or property values. For example, the implementation of single-family zoning laws disproportionately impacted minority communities by making multifamily housing, which is generally more affordable, illegal in vast swaths of cities. This is not just an American phenomenon; similar practices can be observed globally, where urban design has been used to enforce or perpetuate social hierarchies.

The construction of highways in the mid-20th century under the Federal-Aid Highway Act represented another turning point. Often cited as a prime example of structural racism, these highways frequently bisected racially diverse neighbourhoods, segregating communities and disrupting local economies. The placement of these highways was often far from arbitrary; they were explicitly designed to separate white from nonwhite neighbourhoods. This design choice has had a domino effect on community health, local economies, and overall quality of life. For instance, neighbourhoods next to highways often experience higher rates of pollution, which disproportionately affects communities of colour.

The impact of such planning decisions extends to education and healthcare. Schools primarily funded through property taxes will inevitably reflect the economic conditions of their neighbourhoods. In segregated cities, this leads to educational disparities that perpetuate the cycle of poverty and limited opportunity. Similarly, healthcare facilities in underfunded areas often lack the resources to provide adequate services, contributing to health disparities.

Modern urban planners are grappling with these ethical quandaries as they face the challenge of either reinforcing or breaking this cycle. One emerging trend is that of equity planning, which prioritises social justice and attempts to allocate resources more fairly. Tools like Geographic Information Systems (GIS) can be invaluable in this, offering detailed demographic data that helps planners identify and address systemic imbalances. There is also a shift towards participatory planning methods, which include the communities in the planning processes. This ensures that the voices often marginalised in these discussions are heard, and their needs considered. It also goes beyond merely allocating resources and enters the realm of empowering communities to be a part of decisions that affect their lives.

However, well-intentioned plans can still falter due to political roadblocks. Often, It is local governments and vested interests that maintain the status quo, fearing that desegregation and equitable distribution of resources may lead to a drop in property values or introduce "unwanted elements" into certain neighbourhoods. On the technological front, data analytics and machine learning offer promising avenues for assessing the impact of planning decisions, but they also pose risks. Predictive algorithms trained on historical data might perpetuate existing biases if not carefully scrutinised and adjusted. Consequently, the ethical implications of employing these technologies in urban planning cannot be ignored. Land use and property laws further complicate matters. In many cases, legislation may need to be revised to allow for more equitable urban planning practices. The intersection of law and urban planning makes this a complex multidisciplinary issue requiring input from legal experts, policymakers, and planners alike. Sustainability considerations also intersect with issues of racial equity. As cities focus on sustainable urban development, there is an ethical imperative to ensure that the benefits of sustainability—like green spaces, clean air, and access to quality public transport—are equally distributed among all communities. Economic considerations cannot be divorced from this discussion.

While critics may argue that revamping existing structures could be financially draining, the counter-argument centres on the long-term socioeconomic benefits of a more equitable system. Studies suggest that cities with higher levels of racial and economic segregation often experience slower economic growth compared to more integrated cities. The academic community has a role to play in equipping the next generation of urban planners with the conceptual tools they need to think critically about systemic issues. Curricula should incorporate a multidisciplinary approach to problem solving, integrating ethics, sociology, and history along with conventional planning theory and techniques. Such an academic backdrop would encourage prospective planners to question underlying assumptions and inspire innovations that benefit all communities. Beyond educational adjustments, professional institutions should play a more active role in addressing racial disparities. Professional bodies can influence change by setting ethical guidelines and best practices that prioritise equitable outcomes. Their platforms could be used to share successful case studies, provide networking opportunities for like-minded professionals, and advocate for policy change on a larger scale.

Public-private partnerships also represent a promising avenue for change. These collaborations could focus on community-led development projects that aim to balance economic viability with social justice. For example, housing cooperatives or community land trusts can give local communities a voice and stake in the development process, challenging traditional top-down models of urban planning. Transparency and accountability mechanisms must be built into all levels of decision-making. This can include public hearings, community impact assessments, and even the use of blockchain technologies to document and track decisions transparently. Providing a transparent account of how decisions were made and who made them can foster trust and mitigate the damaging effects of past and present discriminatory practices. Moreover, technological innovation should be harnessed to facilitate more equitable planning. We touched upon the use of GIS and data analytics; these can be further supplemented by citizen science initiatives. Such initiatives can empower local communities to collect and analyse data relevant to their living conditions, thereby influencing planning decisions directly. Smart cities technology, which uses data and digital technology to improve urban living, can also be an ally in this cause if applied thoughtfully. Rather than just optimising for efficiency or economic growth, smart city solutions could focus on reducing racial disparities in areas like healthcare access, educational resources, and public transportation.

However, these potential solutions come with their own sets of challenges. Implementing equitable urban planning on a wide scale requires a change in political will, both at the local and national levels. Moreover, the entrenched financial interests tied to the real estate industry often serve as a barrier to significant reform. Activism and grassroots movements can play a crucial role in changing the narrative and pushing for substantial action. In summary, while the challenges of racial segregation and inequality in urban planning are deeply rooted and multifaceted, they are not intractable. A combination of academic rigor, technological innovation, institutional responsibility, community participation, and political activism is essential for moving towards more equitable urban landscapes. Achieving this will not only fulfil ethical imperatives but also build more resilient, harmonious, and sustainable cities, contributing to the wellbeing of all residents.

Subtleties that Add Up

These issues may seem isolated or subtle on their own, but collectively, they contribute to a larger system that consistently disadvantages racial minorities. In the context of a broader society that is grappling with racial inequality, these design decisions can't be viewed as merely unfortunate oversights; they are symptomatic of systemic issues. In discussing systemic disadvantages faced by racial minorities, it is crucial to acknowledge that such disadvantages are often not the result of a single, glaring act of discrimination but rather the cumulative impact of multiple, seemingly minor decisions. These subtleties, which can be as nuanced as a particular font in a design layout or as broad reaching as zoning laws in urban planning, might appear innocuous or irrelevant when examined in isolation. However, when they accumulate and interact within a complex social system, their impact is far more profound and damaging. To start, It is important to conceptualise this idea of subtleties that add up within the framework of systemic or structural racism, which operates through policies, practices, and cultural norms to perpetuate racial inequality. Subtle discriminatory acts can be seen as microlevel manifestations of macrolevel structures. Let us consider the hiring process, for instance. If a resume reviewer unconsciously favours names that appear "Western," they are more likely to pass over resumes from equally qualified candidates with names that are ethnically identifiable. Such a choice may not be overtly racist, but when multiplied across numerous hiring managers and job applications, it upholds a system that systematically disadvantages racial minorities. Moreover, these subtleties often intersect with each other, creating compound effects. For instance, if a qualified candidate cannot secure a well-paying job due to hiring biases, they are less likely to afford housing in areas with good schools and healthcare, which in turn impacts their children's education and long-term prospects. Now consider subtleties in healthcare. Studies have shown that physicians often underassess the level of pain reported by patients of colour, leading to inadequate treatment. Though this might seem like a minor issue in an individual case, when scaled across healthcare systems, it manifests as significant disparities in treatment and health outcomes. Similarly, if medical research predominantly focuses on populations of European descent, the medical conditions that disproportionately affect minorities may be less researched and poorly understood, affecting diagnosis and treatment protocols.

In technology and product design, subtle biases can have extensive consequences. For example, facial recognition software often performs poorly on darker skin tones, a result of being trained on predominantly light-skinned datasets. While this may seem like a technical glitch, the repercussions are significant when such technology is used in law enforcement or border control, disproportionately misidentifying people of colour and subjecting them to unwarranted scrutiny or detention. The idea of subtleties adding up is particularly salient in education. Curricula that predominantly feature Western history and literature implicitly marginalise other cultures and perspectives. When this is combined with other factors like underfunding in schools in minority neighbourhoods, we get a system that perpetuates educational inequalities. These inequalities can limit access to higher education, which in turn narrows job prospects, contributing to a vicious cycle of systemic disadvantage.

When these subtleties intersect across different sectors—employment, healthcare, housing, education, and criminal justice—they contribute to the structural barriers that racial minorities face. It is a cascading effect: subtle biases in education affect job opportunities, which in turn influence housing options, which then affect access to quality healthcare and education for the next generation. Solving these problems involves a multipronged approach. At the institutional level, policies need to be revisited and revised with a focus on eliminating both overt and subtle forms of discrimination. Organisations should invest in regular training that helps employees recognise their unconscious biases. Technological solutions should be scrutinised for equitable performance across different demographic groups, requiring diversified training data and regular audits. Importantly, the communities affected by these issues must be involved in the problem-solving process. A top-down approach rarely addresses the nuances of systemic discrimination effectively. Grassroots initiatives and community advocacy can provide invaluable insights into how subtle biases manifest in everyday experiences and can offer culturally sensitive solutions. In conclusion, the subtleties that perpetuate racial inequality should not be dismissed as minor or isolated incidents. They are interconnected elements in a larger structure of systemic discrimination. Recognizing these nuances and their collective impact is the first step towards dismantling that structure and creating a new social framework based on equity and inclusion.

The Need for Conscious Design

For design to become a force for equity and inclusion, there needs to be a conscious, industry-wide effort to recognise and root out racial biases. This entails a multifaceted approach that includes diversifying design teams, employing inclusive user research, scrutinising design elements for racial sensitivity, and engaging with communities to understand the complex ramifications of design

Politics and the Postcolonial Ideals **159**

decisions better. The call for conscious design in the modern era is not merely an aspiration; It is a necessity. With design influencing nearly every aspect of human life, from the products we use to the cities we inhabit, its impact on social systems and racial dynamics is profound. Conscious design, then, goes beyond aesthetics or functionality; it incorporates an ethical dimension, ensuring that design decisions promote equity and do not exacerbate existing racial disparities.

Firstly, the composition of design teams themselves is critical. A lack of diversity within these teams can result in a narrow perspective that fails to consider the experiences of a broad swath of the population. It is not just about numbers or meeting quotas; it is about enriching the design process with a range of perspectives that can challenge assumptions and broaden creative horizons. Diverse teams are more likely to spot potential racial biases in design elements, whether it is the colour palette used in marketing material that may not be equally appealing or representative across cultures, or an urban planning model that unintentionally reinforces racial segregation. Inclusion should also be a key consideration in user research and testing phases. Traditional research methods often inadvertently centre on majority groups, whether due to convenience, implicit bias, or a lack of awareness of the need for broader representation. Conscious design requires that we diversify our research samples and consider multiple axes of identity, including race, to ensure that the data collected is comprehensive and inclusive. It is crucial to ask: Who are we not designing for, and why? Such a question could open avenues for more inclusive practices, like participatory design, where communities cocreate solutions instead of being mere subjects of research.

Design elements themselves must be scrutinised for racial sensitivity. For example, is a facial recognition system calibrated to accurately identify individuals across a range of skin tones? Are educational materials inclusive in their representation, including illustrations that reflect a diverse student body? Even seemingly minor elements, such as icons and graphics, should be assessed for racial and cultural implications. These elements may appear small in isolation but can have a profound impact when they propagate stereotypes or omit representations of entire communities. Community engagement is another cornerstone of conscious design. While designers bring technical expertise to the table, community members bring lived experiences that can inform more sensitive and effective design. Urban planners, for instance, can work closely with communities to understand their needs and preferences, which can result in public spaces that are not only functional but also equitable. This can also help planners identify how seemingly innocuous decisions, like the placement of a bus stop or the design of a park, can have serious implications for accessibility and inclusivity. Furthermore, industries should consider establishing oversight bodies to review design projects for potential racial biases and social implications. These bodies can operate both internally within organisations and at an industry-wide level. They would be charged with ensuring that design projects adhere to guidelines that prioritise racial equity, and their evaluations should be made public for transparency. The adoption of advanced analytics and machine learning methods presents both an opportunity and a challenge. These technologies can help identify and quantify the impacts of different design choices on various demographic groups, but they can also perpetuate existing biases if not carefully managed. The datasets used should be carefully curated to ensure they are representative, and the algorithms themselves must be transparent and continually audited for bias.

In summary, the design field must engage in critical self-examination and proactive reform to ensure it does not contribute to the perpetuation of racial biases and stereotypes. Each design choice, no matter how small it seems, contributes to shaping the world we live in. Therefore, those involved in design should take their roles as cultural and societal influencers seriously and strive to make choices that are not only aesthetically pleasing and functional but also equitable and inclusive. Continuing from where we left off, It is worth examining the role of education and ongoing professional development in fostering conscious design. Design schools and training programs have a pivotal role to play in cultivating a new generation of designers who are not only proficient in the technical aspects of their field but are also versed in the social and ethical implications of their work. Curricula should be revamped to include courses on social justice, ethics, and the historical context within which design has either perpetuated or challenged societal inequalities. The inclusion of these topics is not merely an academic exercise but a practical necessity. Designers who understand the broader impact of their work are better equipped to navigate the ethical complexities that arise in real-world projects.

Workshops, webinars, and industry conferences should also prioritise discussions on the ethical dimensions of design. These forums provide opportunities for professionals to engage in meaningful dialogues, share best practices, and collectively problem-solve. The focus should not be on abstract ethical principles alone but on case studies that illustrate the tangible consequences—both positive and negative—of various design choices. This approach makes the ethical considerations more immediate and relevant, helping professionals understand the urgency of integrating these principles into their day-to-day work. In the same vein, mentorship programs can be instrumental in imparting the values of conscious design. Experienced designers who have successfully navigated the ethical landscape can provide invaluable guidance to newcomers. They can share insights not only on how to design well but also on how to design responsibly. This type of one-on-one or small-group mentorship can significantly influence the ethical orientation of designers, shaping the industry in a more equitable direction over time.

Moreover, conscious design requires the development and adoption of practical tools and frameworks that help designers operationalise these principles. Checklists, software plugins, or analytical tools could be created to prompt designers to ask the right questions at each stage of the design process: from conceptualisation and drafting to testing and implementation. For instance, a checklist could include items that prompt designers to examine whether their work inadvertently marginalises certain racial or ethnic groups or whether it perpetuates harmful stereotypes. Software plugins could flag potentially insensitive language or visual elements during the design phase, much like spellcheck but for ethical considerations. Finally, the accountability mechanisms in conscious design should be robust. Feedback loops need to be built into every stage of the design process, from the initial sketches to the final product or implementation. This can include public consultations, third-party audits, or transparent impact assessments. Transparency is key here; firms should publicly disclose the steps they are taking to ensure their design processes are inclusive and equitable. This level of transparency not only holds designers accountable but also builds trust with communities and stakeholders, further embedding the principles of conscious design in industry practices.

In summary, the path towards conscious design is multipronged, involving shifts in education, professional development, daily practice, and industry standards. It is a collective effort that requires the commitment of individual designers, educational institutions, professional bodies, and the industry at large. Given the significant and pervasive impact of design on society, there is an ethical imperative to undertake this journey. While the challenges are many, the potential rewards—a more equitable, inclusive, and just society—are well worth the effort.

The Ethical Implications of Politically Engaged Design

The ethical landscape is far from simple or linear. It is a web of challenges and paradoxes that extend beyond aesthetics and functionality. For instance, designers may venture into projects hoping to elevate the voices of marginalised communities. This intention is admirable but brings along with it the risk of paternalism. When designers take it upon themselves to decide what is best for a community, they inadvertently undermine the agency of the very people they aim to uplift. This begs the need for a more collaborative approach, shifting from *designing for* to *designing with*. A practical way to approach this is to adopt frameworks like Participatory Action Research (PAR) that involve the community in the decision-making process from the get-go. By doing so, the outcome is not just something that is done for the community, but something created with them. An example would be the design of healthcare services in rural settings, where community involvement from the start ensures a solution tailored to actual needs and cultural nuances. At the other end of the spectrum lies the issue of virtue signalling. A design might ostensibly embrace political correctness and yet lack genuine engagement with the complexities of social issues. This is where accountability becomes paramount. Going beyond mere client satisfaction or design accolades, there needs to be a set of metrics that can quantitatively and qualitatively measure the impact of the design on the community it serves. In an urban renewal project, for instance, merely including spaces that seem welcoming to diverse groups is not sufficient. The impact must be measurable through actual usage patterns and qualitative feedback from those communities to ensure the design is not merely cosmetically inclusive but substantively so.

Lastly, the commercial constraints under which most design projects operate cannot be ignored. These economic imperatives can easily clash with the altruistic goals that politically engaged design aspires to meet. Balancing the two necessitates creative problem solving. Designers may need to look for alternative funding models or partnerships to ensure that market pressures do not compromise the ethical integrity of the project. A studio aiming to design affordable housing might find it beneficial to collaborate with governmental and nongovernmental bodies to secure subsidies or grants, lessening the need to generate high profits through commercial sales. Politically engaged design is a complex endeavour that requires an iterative, reflexive approach. It involves a fine balance between agency and paternalism, a deep-rooted commitment to ethical accountability, and a reconciling of ethical imperatives with market realities. Each of these dimensions comes with its own set of complexities and considerations that designers must navigate diligently. As we proceed, the next part will delve into operationalising these ethical considerations into actionable strategies.

As we transition from understanding the ethical landscape to focusing on how to operationalise these principles, it becomes evident that concrete frameworks and strategies are required. The first logical step towards this is developing a methodology that incorporates ethical considerations right from the inception of a design project. While traditional design thinking models include empathy as a core element, the focus is generally on the end user. In politically-engaged design, the scope must expand to include broader stakeholders—community members, policymakers, and even future generations who might be impacted. Collaborative methods such as Community-Based Participatory Research (CBPR) offer promising avenues here. CBPR can provide designers with robust ethical frameworks, while simultaneously offering communities a seat at the table.

Once the initial groundwork of stakeholder identification and ethical considerations has been established, the design process can progress into more concrete realms, such as actual prototyping and testing. Here, the importance of feedback loops cannot be overstated. Just like in agile methodologies used in software development, politically engaged design should be iterative. This includes regular milestones where community engagement is fostered to review the project's status. These are not mere checkpoints but opportunities for realignment and even for making significant course corrections. For instance, in designing a public transportation system, ongoing consultations could reveal that the initial designs unintentionally overlooked needs of disabled community members, requiring a redesign to incorporate accessibility features. One challenge that needs particular attention is the translation of ethical accountability into actual design elements. It is easy to state the need for accountability, but what does this look like in the physical or digital product? Here, impact assessment tools can play a crucial role. These tools can measure various dimensions like social inclusiveness, environmental impact, and even long-term sustainability. Specific metrics such as community engagement levels, carbon footprint reduction, or the percentage of underrepresented groups benefiting from the project could be invaluable indicators.

Moreover, documentation becomes critical in this phase. Ethical considerations and community feedback need to be meticulously documented to provide a historical record. This serves two primary purposes. First, it provides transparency, allowing all stakeholders to understand why certain design decisions were made. Second, it acts as a resource for future projects, offering insights into what worked and what did not. Another major concern is the economic sustainability of ethically designed projects. When profit motives cannot be entirely separated from a project—especially one that exists in a commercial ecosystem—designers need to explore alternative economic models that can serve dual purposes. Social impact bonds, crowdfunding, and even government grants could offer solutions. Designers might also consider building a business case for ethical design, focusing on long-term brand reputation and social capital as forms of return on investment. In essence, operationalising ethics in politically engaged design is a multilayered process that demands meticulous planning, constant engagement, and innovative problem solving. With these actionable steps in place, the next part will focus on concluding reflections and future directions in this ever-evolving field.

Balancing Aesthetics, Functionality, and Ethical Considerations

At the intersection of ethical considerations, aesthetics, and functionality lies a complex terrain that often challenges designers to move beyond their comfort sones. Whereas traditional design curricula might concentrate heavily on the latter two, the current era demands an equivalently rigorous focus on ethics. Consider a hypothetical example where an architect designs a visually captivating skyscraper equipped with state-of-the-art facilities. On the surface, it epitomises aesthetic grandeur and functional brilliance. However, the fabric of ethical considerations might unravel this seeming perfection: questions around sustainability, the use of potentially exploitative labour, or the building's gentrifying effect on the local community. Each query introduces the concept of ethical accountability, requiring the design to withstand not just aesthetic and functional scrutiny but also a rigorous ethical evaluation.

The value of an iterative design process comes into sharper focus here. Iteration is not a sign of flawed design but a constructive step in honing the project to align with multifaceted goals. For example, the architect could revisit the design, utilising more sustainable materials and integrating features that support local communities, such as affordable housing units or public spaces. Thus, the iterative process transforms the design journey into a spiral, where each loop enables a more harmonious balance between aesthetics, functionality, and ethics. In our digitally driven age, technology offers new tools and new challenges in achieving this equilibrium. Virtual reality or AI-driven simulations could allow designers to preview how different user demographics interact with their creation, offering invaluable data to refine the project ethically. But a cautionary note is warranted here; these technologies are not devoid of their ethical quandaries. Issues around data privacy or the spectre of algorithmic bias can both inform and complicate the design process. For instance, if AI simulations are used to test a public space design, ensuring the AI algorithms are free from biases becomes crucial to avoid reinforcing existing social inequalities.

Interestingly, the realms of aesthetics, functionality, and ethics need not always be in tension; they can also form a synergistic relationship. Consider a chair made of recycled ocean plastic. Here, the ethical choice of material contributes to the overall aesthetic appeal of the product, attracting a consumer base that values sustainability. At the same time, the chair serves its primary function of providing seating, and its ethical character further adds a dimension of social responsibility to its functionality. This example hints at the transformative potential of designs that succeed in integrating all three pillars into a harmonious whole. Educational frameworks bear an essential role in equipping designers to navigate this triad. Traditional compartmentalisation into isolated modules on aesthetics, functionality, or ethics hardly suffices. A more interconnected educational model is imperative. For example, a curriculum could employ real-world case studies focusing on projects that sought to balance these three elements, dissecting both their successes and shortcomings. This pedagogical approach can arm future designers with the analytical tools needed to make nuanced judgments in their work.

Transparency is the final cornerstone in balancing aesthetics, functionality, and ethics. It adds an additional layer of ethical integrity, opening the door to public scrutiny and, more importantly, to constructive criticism. If our hypothetical architect openly shares the trade-offs and ethical considerations taken into account during the design process, it creates an ecosystem where the design can be critiqued, refined, and even lauded for its ethical considerations. In an age where information flows freely, this openness can only bolster a designer's moral and social standing. Building on the notion that transparency fortifies the ethical integrity of design, let us delve into the entangled aspects of public participation, scrutiny, and the concept of ethical accountability in the design process. An open dialogue between designers and the public serves to enrich the ethical texture of a project, but it also leads to a redefinition of the traditional roles within design.

The democratisation of design is an unavoidable by product of transparency. Gone are the days when designers could be the sole arbiters of taste and functionality. Today's digital platforms enable a collective form of decision-making that necessitates active community engagement. In this scenario, the role of the designer morphs from that of a creator to a facilitator, synthesising public input into a coherent design strategy. To carry forward with the architect example, the involvement of community stakeholders could lead to new design choices. Imagine local artisans contributing to the façade elements, or community groups advising on the use of common spaces to serve public needs better. Such a participatory approach not only enriches the design but enhances its social legitimacy and ethical foundation. However, this does raise a paradox of design democracy: the balance between expert knowledge and public opinion. While participatory models empower communities, the danger exists that the profusion of voices could dilute the expert skills and insights that professional designers bring to the table. In this way, democracy can clash with expertise. Striking a balance requires nuanced methodologies that prioritise inclusive participation while respecting the merits of professional expertise. Techniques such as Delphi methods or design charettes can be employed, allowing for structured interactions that generate constructive dialogues between designers and stakeholders.

The participatory design framework also lays bare the ethical obligation of accountability. It is one thing to consult with stakeholders, but another to be accountable to them. This involves going beyond merely ticking boxes for community engagement; it implies that the designer has a continuing responsibility to ensure the project's ethical compliance and social impact. This might involve setting up long-term monitoring mechanisms or establishing third-party audits to measure the design's effect on various ethical dimensions. The next layer in this dialogue involves virtue signalling, a practice where designs merely pay lip service to ethical considerations. Transparency and accountability become antidotes to such practices. For instance, a transparent design process that details every trade-off and decision making criterion would make it far more challenging to engage in mere virtue signalling. In essence, openness can serve as a self-policing mechanism for ethical sincerity in design. As designs become increasingly complex and politically charged, the issue of impact metrics comes to the fore. How does one measure the ethical success or failure of a design? Here, again, transparency and accountability can play pivotal roles. Robust, open methodologies for assessing social and environmental impact can serve as ethical compasses throughout a design project's lifecycle. It is crucial, however, that these metrics are not merely quantitative but qualitatively rich, capturing the nuanced interactions between the design and its social, cultural, and environmental contexts.

In essence, transparency serves not just as an ideal but as a multifaceted tool that informs, guides, and corrects the ethical trajectory of a design project. In redefining the boundaries between designers and the public, it opens a rich landscape for cocreating designs that are not just aesthetically pleasing or functionally effective, but ethically sound and socially responsible. Through fostering participatory democracy, demanding accountability, curbing virtue signalling, and enabling robust impact assessment, transparency emerges as a linchpin in the complex architecture of modern design ethics. It is no longer just an add-on but an integral element, shaping design as a truly interdisciplinary endeavour that reflects our collective aspirations for a more ethical and equitable world.

Design Systems and Philosophy

I delve into the interaction of humans with design systems, pondering the conscious and unconscious behaviours shaping and shaped by these frameworks. We tackle how design systems can either perpetuate the colonial gaze or liberate us from it, depending on how they are conceptualised and implemented. Central to this discussion is the notion that design is never neutral; it either serves to oppress or liberate. As we wind down this intellectual journey, we will explore the critical interplay between design systems and human consciousness, and how the process of decolonisation can be integrated into the very fabric of these systems. To anchor these insights, I will commence with a poem that attempts to capture the spirit of this intricate dialogue and conclude with a narrative designed to encapsulate the essence of a decolonised future in African design. Both literary devices serve as metaphorical bookends to the complex but necessary discourse this chapter seeks to address, framing it as both a philosophical reflection and a pragmatic guide for the future of African design.

> In the loom of time we weave,
> Kente threads of history grieve.
> Adinkra ink on ancient skin,
> Tales of futures yet begin.
>
> Colonial shades that once confined,
> Are relics in the Afric mind.
> We sew new patterns, carve new grooves,
> In the endless dance, our spirit moves.
>
> From Yoruba lands to Sulu skies,
> A quilt of colours starts to rise.
> In every stitch, a counter-tale,
> Of continents that will not fail.

Ancestral hands guide our art,
Decolonising every part.
Designs once branded "lesser so,"
Are the roots from which we grow.
Our canvas wide, our palette vast,
We reclaim futures from the past.

Building on the discussions that have shaped the previous sections of this book, it becomes imperative to deepen our understanding of the philosophical underpinnings that guide African design. While the technical and aesthetic facets of design have their place, the philosophical dimension serves as the linchpin, anchoring these attributes to the sociocultural and ethical milieu in which they exist. Design, in the African context, is not merely a service or product; It is an intricate worldview that intersects with existential questions of identity, purpose, and community.

Philosophical considerations shape the *why* behind the *what* and the *how* of design. They provide the ethical and conceptual grounding for the aesthetic choices and functionalities we observe. This becomes especially critical in a postcolonial landscape, where design choices can either perpetuate existing power imbalances or actively seek to dismantle them. Therefore, any move towards decolonising design must start with an interrogation of the philosophical commitments undergirding it. In African design systems, the philosophy is often rooted in the community. The Ubuntu philosophy from Southern Africa, for instance, emphasizes communal values over individualistic pursuits. Ubuntu states, "I am because we are," framing the individual not as an isolated entity but as part of an interconnected web of relationships. When this philosophical concept influences design, it encourages collaborative, participatory approaches. It emphasizes designing *with* the community rather than *0* them, breaking away from the patronising undertones that often accompany Western paradigms of design.

Another critical philosophy is the Yoruba concept of Ase, which refers to the power to make things happen and produce change. It acknowledges that every individual has the agency and responsibility to cocreate their world. When integrated into design, Ase empowers local artisans, encourages community participation, and leads to design solutions that are not only functional but also spiritually and emotionally fulfilling for the community. Further, philosophies like Ujamaa, which means familyhood in Swahili, champion collective economics and social cooperation. When such ideas influence design, they direct attention towards equitable resource distribution and community benefit rather than mere profit-maximisation. This could manifest in various ways: from encouraging the sourcing of local materials and labour to setting up design education scholarships for young people in the community.

Of course, the interaction between philosophy and design is not unilateral. As we work to decolonise African design, there is a symbiotic relationship where each informs and evolves the other. Philosophical concepts are not static; they interact with contemporary challenges and reinterpretations, sometimes even being transformed by the act of design itself. Designers, therefore, bear the weighty responsibility of ensuring that these philosophies are not just appropriated but genuinely integrated into the design process, reflecting both their letter and spirit. Thus, as we navigate the intricate task of decolonising African design, the role of philosophy cannot be relegated to a mere footnote. It must be central to our conceptual framework, shaping our methodologies, guiding our ethical commitments, and moulding our aesthetic choices. It is a complex task but one that is necessary if the design is to serve as a vehicle for social change, embodying the dreams, aspirations, and lived realities of the communities it aims to serve.

The Structure and Influence of Design Systems

In the realm of design, systems serve as the scaffolding that holds together disparate elements, aligning them toward a coherent objective. In a decolonised African context, design systems are more than mere guidelines for consistency; they are powerful vehicles for cultural representation, social justice, and ethical considerations. Design systems manifest in various forms—be it in architecture, graphic design, textiles, or digital interfaces—and their influence permeates different levels of human interaction. These systems, imbued with philosophies, aesthetics, and functionalities shaped by unique cultural perspectives, become expressions of collective identity. Understanding the structure of these design systems is fundamental for their effective application. A typical design system comprises components like typography, colour palettes, space utilisation, patterns, and more. Yet, in a decolonising context, these components acquire new dimensions. Typography may involve the incorporation of indigenous scripts; colour palettes may draw from culturally significant symbology; spatial designs may align with traditional understandings of community and habitat. This culturally embedded structuring elevates the design system from being a mere toolkit to becoming a narrative device that speaks to the histories, philosophies, and values of the community it emerges from.

The intersection of traditional cultural expressions and modern design frameworks presents both an opportunity and a challenge. Take Ndebele mural art as a case in point. This vibrant visual language is steeped in the history and cultural identity of the Ndebele people, with each pattern and colour imbuing the art with community-specific narratives and values. These murals do much more than beautify; they communicate, educate, and preserve the intangible heritage of the Ndebele culture. When elements of Ndebele art are thoughtfully integrated into contemporary design projects—such as urban spaces or digital platforms—they can enhance the user experience by adding layers of cultural significance and engagement. For instance, an urban space that incorporates Ndebele patterns can transform a mundane walkway into a storytelling journey, fostering a sense of community and historical continuity.

The digital realm offers an even broader canvas. A website or app that skilfully includes Ndebele designs can break the monotony of standardised interfaces, offering users a unique and culturally enriched interaction. Such applications can make technology more approachable and relatable to local communities, embedding local identity within the global digital narrative. However, there is a delicate line to tread. The global design language—characterised by the likes of Google's Material Design and Apple's Human Interface Guidelines—promotes a certain uniformity that ensures usability and familiarity but often at the expense of local uniqueness. The real challenge is to harmonise these global standards with local design idioms, ensuring that the adoption of Ndebele or any other indigenous design philosophy enhances rather than overrides the cultural essence. This balance is not merely an aesthetic consideration; it is a dialogue between global design principles and local cultural imperatives. It calls for designers to be culturally sensitive and creative, not just in the aesthetic rendition but also in conceptualising how these designs function within modern frameworks. This could mean creating design systems that are flexible enough to incorporate local motifs and philosophies without compromising on functionality or losing the narrative power inherent in traditional designs.

One way to navigate this tension is to approach design systems as living, evolving entities rather than static repositories. For instance, the application of African fractal geometry in modern architecture or digital algorithms offers exciting opportunities for innovation while remaining grounded in indigenous knowledge systems. This form of cultural hybridity allows for the expansion and evolution of traditional systems within modern contexts, embracing technological advancements for societal benefit without losing the essence of cultural identity. Moreover, design systems are not isolated constructs; they interact in complex ways with sociopolitical structures, economic systems, and ethical frameworks. A design system that embraces ethical sourcing, for example, is not just a stylistic choice but a deeply political act that resists exploitative global economic structures. Likewise, a system that prioritises accessibility challenges the societal norms that marginalise certain user groups, contributing to greater social inclusion. In sum, the structure and influence of design systems in a decolonising African context are multilayered and dynamically intertwined with cultural, ethical, and sociopolitical considerations. Understanding this complexity is key to developing design systems that are not only visually compelling and functionally effective but also serve as powerful agents for cultural preservation and social change.

The Ethics of Inclusion

Before diving into the content, it is important to acknowledge that this section aims to extend the ongoing discussion on the ethics of inclusion in design. This is not a standalone debate but is deeply integrated into the broader context of decolonising African design, which we have already examined in earlier parts of the book. Inclusion in design is not just an afterthought; it is a moral imperative and an ethical stance. It is often treated as a buzzword or a box to check off, but what does it truly mean? Inclusion goes beyond just making room at the table for people who have historically been excluded. It means rethinking the shape of the table, reconsidering who sets the table, and critically evaluating the menu itself. This deeper level of inclusion, consequently, carries several ethical considerations.

Addressing inclusion within African design necessitates a critical examination of postcolonial power dynamics that continue to shape which perspectives are amplified and which are marginalised. Colonial history has, in many instances, entrenched a hierarchy that valorises Western educational pedigrees and certain forms of knowledge over others, often overshadowing local expertise and indigenous methodologies. This legacy has profound implications for who is considered an expert and whose contributions are deemed valuable or innovative within the design landscape. Confronting this challenge involves active and deliberate efforts to dismantle these ingrained hierarchies. For example, integrating local artisans and their crafts into academic syllabi not only enriches the curriculum but also serves to re-evaluate and elevate indigenous knowledge systems. Such actions disrupt the traditional academic canon, expanding it to include a diversity of voices and skills that have been historically overlooked or undervalued due to colonial biases.

Intersectionality further complicates the pursuit of inclusivity, as it intersects with various axes of identity, including race, class, gender, and sexual orientation. Each axis brings unique ethical considerations into play, particularly in settings where resources and opportunities for inclusion are finite. Decision makers are faced with the ethical dilemma of determining whose voices are prioritised and on what basis these decisions are made. Is it the marginalised artisan whose craft tells a story of cultural survival, or the urban designer whose work has the potential to reach a wider audience and drive economic growth?

The criteria for these decisions should be carefully considered and transparently communicated, ensuring that the process of inclusion is as equitable as possible. This could involve creating platforms for dialogue and collaboration that allow for a multiplicity of voices to be heard. For example, community-based design initiatives that pair local artisans with emerging designers can foster an environment where traditional knowledge is not only preserved but also evolved in conversation with contemporary practices. Moreover, inclusion must be more than tokenistic; it should empower those involved to have a tangible impact on the design process and outcomes. This means not only inviting diverse participants to the table but also reconfiguring the table itself to ensure that it is shaped by a plurality of influences. Ultimately, the goal is to cultivate a design ethos that is reflective of the multifaceted social fabric of Africa, one that celebrates and utilises the richness of its diverse cultures, experiences, and histories.

Furthermore, the challenge of inclusion extends to technology. The digital divide is an ethical issue that design must grapple with. In African contexts, where access to highspeed internet and advanced computing technologies might be limited, designing digital platforms that are inclusive by default becomes a key ethical consideration. Lastly, the term *inclusion* itself needs to be scrutinised. It risks becoming a performative action if not deeply rooted in the objectives of the project. Performative inclusion is akin to tokenism, and the design community must steer clear of this trap. Rather, ethical inclusion is a commitment to continually reassess, recalibrate, and reform to ensure all voices are heard, valued, and integrated into the design process. In conclusion, the ethics of inclusion in design form a complex web of considerations, each demanding its own nuanced approach. It is not about finding the perfect solution but about earnestly striving for a more equitable design landscape. As we talk about decolonising African design, the ethics of inclusion stand as a cornerstone, urging us to look past superficial practices and dive into transformative change.

Human Interaction with Design Systems

In this section, we examine another critical layer of the design universe: how humans interact with design systems. These interactions often happen at the crossroads of aesthetics, functionality, and ethics, and are coloured by the existing social structures, which can be colonial, patriarchal, or exclusionary in nature. Given that design systems are not neutral but carry implicit values, reengineering human interactions with these systems becomes vital.

Let us begin by understanding that each design system, be it digital, architectural, or social, essentially carries a coded language. This code manifests in user interfaces, spatial layouts, or social norms dictated by design. Often, these codes implicitly reaffirm colonial or Western-centric notions. For example, the predominance of English in digital interfaces can alienate non-English speakers, thus perpetuating linguistic imperialism. To reengineer this, we can start with localising design languages. Imagine a digital platform that automatically adopts the visual and linguistic elements reflective of African cultures when accessed from an African IP address, without compromising on usability. This not only pays homage to local cultures but also enhances accessibility.

On a psychological level, we need to consider both conscious and unconscious engagements with design systems. The conscious engagement is more straightforward to address because it involves explicit choices like opting for eco-friendly materials in a product. The unconscious part is trickier, as it involves changing deep-rooted perceptions or biases. For instance, colour psychology, deeply embedded through cultural narratives, influences our emotional response to design elements. Decolonising these unconscious biases could involve a long-term societal education plan that starts in design school, aiming to replace colonial colour narratives with local, historically rich narratives of colour in African societies. Another arena is the ethical engagement with design systems. Take, for example, a shared community space designed to be accessible only by facial recognition technology. While on the surface this appears to be a functional and aesthetic design system, it is fraught with ethical issues, from data privacy to the potential for racial bias in facial recognition algorithms. A decolonised design system would involve the community in the design decision-making process, possibly leading to more inclusive, ethical solutions.

In the realm of artificial intelligence, algorithmic decision-making in design often perpetuates societal biases. Decolonising this aspect would entail using data sets that are balanced and representative, and algorithms that are transparent and adjustable by the end-users. Thus, reengineering the way humans interact with these algorithms is both an ethical and a functional concern. Lastly, let's consider the notion of ownership in design systems. The Western paradigm often enforces a sense of individual ownership or copyright, whereas many African societies have communal or collective views of ownership. Respecting these notions in the design of digital platforms or community spaces can influence how humans interact with them, turning users into stakeholders. In summary, the human interaction with design systems is multilayered and rich in context. Decolonising this interaction demands that we consider the coded languages of design, the conscious and unconscious ways people engage with these codes, and the ethical dimensions of such engagements. By doing so, we can transform design from a mere discipline to an inclusive dialogue, enriching not just the field but also the societies it serves.

Reengineering Conscious and Unconscious Engagement

In the quest for decolonising African design, one of the most intricate yet indispensable tasks is to reengineer both the conscious and unconscious ways in which individuals engage with design systems. The term reengineering implies a foundational shift, a need to reconstruct existing frameworks from the ground up, keeping the nuances of diverse African cultures and philosophies at the centre. This task transcends mere changes in aesthetics or functionality and delves deep into the realms of psychology, sociology, and ethics. Let us start with conscious engagements, the more visible, measurable interactions that users have with a design system. This includes everything from the user choices in a digital interface to the paths pedestrians take in a public space. One straightforward approach to decolonise conscious engagement is through the choice architecture. In a digital context, for example, instead of defaulting to a Western set of privacy settings or language preferences, a system could prompt the user to make an active choice, perhaps even recommending settings that are tailored to local norms and laws. Such deliberate configurations enforce the agency of the user, reducing the scope for colonial default settings to dictate the interaction.

Similarly, in urban design, instead of replicating western city layouts that prioritise cars, urban planners could involve local communities in choosing to build cities that prioritise pedestrians or nonmotorised vehicles, aligning better with the lifestyle and ecological philosophies of many African societies. This shifts the locus of control, placing the community—not just a set of external experts—in the driver's seat. Conscious reengineering, therefore, is about acknowledging the existing landscape of choices and then reshaping this landscape to amplify local voices and preferences. Shifting to unconscious engagements, we venture into the implicit attitudes, inherited perceptions, and cultural biases that most individuals are not even aware they possess. Here, design plays a powerful yet subtle role in either reinforcing or challenging these biases. Take, for example, the unconscious bias in associating certain shapes or colours with gender. In many societies influenced by colonial narratives, a colour like pink is associated with femininity. In reengineering unconscious engagements, designers could choose to reclaim local colours that have historic or cultural significance, perhaps employing them in gender-neutral contexts, thereby chipping away at the colonial gender norms. The concept of nudging can also be adapted to steer unconscious interactions. These nudges can be based on localised behavioural insights to subtly guide user behaviour towards more equitable or sustainable outcomes. However, the ethical aspects of nudging must be considered to ensure that it aligns with the collective values of the community it serves.

Narratives also wield immense power in shaping unconscious thought. As discussed in earlier sections, storytelling rooted in indigenous wisdom can serve as a counternarrative to colonial stereotypes. Incorporating these stories into design elements—be it through visual motifs or augmented reality experiences—can subtly influence unconscious perceptions. However, it is important to note that reengineering unconscious engagement is not a one-time fix but an ongoing process of unlearning and relearning. Therefore, alongside design interventions, educational systems must be revised to include curricula that instil critical thinking, empathy, and a deep understanding of the local cultural milieu from an early age. This fosters an environment where unconscious biases are less likely to be formed in the first place.

In conclusion, reengineering conscious and unconscious engagements in design requires a multipronged approach that revaluates both the visible and invisible aspects of how humans interact with systems. The aim is not just to shift behaviours but to redefine the very paradigms through which design is perceived and experienced, setting the stage for a genuinely decolonised and inclusive future. In this final chapter, we have journeyed through the complex layers that make up the design landscape in the context of decolonising African design. From the philosophical foundations that guide our understanding of aesthetics, functionality, and ethics, to the structured influence of design systems, we have explored how these elements can either reinforce or dismantle colonial legacies. The crux of our discussion has also emphasized the necessity of reengineering both the conscious and unconscious ways humans interact with these systems—a task that requires us to venture into the realms of psychology, sociology, and ethics. The push for decolonisation is more than a theoretical exercise; it is a call to action that seeks to redistribute power, decentre Eurocentric perspectives, and uplift local voices and wisdom. By incorporating anticolonial frameworks and indigenous epistemologies, we can envision a more inclusive, socially responsible, and culturally resonant design landscape. The ethics of inclusion must be more than a mere tagline; they need to be meticulously integrated into our educational systems, professional practices, and social interactions. The road ahead is undeniably arduous, fraught with complexities and challenges that defy easy solutions. But the potential rewards—a design ethos that is as diverse as it is inclusive, as culturally rich as it is universally accessible—are too significant to ignore. As we reimagine the future of design, let us strive for an ecosystem that honours both the individual and collective, the modern and the traditional, the functional and the beautiful, all within an ethical and socially conscious framework.

By consciously choosing to engage in this intricate balancing act, we commit to a continual process of learning, unlearning, and relearning. And in doing so, we sow the seeds for a future where design is not just an instrument of aesthetics or functionality but a potent tool for social transformation. It is a future well worth striving for.

In a bustling market square, shaded by ancient baobab trees and enlivened by the laughter and chatter of traders, stood Ama, a market woman in her late sixties. She was an institution in the community, known for her vibrant fabrics, colourful beads, and spices that could make even the dullest meal come alive. The square was more than a market; it was a living tapestry of culture, history, and intergenerational wisdom. But it was also a space of systemic inequality, entrenched by decades of colonial rule and its long-lasting impacts.

Ama had heard whispers of digital currencies, online marketplaces, and smart devices. She was intrigued but also overwhelmed. The digital world seemed constructed in a language she did not speak, designed for lives she did not live. It was, in essence, another form of colonisation—a space crafted by the young, the urban, and the Western-educated, with little thought to women like her.

Then came Chijioke, a young man passionate about decolonising design and technology. Upon returning from his studies abroad, he was determined to create systems that empowered local communities rather than perpetuating existing divides. The market square, the epicentre of local commerce and culture, seemed like the perfect place to start. His approach was rooted in participatory design, a method that involved the end-users—the market women, the rural elders—in the design process from the get-go.

With deep respect for Ama's wisdom and experience, Chijioke and his team set out to codesign a digital marketplace tailored to her needs. They ditched jargon for local languages and used symbols familiar to the community. The application featured an audio option that described each screen and gave voice commands in indigenous languages. It incorporated existing trust systems like communal saving circles into its economic model. The interface was simple, intuitive, and accessible even for those with limited digital literacy.

To bridge the energy gap in rural areas, the system was designed to be low-energy, functioning on solar-powered community tablets available at various points in the market. This eco-centric design also aligned with the community's long-standing respect for the environment—a counternarrative to the often wasteful design of modern tech.

Ama could now upload photographs of her products, set prices, and connect with customers far beyond her small town—all while being seated at her market stall. The app even had a feature that allowed bartering, a practice deeply rooted in African trading history. It was more than just an app; it was a decolonised space that honoured her culture, respected her age, and valued her wisdom.

Over time, this project became a beacon for what design decolonisation could look like. It was an emancipatory act, proving that technology could be a tool for empowerment if designed with a respect for context, history, and the plurality of human experience.

As Ama surveyed her digital stall on the community tablet, she felt a deep sense of pride and empowerment. Here she was, a woman of her age and background, navigating the digital world not as a visitor but as a native. She turned to Chijioke and, with tears of joy in her eyes, said, "You see, we are not just surviving in this new world; we are thriving."

This was the design of freedom, an architecture of dignity. It was a small but radical act of reclaiming space and, in doing so, rewriting history.

Responsibility of Design Educators to Impart these Values

The onus of cultivating ethically responsible designers does not fall solely on the industry; it starts with design education. Educators have a crucial role to play in broadening the horizons of what design can and should be. The curriculum should extend beyond technical skills and aesthetic principles to include courses on ethics, social justice, and the history of design's role in societal structures. These courses should not exist in isolation but be integrated into the larger design curriculum, encouraging students to apply ethical reasoning in real-time as they work on design projects. Moreover, educators can utilise project-based learning to simulate real-world ethical dilemmas that designers might face. This experiential approach not only solidifies ethical principles but also trains students in the practical skills needed to navigate complex moral landscapes. Case studies can offer valuable insights into both successful and failed attempts to integrate ethics into design, serving as cautionary tales or inspirational benchmarks.

Internships and partnerships with organisations and firms committed to ethical design practices can provide students with the mentorship and hands-on experience they need to apply their skills in a real-world context. In turn, these organisations benefit from fresh perspectives that can challenge established norms. Additionally, educators can actively cultivate a classroom environment that encourages critical discussion and debate. This promotes an understanding that ethical considerations are often complex and nuanced, requiring thoughtful engagement rather than straightforward solutions. It is important that students learn not just to identify ethical issues but also to articulate their thought process in addressing them, refining their skills in ethical reasoning and moral justification.

There is a growing movement within design education towards interdisciplinary collaboration. Including courses from sociology, psychology, and political science, for example, can provide a multifaceted understanding of the broader impact of design decisions. It is crucial for design students to recognise that their work exists within a societal framework and can significantly affect communities, often in ways that are not immediately apparent. It is also important for educators to be self-critical and open to evolution. The ethical landscape is not static; it shifts with societal changes, technological advancements, and evolving understanding of social justice issues. As such, curricula need to be regularly updated to reflect these changes. Educators themselves should engage in ongoing professional development and education in these areas, ensuring that they are not just disseminating information but also continually learning. Furthermore, educational institutions should take active steps to diversify both faculty and student bodies. A more diverse environment naturally fosters a broader range of perspectives, enriching the discourse around ethical considerations in design. Such diversity can lead to design solutions that are more inclusive and considerate of different lived experiences.

Lastly, the value of mentorship in shaping ethical designers cannot be overstated. Senior designers and faculty members act as role models, setting the tone for what is considered acceptable practice. Through their behaviour, they send strong signals to students about the importance of ethical considerations. Their commitment to ethical practices in their own work serves as a living example to aspiring designers. In conclusion, the role of design educators in shaping the next generation of ethically responsible designers is crucial. Through an integrated curriculum, experiential learning, critical dialogue, and a commitment to continuous learning and diversity, educators can significantly influence how future designers will approach the ethical dimensions of their work. This is not just beneficial for the students and the industry but also for society at large, which increasingly demands designs that are not just functional and beautiful, but also ethically sound.

Integrating Postcolonial Theory into Design Curricula

The integration of postcolonial theory into design education heralds a sea change in how we approach the teaching and practice of design, offering a critical lens to dissect power dynamics, subjugation, and marginalisation in the domain. Grounded in the ideological struggle against Western imperialism and its associated cultural paradigms, postcolonial theory does not just advocate for a rethinking of design but a complete recontextualization.

A crucial component of this integration is challenging the fundamental underpinnings of what is considered standard or canonical in design. Traditional design principles, often rooted in Eurocentric ideals, inadvertently perpetuate a singular view that marginalises other cultural perspectives. postcolonial theory exposes these biases and challenges the status quo, calling for a more diversified, inclusive approach that accommodates multiple narratives. Here, the concepts of coloniality are expanded to include not only physical colonisation but also more insidious forms like the colonisation of thought, of representation, and of cultural narratives. This is particularly salient when we consider that coloniality extends beyond the boundaries of formal empire to shape perspectives along various axes, including race, gender, and sexuality.

Historicising design principles through a postcolonial lens allows us to see the perpetuation of stereotypes, especially in the representation of African cultures. African aesthetics, for example, have often been cast as exotic, primitive, or otherworldly in mainstream design narratives. These notions do not simply arise in a vacuum; they are a continuation of colonial ideologies that have categorised African cultures as inferior or lesser than. postcolonial theory offers the tools to deconstruct these narratives and reconstruct them in a way that acknowledges the richness and diversity of African cultural heritage. It provides a methodological foundation to challenge systemic biases, not as a one-off exercise, but as a continuous, integral part of design pedagogy.

Incorporating Indigenous ontologies and epistemologies serves as a significant methodological shift, particularly when it comes to narrative frameworks like storytelling. Far from being a simple act of recounting tales, storytelling in African cultures often serves as a repository of communal wisdom, moral codes, and aesthetic principles. It is a dynamic, interactive medium that has been used for generations to preserve history, instil social values and galvanise communities. When integrated into the design curriculum, storytelling offers an alternative to dominant, linear ways of thinking. It provides a textured, multidimensional lens that values experiential knowledge and communal wisdom, and it serves as a potent counternarrative to colonial discourse. Storytelling, in this context, acts as a vehicle for metaphors of resistance. These metaphors break down the binary worldviews often perpetuated by colonial narratives, such as civilised vs. uncivilised or modern vs. traditional. They enable a more nuanced understanding that embraces the complexities of African societies as they are, rather than through a colonial lens that imposes simplifications or stereotypes. Storytelling thus becomes a form of intellectual and cultural activism, a way to reclaim agency over the representation of African cultures in design.

The integration of storytelling and other Indigenous methods into design education also creates a more participatory pedagogical model. Students are not merely passive recipients of information but active contributors to a collective knowledge base. They become cocreators of a curriculum that is ever evolving, adapting to include a broader range of perspectives and experiences. This aligns with the pedagogical aims of postcolonial theory, which seeks to decentralise education, making it more democratic and less hierarchical. Moreover, a postcolonial approach encourages a more ethical form of design practice. When design students are trained to question systemic injustices and to consider the sociopolitical dimensions of their work, they are more likely to engage in design that is not just aesthetically pleasing but also socially responsible. This represents a fundamental shift from a design philosophy centred on form and function to one rooted in ethics and social justice.

Incorporating storytelling into a postcolonial design curriculum presents an opportunity to breathe life into abstract theories, providing tangible examples that students can relate to. For instance, consider the story of Nia, a young designer who travels to a small village in Ghana to assist in building a community centre. Influenced by mainstream design principles, she initially proposes a sleek, glass-encased structure. The villagers are hesitant but do not express their concerns outright.

Now, let us introduce a layer of postcolonial storytelling into this scenario. In the village, the elder Kwame invites Nia to a communal storytelling session. He recounts the tale of Anansi, the spider, who wanted to hoard all the world's wisdom into a pot. Anansi quickly realised that wisdom was too vast and too communal to be contained. The moral, Kwame shares, is that wisdom should be collectively owned and spread, not isolated within glass walls—a pointed metaphor for Nia's initial design.

Nia then rethinks her approach, inviting the villagers into codesign sessions. They collectively decide on a circular, open-air structure that accommodates communal gatherings, built with local materials. This narrative methodology resonates with the students because it is more than just a case study; it is a lived experience, enveloped in the rich cultural fabric of African storytelling. It epitomises the idea of designing *with* rather than designing *for*, and it instils the critical lesson that design is not just about physical structures but also about the narratives that those structures house. Another example employs a technique known as in media res, starting the story in the middle of the action to captivate interest. Let us dive into the high-pressure situation of Maria, a designer at a tech company tasked with developing a new user interface. Her team is predominantly male and influenced by gamified designs that studies indicate are generally more appealing to men. Maria is uneasy but cannot immediately pinpoint why. She recalls a story from her postcolonial design course, where a Native American woman successfully campaigned against a harmful dam construction by sharing river stories that reconnected the engineers with the sanctity of natural flow.

Motivated by this, Maria disrupts a team meeting with her own form of storytelling. She shares a day in the life of her grandmother, who struggles to navigate the existing app with its adrenaline-pumping, complex interface. Her grandmother, Maria narrates, finds solace in the simple beauty of her garden, where each path and plant serves a purpose, guided by the simplicity of nature. Maria then correlates this to user interface design, making a case for simplicity and natural flow over gamified complexity. The story is both a disruption and a connection, emphasising the need for inclusivity and questioning the paradigms under which her team operates.

In both instances, storytelling serves as a practical teaching tool. It aligns with the objectives of postcolonial theory by dismantling preconceived notions and injecting a diverse range of perspectives into the design process. The stories, rich in cultural context and nuance, act as counternarratives to established design norms. They serve as metaphorical vessels carrying complex theories, ethical considerations, and alternative methodologies, making them more accessible.

Through the art of storytelling, design education can transform from a rigid discipline into a vibrant, evolving conversation that engages both the intellect and the imagination. It lays the groundwork for a more empathetic and socially conscious generation of designers, capable of seeing beyond their own worldviews and appreciating the rich tapestry of human experience that informs truly inclusive design.

Conclusion

The journey toward a politically conscious design approach necessitates the integration of postcolonial and anticolonial frameworks, participatory design involving marginalised communities, and a commitment to continuous learning and political awareness. postcolonial theory offers a disruptive conceptual lens to critique and reshape design curricula. It serves as a vehicle for questioning Western-centric design principles, bringing in Indigenous ontologies and epistemologies, notably through storytelling, which emerges as a potent methodological tool. Engaging with marginalised communities, particularly local artisans, is not merely ethical but essential. Their unique perspectives offer an invaluable layer of context that challenges the norms of design professionalism, which often perpetuate colonial codes. Through such engagement, we can begin to decolonise the design landscape, offering more inclusive, relevant, and socially just designs. Fostering a culture of continuous learning and political awareness is an ongoing task. It requires adopting an anticolonial perspective that transcends the typical parameters of land and space to integrate spirituality and political resistance. Furthermore, a decolonised design education must be ecologically sensitive, aligning with Indigenous environmental philosophies to produce designs that are sustainable and harmonious with the land and its inhabitants. The urgency for a politically engaged design education cannot be overstated. As the social and political landscape continues to evolve, staying anchored in outdated, colonial, and oppressive design frameworks is both anachronistic and harmful. Academics, professionals, and students alike must urgently work to decolonise design education.

This begins with a curriculum overhaul that integrates postcolonial and anti-colonial theories, emphasising methodologies like storytelling that reflect African cultural and historical contexts. It means that design schools must actively involve marginalised communities, giving them a voice in both curriculum development and the broader design process. Educators and designers should be committed to ongoing learning and political awareness, adapting and evolving to the changing contexts around them.

But it is not merely an academic or professional endeavour; it is a collective societal responsibility. The designs we create shape our world; they influence perceptions, behaviours, and ultimately, societies. It is imperative, then, that design education moves away from an oppressive status quo to become an active participant in social justice and political activism.

While this discourse begins to outline the contours of a politically conscious design education, there is ample room for future research and conversation. To start, empirical studies that involve local artisans and marginalised communities in design education can offer quantifiable data on the benefits and challenges of such an approach. Further study into the convergence and divergence between postcolonial, anti-colonial, and decolonial frameworks in design education would add nuances to the current discourse.

Other areas include the exploration of how African Indigenous environmental philosophies can be integrated into design curricula to create more sustainable and socially responsible designs. Moreover, how do notions of Africanisation and Indigenisation intersect in practical applications? How can design education be assessed and evaluated in this new, more inclusive context? Lastly, the role of digital technologies in promoting or impeding a decolonised design space needs to be scrutinised. Technology is a double-edged sword; it can either amplify existing inequalities or become a tool for liberation. Investigations into how digital platforms can either inhibit or facilitate politically conscious design could serve as a crucial research frontier. In sum, adopting a politically conscious design approach is not an endpoint but a continuous journey requiring active engagement from all stakeholders. It is a complex, interdisciplinary challenge that promises rich rewards in fostering a more equitable, inclusive, and sustainable future.

Note

1 The halo effect is a cognitive bias where an individual's overall impression of a person, brand, product, or entity positively influences their feelings and thoughts about that entity's character or properties. This bias was first identified by psychologist Edward Thorndike in 1920. Essentially, if someone likes one aspect of something (or someone), they will l have a positive predisposition towards everything about it (or them). In practical terms, if someone perceives a particular brand or person as good in one aspect, they are likely to assume that everything about that brand or person is good. For example, if a celebrity is attractive, people might also automatically believe they are more intelligent, kind, or talented, even without concrete evidence to support these traits. The halo effect can significantly influence decision making and judgments in various areas, including marketing, branding, hiring practices, and social interactions. The halo effect, in the context of design education, refers to a cognitive bias where the perceived positive attributes of Western designs (such as their prominence, prestige, or financial success) influence individuals' overall perception of these designs as superior. This effect leads to a generalized favourable attitude towards Western aesthetics, often at the expense of appreciating and valuing non-Western design traditions. As a result, designs aligning with Western aesthetics are not only more likely to be showcased and financially supported but are also perceived as inherently better or more desirable, reinforcing a narrative of Western superiority in design. The halo effect thus contributes to shaping a biased view of design excellence, often marginalizing, or undervaluing the richness and diversity of non-Western design philosophies and practices.

References

Albarrán González, D. (2020). *Towards a buen vivir-centric design: Decolonising artisanal design with Mayan weavers from the highlands of Chiapas, Mexico*. PhD thesis. Auckland University of Technology.
Andreotti, V. (2011). *Actionable postcolonial theory in education*. Springer. https://doi.org/10.18546/IJDEGL.04.3.05
Aravena, A. (2005). *Alejandro Aravena*, vol. 33. Servicio Publicaciones ETSA.
Arnold, M. (2021). Sarr, Felwine. 2021. Traces. Discours aux nations africaines. *French Studies in Southern Africa*, *51*(1): 1711–1776.
Bakker, J. P., Goldsack, J. C., Clarke, M., Coravos, A., Geoghegan, C., Godfrey, A., Heasley, M. G., Karlin, D. R., Manta, C., & Peterson, B. (2019). A systematic review of feasibility studies promoting the use of mobile technologies in clinical research. *NPJ Digital Medicine*, *2*(47). https://doi.org/10.1038/s41746-019-0125-x
Begum, T. (2015). A postcolonial critique of industrial design: A critical evaluation of the relationship of culture and hegemony to design practice and education since

the late 20th century. PhD thesis. University of Plymouth. https://doi.org/10.1162/leon_a_01297

Bourdieu, P. (1986). The force of law: Toward a sociology of the juridical field. *Hastings Law Journal, 38*(5): 814–853.

Breidlid, A. (2013). *Education, indigenous knowledges, and development in the global south: Contesting knowledges for a sustainable future.* Routledge.

Brock-Utne, B. (2005). Language-in-education policies and practices in Africa with a special focus on Tanzania and South Africa—insights from research in progress. In J. Zajda (Ed.), *Third International Handbook of Globalisation, Education and Policy Research.* Springer. https://doi.org/10.1007/978-3-030-66003-1_35

Dache-Gerbino, A., Aguayo, D., Griffin, M., Hairston, S. L., Hamilton, C., Krause, C., Lane-Bonds, D., & Sweeney, H. (2019). Re-imagined postcolonial geographies: Graduate students explore spaces of resistance in the wake of Ferguson. *Research in Education, 104*(1): 3–23.

Dahmani, N., Belhadi, A., Benhida, K., Elfezazi, S., Touriki, F. E., & Azougagh, Y. (2022). Integrating lean design and eco-design to improve product design: From literature review to an operational framework. *Energy & Environment, 33*(1): 189–219.

Dennis, C. A. (2018). Decolonising education: A pedagogic intervention. In K. Bhambra, Gurminder, K. Nişancioğlu, & D. Gebrial (Eds.), *Decolonising the university.* 190–207. Pluto Press.

Dorner, L. M., Kim, S., Bonney, E. N., & Montes, I. C. (2023). Using critical discourse analysis to challenge and change educational practice and policy. In *Handbook of Critical Education Research.* 356–376. Routledge.

Dourish, P., & Bell, G. (2011). *Divining a digital future: Mess and mythology in ubiquitous computing.* Mit Press.

Enwezor, O., & Okeke-Agulu, C. (2009). *Contemporary African art since 1980.* Damiani Bologna.

Friedman, B., & Nissenbaum, H. (1996). Bias in computer systems. *ACM Transactions on information systems (TOIS), 14*(3): 330–347.

Gammage, M. M. (2015). *Representations of black women in the media: The damnation of black womanhood.* Routledge.

Giroux, H. (1983). Critical theory and educational practice. *ESA 841, Theory and Practice in Educational Administration.* ERIC.

Gulliksen, J., Göransson, B., Boivie, I., Blomkvist, S., Persson, J., & Cajander, Å. (2003). Key principles for user-centred systems design. *Behaviour and Information Technology, 22*(6): 397–409.

Hartley, J., & McWilliam, K. (2009). *Story circle: Digital storytelling around the world.* Wiley-Blackwell. https://doi.org/10.1002/9781444310580.ch1

Haugtvedt, C. P., Herr, P. M., & Kardes, F. R. (2018). *Handbook of consumer psychology.* Routledge.

Herman, D. (2004). *Story logic: Problems and possibilities of narrative.* University of Nebraska Press.

Keen, S. (2006). A theory of narrative empathy. *Narrative, 14*(3): 207–236. http://www.jstor.org/stable/20107388

King, J., & South, J. (2017). Reimagining the role of technology in higher education: A supplement to the national education technology plan. *US Department of Education, Office of Educational Technology.*

King, P. E. (2019). Religion and identity: The role of ideological, social, and spiritual contexts. In J. L. Furrow, L. M. Wagener (Eds.), *Beyond the self: Perspectives on Identity and Transcendence Among Youth:a Special Issue of Applied Developmental Science.* 197–204. Routledge.

Kotok, S., & Kryst, E. L. (2017). Digital technology: A double-edged sword for a school principal in rural Pennsylvania. *Journal of Cases in Educational Leadership*, *20*(4): 3–16.

Kumar, R. (2018). *Research methodology: A step-by-step guide for beginners*. Sage.

Levin, D. T. (2000). Race as a visual feature: using visual search and perceptual discrimination tasks to understand face categories and the cross-race recognition deficit. *Journal of Experimental Psychology: General*, *129*(4): 559–574. doi: 10.1037//0096-3445.129.4.559.

Manzini, E. (2015). *Design, when everybody designs: An introduction to design for social innovation*. MIT press.

Mbembe, A. (2001). *On the postcolony*. University of California Press.

Mbembe, A. (2017). *Critique of black reason*. Duke University Press. https://doi.org/10.2307/j.ctv125jgv8

McPartlan, P., Rutherford, T., Rodriguez, F., Shaffer, J. F., & Holton, A. (2021). Modality motivation: Selection effects and motivational differences in students who choose to take courses online. *The Internet and Higher Education*, *49*: 100793.

Moreton-Robinson, A. (2015). *The white possessive: Property, power, and indigenous sovereignty*. Univeristy of Minnesota Press.

Nelson, H. G., & Stolterman, E. (2014). *The design way: Intentional change in an unpredictable world*. MIT Press.

Nickerson, R. S. (1998). Confirmation bias: A ubiquitous phenomenon in many guises. *Review of General Psychology*, *2*(2): 175–220. https://doi.org/10.1037/1089-2680.2.2.175

Nwagwu, W. E., & Akintoye, A. (2023). Influence of social media on the uptake of emerging musicians and entertainment events. *Information Development*. https://doi.org/10.1177/02666669221151162

Nzegwu, N. (1994). Gender equality in a dual-sex system: The case of Onitsha. *Canadian Journal of Law & Jurisprudence*, *7*(1): 73–95.

Ofosu-Asare, Y. (2023). *Sankofa: Stories of a postcolonial space, African philosophy, Decolonisation and Practice in Design Education in Ghana*. PhD thesis. Southern Cross University.

Papachristodoulou, A. (2023). *Visual poetry in the anthropocene: Sculpting & materialising language as a social, ecological and feminist gesture*. PhD thesis. University of Surrey.

Porter, M. E. (2011). *Competitive advantage of nations: creating and sustaining superior performance*. Simon and Schuster.

Ramkelewan, R. (2020). *Personal-professional identities: stories of teachers' lived dilemmatic experiences in the context of school quintiles*. PhD thesis. University of KwaZulu-Natal, Durban.

Rigon, A., & Broto, V. C. (2021). *Inclusive urban development in the global south: intersectionality, inequalities, and community*. Routledge.

Robin, B. (2008). Digital sorytelling: A powerful technology tool for the 21st century classroom. *Theory Into Practice*, *47*: 220–228. https://doi.org/10.1080/00405840802153916

Rodrigues, A. P. A. (2018). *Pop-up pedagogy: Exploring connections between street art, feminist literacy practices and communities*. PhD thesis. York University.

Sanders, E. B.-N., & Stappers, P. J. (2008). Co-creation and the new landscapes of design. *Co-design*, *4*(1): 5–18.

Sarr, F. (2023). *African meditations*. University of Minnesota Press.

Smith, L. T. (2021). *Decolonizing methodologies: Research and indigenous peoples*. Bloomsbury Publishing. https://doi.org/10.2307/j.ctv19m61z3.10

Sun, H. (2012). *Cross-cultural technology design: Creating culture-sensitive technology for local users*. Oxford University Press.

Tacchi, J. (2020). Digital engagement: Voice and participation in development. In H. A. Horst & D. Miller (Eds.), *Digital anthropology*. 225–241. Routledge.

Taras, V., Steel, P., & Stackhouse, M. (2023). A comparative evaluation of seven instruments for measuring values comprising Hofstede's model of culture. *Journal of World Business*, 58(1): 101386.

Utuk, B. (2018). *Instructional strategies for culturally diverse learners: a case study of instructional designers*. PhD Dissertation. Capella University.

Woolman, D. C. (2001). Educational reconstruction and postcolonial curriculum development: A comparative study of four African countries. *International Education Journal*, 2(5): 27–46.

INDEX

Accra, Ghana, 6, 21, 28, 174
Adeyemi, Kunlé, 17
Africanisation, 180
Afrocentricity, 32
Afrofuturism, 127
Akan gold weights, 75, 108
Algorithmism, 16, 119, 150–153
Anticolonial theory, 180
Appiah, Kwame Anthony, 28–29, 30, 36, 83
Architectural design, 92, 112–114, 128–129, 139
Armah, Ayi Kwei, 4
Ase concept, 90, 167
Ashanti Region, Ghana, 2–3
Augmented reality, 121
Abiodun, R., 71
Achebe, Chinua, 43, 48
Adinkra symbols, 3, 75, 108
African design: Decolonising, 7–8, 32–33, 100–101, 126–127; History of, 105–107; Indigenous aesthetics, 123–125; Politics, 103–105; Postcolonial ideals, 104–105; Reclaiming cultural narratives, 126–127; Spirituality, 69–71, 92–93
African education: Colonial impact, 3–7, 105–107; Decolonising, 29–32, 36–37; Design education, 32–33, 36–37; Historical context, 105–107; Politics, 103–105; Reforms, 29–32

African philosophy, 18–19, 27–28
African Virtual University, 30
Agyekum, Kofi, 6
Akyeampong, Kwame, 6
Aravena, Alejandro, 128
Art, African, 71–73, 123–125
Asante Twi, 37
Asante, Molefi Kete, 31–32

Black Lives Matter movement, 134–135
Botho concept, 79
Bourdieu, P., 49, 118
Buolamwini, Joy, 148
Bennett, Audrey, 7–8
Bhabha, H. K., 83

Cape Town, South Africa, 55
Collaborative design, 96, 162
Community-based design, 141
Community centres, 130, 137
Confirmation bias, 118
Conscious design, 158–162
Critical theory, 152
Cross-cultural design, 152
Crowdfunding, 9
Cultural heritage preservation, 111, 127
Cultural sustainability, 110
Culturally relevant pedagogy, 12, 34, 44–46
Colour psychology, 172
Community engagement, 88–90, 135, 137, 140–141

Critical consciousness, 47–48, 51–53
Cultural appropriation, 83–85, 97–98
Cultural capital, 14, 47–49
Cultural sensitivity, 140–141
Culture and design education, 76–78; and spirituality, 70–71, 92–93
Curriculum 2005 (South Africa), 35

Dakar, Senegal, 21
Decolonial Aesthesis, 100
Decolonised space, 26–27
Design ethics education, 175–177
Design for social innovation, 122
Design thinking methodologies, 179
Digital divide, 135, 140
Data analytics, 144–145
Decolonisation of African education, 29–32, 36–37; of design education, 7–8, 32–33, 36–37, 100–101, 126–127; and politics, 103–105; and spirituality, 69–71, 92–93
Decolonising methodologies, 4, 19–20
Design education: Decolonising, 7–8, 32–33, 36–37, 100–101, 126–127; Culture, 76–78; Politics, 103–105; Spirituality, 69–71, 80–82, 92–93
Design thinking, 4, 34, 57
Design: Activism, 133–135; Culture, 76–78; Decolonising, 7–8, 32–33, 100–101, 126–127; Definition, 14–16; Ethics, 142–143, 162–163; Politics, 103–105, 128–131; Social justice, 127–131, 141–142; Spirituality, 69–71, 80–82, 92–93; Sustainability, 142–143

Ecological design, 90, 143, 180
Embodied cognition, 52
Empathy-driven design, 147
Engaged pedagogy, 95
Epistemic injustice, 58
Ethical accountability, 164–165
Experiential design, 74
Ehn, P., 96
Escobar, A., 8
Eseanya-Esiobu, C., 6
Ethical design, 159–162
Experiential learning, 95–96, 100

Facial recognition bias, 148–150
Festinger, Leon, 12

Fractals, African, 3, 169
Fwenso Hills, Nigeria, 21
Fanon, Frantz, 20–28, 48
Freire, Paulo, 56–57, 95

Ga language, 6, 38
Gamification in education, 179
Gender studies, 148
Globalisation and African design, 17, 126; and education, 30, 58, 107
Green design, 142–143
Gupta, Deepak, 57
Gender-neutral design, 130–131
Gyekye, Kwame, 18

Halden Prison, Norway, 132–133
Halo effect, 117, 181
Harare, Zimbabwe, 21
Holistic education, 100
Human-centred design, 132, 158
Half-houses, 128
Hooks, bell, 8, 95

Identity, African, 29, 36
Inclusive design, 138–142, 147
Indigenous environmental philosophies, 180
Indigenous futurism, 127
Indigenous technologies, 4, 13
Intellectual property rights, 107, 127
Intercultural design, 96
Indigenous aesthetics, 123–125
Indigenous knowledge, 6–7, 29–32, 123–125
Indigenous languages, 6, 29–30, 54–55

Johannesburg, South Africa, 21

Kampala, Uganda, 21
Kikuyu language, 54
Kinshasa, Democratic Republic of Congo, 21
Kente cloth, 2–3, 108–111
Knowledge diversity, 31
Kumasi, Ghana, 8, 19
Kwame Nkrumah University of Science and Technology, 19

Lagos, Nigeria, 55
Land-based education, 78

Language revitalisation, 6, 29–30
Linguistic imperialism, 171
Lusaka, Zambia, 21
Ladson-Billings, Gloria, 12, 47
Laenui, P., 19
Language policies, 4, 6, 29–30

Maasai, Kenya, 85
Machine learning bias, 150
Marginalisation in education, 106–108
Mombasa, Kenya, 21
Morvan, C., 12
Maasai beadwork, 85
Mbembe, Achille, 106
Meadows, D. H., 4–5, 16
Mentor-apprentice systems, 87–88
Mignolo, W. D., 7

Nairobi, Kenya, 21, 54–55
Narrative inquiry, 65
Neocolonialism, 5
Nigerian design, 92–93
Nkrumah, Kwame, 2–3, 20
Nok sculptures, Nigeria, 72
Nairobi, Kenya, 54–55
Narrative psychology, 120–121
Ndebele, South Africa, 55–56
Ndlovu-Gatsheni, S. J., 5, 30
Ngũgĩ wa Thiong'o, 6, 29–30, 48
Nkrumah Educational Centre, 2–3
Nsibidi scripts, 3
Nussbaum, M., 67
Nzegwu, N., 106

Open education resources, 16
Open-source technology, 16
Orientalism, 47, 83, 96
Ofosu-Asare, Y., 108
Okri, Ben, 18
Opoku, Francis, 7
Orientalism, 83

Papert, S., 8
Participatory action research, 161
Planck, Max, 114
Placemaking, 140
Postcolonial design, 104–105, 126–127
Prison design, 132–133
Problem-based learning, 35
Problem-posing education, 6–7

Participatory design, 95–96, 135
Pogoson, O. I., 71
Postcolonial ideals, 104–105
Postcolonial theory, 26–28, 177–180

Qwabe, Sihle, 57

Racialised design, 145–146, 151–154
Reflective practice, 96–97, 100
Restorative design, 141–142
Restorative justice design, 141–142

Said, Edward, 13, 47, 83, 96
Self-efficacy theory, 118
Shona sculpture, Zimbabwe, 21
Smart cities, 139, 156
Social capital, 14
Social identity theory, 118
Sociology of education, 152
South Africa, 30, 35, 55–56, 92
Spivak, G. C., 13
Stereotype threat, 151
Storytelling in education, 43, 79–80, 178–179
Swahili language, 29
Systems thinking, 4–5, 16, 166–174
Sankofa, 3, 90
Senghor, Leopold, 18
Social justice, 127–131, 141–142
Social media activism, 134–136
Spirituality and African design, 69–71, 92–93; and design education, 69–71, 80–82, 92–93; definition, 70
Storytelling, 43, 79–80, 178–179
Sustainability, 142–143

Tamale, Ghana, 10
Technological determinism, 166
Transdisciplinarity, 176–177
Takoradi, Ghana, 7
Technology and decolonisation, 30–31; and design, 15–16, 31, 135–136, 147–150
Traditional architecture, 112–114
Typography, 151–154

Ujamaa philosophy, 88
Universal design, 138–139
Urban acupuncture, 128
Urban informality, 128
User-centred design, 119, 129

Ubuntu philosophy, 18, 78–79, 88, 90, 124
Urban planning, 8, 154–157

Vastu Shastra, 140
Virtual reality, 74, 121

Wangari Maathai Institute for Peace and Environmental Studies, 21
Wicked problems, 132
Wodehouse, P. G., 113
Wolof language, 21

Wa Thiong'o, Ngũgĩ, 6, 29–30, 48
Walker, S., 72–73, 82
Western-centric design, 7–8, 60–61, 151–154

Xhosa language, 21

Yoruba art, 71, 92–93
Yoruba philosophy, 74, 90, 92–93

Zulu language, 21

Printed in the United States
by Baker & Taylor Publisher Services